ADVANCED
CAREER
INTELLIGENCE

RAY BLASING

ADVANCED
CAREER
INTELLIGENCE

Master *your* **Journey** *with*
Purpose, Integrity, *and*
Grace

RAY BLASING

Book Layout ©2017 BookDesignTemplates.com

Advanced Career Intelligence/ Ray Blasing. —1st ed.

Published in the United States by WWIT Press.
ISBN 979-8-9918093-3-7

To Cori and Kyler—I wrote this book for you.

And to Elaine—my partner, best friend, and the love of my life. Every day with you is a priceless gift.

Contents

Introduction

Welcome to *Advanced Career Intelligence*, a comprehensive career guide for navigating the evolving landscape of today's working world. This book, the second in a two-volume series, is designed to equip you with the additional knowledge and skills necessary to thrive in your career and personal life.

In *General Career Intelligence,* we established a solid foundation and explored how to navigate the various stages of your career in a rapidly changing world. In *Advanced Career Intelligence*, we focus on additional echelons of your job, where leadership, innovation, and strategic thinking come to the forefront.

As you ascend the career ladder, your challenges become increasingly complex. Executive leadership, for example, demands strategic vision and the ability to inspire and guide diverse teams toward common goals. Effective conflict resolution processes are crucial for sustaining a culture of safety and respect that enhances continuous improvement and innovation. Influence and mentoring become essential tools for nurturing talent and driving organizational success. Entrepreneurship requires a unique blend of creativity, resilience, and strategic planning, whether pursued within established companies or through new ventures. Building a positive work culture and achieving work-life balance is critical for long-term success and well-being. Avoiding toxicity while nurturing cross-functional teamwork presents challenges and opportunities that must be navigated with care and intentionality.

In addition to these common work themes, *Advanced Career Intelligence* addresses the importance of corporate citizenship and philanthropy, highlighting how impactful contributions to society can enhance personal fulfillment and professional reputation. As you approach the later stages of your career, considerations around joyful living and retirement planning become increasingly significant, offering a chance to reflect on your legacy and the enduring significance of your life's work.

As I approached the completion of this multi-year writing journey, I concentrated on creating a tagline for this book that encapsulates the primary themes of career intelligence worthy of highlighting. I eventually arrived at this tricolon:

Ambition with Purpose
Achievement with Integrity
Legacy with Grace

Ambition with Purpose reflects the critical balance between striving for success and ensuring our efforts are grounded in meaningful goals. Ambition alone can lead to unfocused energy, wasted potential, and even burnout if it lacks clear direction. Purpose transforms ambition into a constructive force by anchoring it to a vision that aligns with personal values and long-term objectives.

In career development, having purposeful ambition means planning thoughtfully, setting actionable goals, and consistently evaluating whether your pursuits align with your broader aspirations. It's about moving beyond chasing promotions or accolades to consider the deeper "why" behind your actions. Purpose drives initiatives that advance careers and contribute positively to teams, organizations, and society.

Therefore, it's important to take initiative, not merely waiting for opportunities but actively creating them, and use ambition to build a fulfilling and impactful career. With purpose, ambition is no longer chaotic or reactive; it becomes strategic, inspiring, and ultimately transformative.

Achievement with Integrity emphasizes the profound value of attaining success through moral principles, ethical conduct, and a commitment to benefiting others. Achievement isn't about winning at all costs or exploiting opportunities solely for personal gain; it's about contributing to collective progress while staying true to your values and positive character traits.

When individuals approach their goals with integrity, they advance their careers and elevate the people and systems around them. By applying empathy, honesty, and fairness in every interaction, we create environments where mutual success is possible. Integrity ensures that the journey toward achievement uplifts teams, supports peers, and leaves a positive mark on the organizations and communities we serve.

Far from being a zero-sum game, achievement with integrity reframes success as a shared endeavor. When we help others excel—whether through mentorship, collaboration, or simply leading by example—we multiply the impact of our efforts. This mindset contributes to a society that values connection, fairness, truth, and trust, advancing us toward a brighter future. Through integrity, achievement becomes a personal milestone and a catalyst for broader, meaningful change.

Legacy with Grace captures the essence of our lasting impact on the world, shaped by our values and actions. Initially, I struggled between the terms grace and virtue, as both contribute to this legacy, but they do so in distinct yet complementary ways. While virtue reflects moral excellence, grace captures the nuanced ability to inspire, forgive, and uplift others, inspiring unity and understanding.

Grace transcends the mechanics of doing what is right and focuses on how we carry ourselves and interact with others. Grace reflects humility, compassion, forgiveness, and the ability to inspire through kindness and empathy. Where virtue provides the ethical framework, grace softens its edges, allowing for understanding, connection, and healing in a divided world.

In the chapter *Dent the Universe*, the idea of legacy takes center stage. It celebrates how even small, individual acts can ripple outward, building upon the ripples of others to create meaningful change. Every person has the potential to contribute to the common good, whether through acts of kindness, mentorship, innovation, or service. A legacy built with grace is not about fame or grandeur but our subtle yet profound influence on others' lives.

Our career journeys are continuous and ever-evolving, shaped by the lessons we learn and the experiences we encounter. Like its predecessor, *Advanced Career Intelligence* encourages active engagement, reflection, and application of the knowledge shared within these pages.

As you immerse yourself in the contents of this book, remember that each chapter is a step toward mastering the complexities of your career and life. Embrace the challenges, leverage the opportunities, and let the insights within this book empower you to reach new heights in your professional and personal journey.

> *Life isn't about finding yourself. Life is about creating yourself.* —George Bernard Shaw, Irish playwright, critic, polemicist, and political activist.

CHAPTER 1

Executive Leadership

Some are born great, some achieve greatness, and some have greatness thrust upon them. —William Shakespeare, English playwright, poet, and actor.

Executive leadership demands a unique blend of strategic insight, vision, and the ability to drive effective organizational execution. At the highest levels, leaders must balance decisiveness and assertiveness with approachability and relatability, understanding that their actions and decisions shape the company's culture. A successful executive embodies technical expertise, industry knowledge, and the ability to inspire, motivate, and guide diverse teams toward a common goal.

Executives set the tone for excellence, navigating complex challenges and opportunities with a clear vision while maintaining the agility to adapt and innovate. Whether leading with a firm hand or adopting a more inclusive approach, executives understand that effective leadership combines strength with empathy, strategy with execution, and ambition with integrity and morality. In doing so, they achieve their organizational goals and set a standard for superior leadership in the modern world.

The role of an executive can be demanding and challenging, often shaped by the expectations set by the CEO and the Board of Directors. The responsibilities can be immense, requiring a unique blend of skills, temperament, and dedication. The CEO, for example, shoulders a tremendous responsibility as their decisions ripple through the lives and livelihoods of employees, stakeholders, and communities. The weight of steering an organization toward success while navigating risks and uncertainties amplifies the gravity of their role and the stress inherent in making choices that can shape futures and legacies.

The dynamics within the executive team play a prominent role in determining the overall experience as an executive. A supportive, collaborative, and cohesive team can transform challenges into opportunities for growth and fulfillment. In contrast, a dysfunctional or combative team can amplify the burdens of the role, leading to a toxic and draining experience.

Not surprisingly, executive arrogance or ego can poison the workplace environment, making collaboration and progress challenging. When executives prioritize individual success over collective goals or encourage an environment of competition and turf wars, it erodes trust and undermines the organization's culture. Further, when a CEO promotes chaos or unhealthy competition among executives, it can create a toxic atmosphere that can harm the well-being of the entire executive team. In such environments, it becomes challenging for executives to thrive and fulfill their roles effectively.

Executive Excellence

Successful CEOs understand the importance of building strong executive teams, as they constitute the backbone of successful companies. They meticulously select exceptional partners whom they can trust and engage in honest communication. An exceptional leadership team goes beyond individual performance; it inspires collaboration, makes sound decisions, introduces innovative ideas, and offers constructive upward feedback. CEOs should resist surrounding themselves with sycophants and loyal followers within their executive team, as this can undermine the company's success in various ways.

The best executive is the one who has sense enough to pick good people to do what needs to be done, and self-restraint to keep from meddling with them while they do it. —Unknown.

Below is an abbreviated list of attributes that further describe exceptional executives and CEOs:

- Integrity and ethics: They demonstrate honesty, integrity, and ethical behavior in all aspects of their leadership.

- Visionary leadership: They have a clear vision for the company's future and inspire others to follow it.

- Strategic thinking: They develop and execute effective strategies to achieve long-term goals.

- Communication excellence: They communicate clearly, transparently, and effectively with employees, customers, stakeholders, and the public, facilitating understanding and engagement.

- Decision-making: They make informed decisions based on data, analysis, experience, and intuition.

- Empowering leadership: They empower and trust their team members, creating a culture of accountability and innovation.

- Positive influence: They leverage their position, power, and exceptional communication skills to drive positive progress beyond what authority alone can achieve.

- Results-driven: They set ambitious and compelling goals that align everyone toward a joint mission. Leveraging their position of influence, they model positive examples for others to follow and eliminate barriers that hinder progress. They hold themselves and their team accountable for achieving results.

- Adaptability: They adapt to changing market conditions and embrace new technologies and trends.

- Patience: As new hires, they carefully evaluate the business and seek input from team members before making any substantial changes. They proceed cautiously, ensuring their actions align with the company's goals.

- Financial acumen: They possess a deep understanding of the company's financials. They avoid rushing into contracts or making hasty decisions under pressure. CEOs often demonstrate financial acumen comparable to that of their CFOs.

- Diversity: They value a robust, independent board and advisory team and welcome candid feedback and honest discussions. While they seek and consider advice, they understand that final decisions rest with them and embrace the responsibility that comes with it. Transparent in their methods, they recognize the value of diverse perspectives.

- Confidence: Great executives are confident in their leadership and style. They work to cultivate a personal brand that aligns with the company values and then model it for others.

- Fundamentals: They understand company fundamentals, including levers of influence, sustainable profitability, and critical concerns of other executives. They grasp customer motives and know when to reject unprofitable pursuits.

- Self-awareness: They exhibit self-awareness and emotional intelligence, building solid relationships and modeling organizational values. They demonstrate proactive, consistent leadership, inspiring greatness, and nurturing a positive work culture centered on employee well-being. They actively contribute to building an inclusive, inspirational, and sustainable workplace environment.[1]

- Storytelling: They possess exceptional storytelling skills and are adept at articulating their company's mission and story to employees, investors, customers, and beyond. Their stories energize and inspire others, compelling them to align with the company's vision.

- Role model: Great executives embody creativity, energy, and receptiveness to learning and growth. They actively listen to feedback, adapt their plans accordingly, and lead by example, demonstrating hard work, grit, and resourcefulness.

- Teambuilding: The best leaders build great teams that appreciate camaraderie and collaboration. Team participants know how and where they fit in, and they understand how their efforts contribute to the greater good.[2]

- Metrics: Great leaders measure what matters most. They understand the differences between ROI, ROE, and ROA and use them effectively to inform decisions, clarify resource efficiency, and drive strategic outcomes.

When searching for an executive role, selecting the right leadership environment is crucial for your professional growth and well-being. When interviewing, be sure to thoroughly research the incumbent executives, evaluating their professional reputation, interpersonal dynamics, and behavior under pressure. Supportive and non-combative executive leaders promote positive work environments conducive to personal and organizational success. Finding the right fit ensures you align yourself with leaders who inspire and empower you to thrive in your role.

You may find it helpful to focus your research and interview assessments by asking yourself the following questions:

- Do the executives embrace kindness and flexibility towards their workers? Great executives value work-life balance and respect employees' personal lives and priorities.

- Do they genuinely understand how important it is for people to feel happy and satisfied personally and professionally?

- Are they focused on creating an "us" environment where one supports the other, inside and outside the office, and where making human connections with other workers is the glue that binds them together?

- Do they emphasize caring and teamwork, which provide employees with a sense of purpose in their work?

- Do they care about their employees' personal and professional development by allocating resources to improve their mental and physical health, career progression, and personal growth?

- Do they excel in leading, mentoring, and developing their employees, including high-potential, next-gen executives?[3]

Executive excellence drives strategic vision, promotes innovation, and achieves sustainable organizational success. By embodying integrity, visionary leadership, and a commitment to continuous learning and growth, executives can inspire teams, navigate complexity, and deliver exceptional results that propel their organizations forward.

Leadership is about making others better as a result of your presence, and making sure that impact lasts in your absence.
—Sheryl Sandberg, American business executive, author, philanthropist, and women's rights advocate.

Brutal CEOs

While most experts advocate for essential leadership qualities such as kindness, humility, and empathy, we continue to witness immense success from leaders who disregard these behaviors entirely. The toxic blend of money, power, and hubris has long existed in the corporate landscape. Leadership arrogance often prevails in the most influential companies, as investors and shareholders shower their ruthless CEOs with excessive wealth.

How you make others feel about themselves says a lot about you. —Unknown.

Many founders have exhibited terrible and even tyrannical behavior, later becoming infamous for their actions. Take Steve Jobs, known for his arrogance, dictatorial tendencies, and occasional dishonesty. Despite this, he's widely regarded as having been an exceptional leader. Zuckerberg infamously ousted his friend and co-founder Eduardo Saverin from Facebook, while Twitter's co-founders repeatedly backstabbed each other. Jeff Bezos of Amazon was notorious for sending terse, single-character emails ("?"), and Bill Gates was known for his aggressive style, berating Microsoft employees for what he perceived as bad ideas or stupid questions. Elon Musk has trolled, abused, lashed out, and bullied more people, or classes of people, than one can count, especially since acquiring Twitter.

It's deeply troubling that society often excuses bad leadership behavior. Many industry titans exhibit entitlement, arrogance, and a belief that normalized leadership expectations don't apply to them. Unfortunately, this permeates other spheres, including politics, where being abrasive and disrespectful is sometimes seen as a prerequisite for power and influence. Political leaders often exploit intimidation and hard power to assert dominance, disregarding traditional norms, conventional wisdom, and basic decency. However, this doesn't mean that corporate leaders should follow suit. Embracing ruthlessness and disrespect in the workplace goes against the fundamental principles of ethical leadership and can lead to toxic work environments.

The culture of any organization is shaped by the worst behavior the leader is willing to tolerate. —Steve Gruenert and Todd Whitaker, professors of education.

When a biographer asked Steve Jobs to explain his mean streak, he replied, "This is who I am, and you can't expect me to be someone I'm not." This raises serious questions about authenticity in the workplace. While individuals should bring their authentic selves to work, it's equally important to cultivate and emphasize positive values like integrity, humility, and empathy. The challenge lies in reconciling our authentic selves with the expectations of a professional environment. While certain traits may drive remarkable performance, it's worth considering the impact of harmful behaviors on workplace culture and relationships. Authenticity shouldn't be an excuse for destructive behavior; rather, it should be a commitment to embodying the *best* aspects of ourselves while striving for growth and positive impact.

Steve Jobs and Elon Musk exemplify different leadership styles and approaches to achieving extraordinary results. Jobs was known for his keen ability to assess and motivate employees to achieve remarkable outcomes. He had a knack for pushing boundaries and challenging conventional thinking. On the other hand, Musk is driven by a vision to revolutionize entire industries through ambitious goals and technological innovation. He prioritizes logic and rationality over emotion, which can sometimes be perceived as heartless. However, his commitment to bold action and willingness to take extraordinary risks have propelled his ventures forward, inspiring others to push the boundaries of what's possible.

Cleverness is a gift. Kindness is a choice. —Jeff Bezos, American entrepreneur, media proprietor, investor, computer engineer, and commercial astronaut.

The successes of companies led by individuals like Jobs and Musk have undoubtedly been significant, but at a cost. Many personnel relationships have been injured, and large swaths of employees have suffered burnout, given the constant, almost ruthless push to succeed at the hands of their overly demanding CEOs.

Despite their considerable successes, Jobs and Musk may have achieved even greater success if they had exhibited compassion, empathy, and humility. Their harsh leadership tactics created substantial turnover, which may have resulted in lost opportunities for increased innovation and productivity. Work environments characterized by fear and intimidation as primary motivators stifle creativity and collaboration, potentially limiting the full potential of their organizations. By cultivating healthier and happier workforces, free from fear and undue stress, Jobs and Musk might have unlocked even more success and innovation within their companies.[4]

That said, leadership style is often contingent upon the situation, and what may work effectively in one context might not be suitable in another. Jobs' and Musk's perceived mean-streaked leadership approaches were usually employed selectively, based on what they deemed necessary for specific situations. Despite their shortcomings, they compensated with abundant positive traits such as exceptional vision, passion for their companies, and the ability to inspire trust. Jobs, for instance, instilled a higher purpose within Apple that resonated with employees and customers alike, while his passion for the company's products was renowned. Although his interpersonal style may have been caustic, his leadership qualities remained unparalleled, leading many to overlook his occasional abrasive behavior in light of the company's extraordinary success. As Jobs famously stated, "My job is not to be easy on people. My job is to make them better."[5]

While some may argue that being mean but successful justifies negative behavior, there's almost always a better approach. Most leaders recognize that eliciting the best from their employees involves demonstrating positive behavioral traits, particularly emotional intelligence rooted in kindness. Employees are unlikely to tolerate bullying from a CEO unless the company is experiencing remarkable success in ways that align closely with their values and goals.

While it's preferable not to work under a tyrannical boss, the reality is that, in some instances, enduring such leadership may compel you to produce the best work of your career.

> *One of the most underrated skills in business right now is being nice. Nice sells.* —Mark Cuban, American entrepreneur, executive, television personality, and media proprietor.

Strategy, Execution, and Vision

When we think about executive leaders, specific leadership profiles like "visionary," "operator," and "strategist" come to mind. Visionaries and strategists contemplate and resolve what the company will do, while operators know how to do it. Unfortunately, many executives aren't great at all three. Successful leaders don't view strategy/vision and operation/execution as separate skill sets. Instead, they understand that they're substantially linked.

Steve Jobs' remarkable return to Apple and his subsequent company transformation provide a compelling illustration of aligning a bold vision with flawless execution. Under his leadership, Apple orchestrated a highly aligned and inspired organization, ensuring that every necessary innovation was fully funded, supported, and executed. Unlike companies that rely on historical incrementalism to shape their annual budgets, Apple invested substantially in new and innovative pursuits that directly advanced its strategic objectives.

This approach ensured that Apple's vision and strategy were established and optimized within the context of achievable outcomes.

Ensuring everyone understands and connects to the company strategy in tangible ways is critical to success and achievement. Facebook exemplifies this objective by sustaining a highly collaborative and communicative culture, providing numerous opportunities for employees to learn about the company's direction, rationale, and plans for the future. Regular all-hands meetings and smaller gatherings feature talks from employees who share their project experiences, humanizing challenges, and celebrating successes. Summary presentations are regularly delivered to communicate program progress and status, with a continuous cycle of preparation for upcoming presentations on various projects or subjects. The cross-pollination of information is actively embraced, with videos from the field and customer testimonials reinforcing the significance of employees' work by showcasing real-world impacts. This inclusive approach ensures that every employee, from top to bottom, feels inspired and connected to the company's overarching mission, fueling pride in their contributions.

Leaders who seamlessly transition between strategy and execution and who are visionaries and operators are most likely to drive exceptional corporate success. Their strategies are achievable and effectively communicated. Critical skills and processes necessary to execute effectively are identified, funded, and secured. Budgets are realistic and adequate. Employee and organizational goals are established and communicated, and employees are motivated, recognized, and rewarded for excellence.[6]

> *Most leaders would agree that they'd be better off having an average strategy with superb execution than a superb strategy with poor execution.* —Stephen Covey, American educator, author, businessman, and motivational speaker

It is interesting to observe how leaders often forecast future revenues and profits. Frequently, executives generate optimistic projections, envisioning future success based on comparisons to past performance, slight technological advancements, and ambitious sales expectations while overlooking changes in the competitive landscape. Competing agendas and inflated egos often influence this process. However, once these "hockey stick" projections are finalized, unexpected realities inevitably challenge their validity.

Nobel laureate Daniel Kahneman has highlighted how individuals often rely on their own experiences and data when attempting new endeavors—a phenomenon he calls the "inside view." However, this perspective is susceptible to contamination from overconfidence, cognitive biases, and internal politics, which can compromise the accuracy of their projections and strategies.

When leaders with shared goals and experiences come together in a strategy session, they often reinforce their collective biases, leading to an exaggerated assessment of their product against their competition—an opinion not widely shared by their customers. Presenters and stakeholders, in their pursuit of plan approvals, overestimate projected market share in optimistic terms, emphasizing the positives while downplaying the negatives or risks. Team leads advocate for budgets and headcounts that exceed their needs, anticipating that they'll get negotiated down to a fraction of what they ask for.

Conversely, successful strategists outperform their peers by embracing the following mindsets, which steer strategic conversations away from old and stale rehashing while mitigating the negative impacts of fear, ambition, rivalry, and bias:

-   Market forces: They understand the fierce nature of market forces and competition. They prioritize realism and conduct thorough research on competitors and market trends. They recognize that companies in the top quintile often capture nearly 90% of economic profit creation, while those in the bottom 20% suffer significant losses. These dynamics intensify over time.

- Size matters: They understand that economic profit depends on a company's ability to scale. Return on capital isn't the only factor—the amount invested can strongly influence yearly net profit.

- Industry matters: They understand that a company's position on the profit curve is dependent, at least partially, on the industry in which it operates. Sometimes, it's better to be an average company in a great industry than a great company in an average industry.

- Lever manipulation: They believe the best strategies are grounded in thoroughly understanding the attributes and actions necessary to achieve top-tier market results. Gauging the optimal intensity for each lever, such as revenue (size), debt level (leverage), and R&D (innovation), is essential.

- Industry trends: Understanding industry trends and competitive dynamics is also essential. Successful companies excel at judiciously allocating resources and swiftly reallocating them when needed to mitigate risks or capitalize on opportunities.

- Robust capital expenditure: They understand that successful companies don't save their way to success—they're willing to expend substantial capital to meet their aggressive goals.

- Focus on productivity: They know that the most profitable companies are at the top of their industry in terms of productivity and gross margin. They're also the leanest in terms of G&A.

- Innovation and differentiation: They focus on innovating products and services and ensuring that they are the most highly differentiated in the industry, which is essential for a company's long-term survival and profitability. Mediocrity kills companies.

- Action beats inaction: They understand that failing to make bold moves is often the worst strategy. Timid leaders risk corporate stagnation and miss out on the reward of growth capital, which primarily flows to the winners.[7]

Great leaders also learn to strategically leverage the right tools to enhance their effectiveness and impact. For example, AI tools can help scale a leader's natural abilities when utilized effectively. Here are just a few possible applications:

- Perspective analysis: AI can emulate a personal Board of Directors, providing insights and exposing blind spots.

- Enhanced communications: AI can refine emails, reports, and presentations, ensuring persuasive and impactful messaging.

- Predictive market and industry trends: AI can analyze patterns in consumer behavior, market shifts, and competitor activities, enabling executives to anticipate changes and optimize strategies.

- Risk assessment and crisis management: AI-driven risk models help identify threats and provide recommendations for mitigation.

Successful executives focus on cultivating their strategic and execution skills. They understand that they're substantially linked and intertwined—both are critical for aligning organizational goals with effective decision-making and resource allocation while ensuring sustainable growth and competitive advantage. Executives can steer their organizations toward long-term success and market leadership by crafting and executing strategic plans that anticipate market trends, capitalize on opportunities, and mitigate risks.

Manage the top line: your strategy, your people, and your products, and the bottom line will follow. —Steve Jobs, American entrepreneur, industrial designer, business magnate, media proprietor, investor, and co-founder and CEO of Apple.

Likability vs. Agreeability

Discussions about leadership often question whether executives need to be "likable" to be successful. While stories abound of tyrannical CEOs who achieve success despite their abrasive behavior, it's worthwhile to consider whether success and accomplishment should be the sole metrics by which executives are evaluated.

If you set out to be liked, you would be prepared to compromise on anything at any time, and you would achieve nothing. —Margaret Thatcher, British politician, and prime minister.

In my experience, the companies I enjoyed most were those led by charismatic, empathetic, and likable CEOs and executives. Working for such leaders creates a sense of pride and confidence among employees. In workplaces where we spend significant time with coworkers, cultivating positive relationships and mutual respect contributes to building a loyal and supportive organization underpinned by a nurturing, safe, supportive, and sustainable culture.

While authoritarian bosses may extract performance from their subordinates through power, being likable fuels a more positive and enduring energy that encourages greater commitment and loyalty from employees. Likable leaders engage with their workers personally, compassionately, and empathetically, which builds trust and enhances leadership effectiveness and organizational performance. Recent studies suggest that while likability isn't the primary determinant of leadership success, employees tend to perform better when they like their bosses. However, achieving likability requires more than a desire; it necessitates genuine connection and rapport-building efforts.[8]

Unfortunately, likability has lost significance in today's public sphere, particularly politics. Many political leaders no longer prioritize being appealing or likable. Instead, a trend toward embracing an abrasive and aggressive demeanor has elevated formerly unknown political operatives to quasi-celebrity status. Their readiness to engage in aggressive rhetoric and combativeness is now perceived as a display of strength and desirability, especially among those who favor an authoritarian leadership style. This shift towards smugness and disregard for how they are perceived, coupled with the abandonment of respectful and civil discourse, is fast becoming the new norm.[9]

Bullies and jerks can harm our ability to establish unity as a society and, more importantly, our mental well-being. Conversely, being liked is a timeless quality that speaks to our higher nature. Striving to be likable is an endeavor worthy of our effort—it's a winning strategy.

That said, while likability can be advantageous in the workplace, research suggests that individuals who tend to be less *agreeable* often ascend the corporate hierarchy more rapidly and effectively. Consider the executives you've encountered. They likely possess a streak of individuality, unmoved by conventional wisdom. They challenge the status quo and offer alternative perspectives, distinguishing themselves as contrarians. However, being less agreeable doesn't equate to being a bully or engaging in pointless arguments. There's a distinction between constructive dissent and abrasive behavior.

Leaders are obligated to respectfully challenge decisions when they disagree, even when doing so is uncomfortable or exhausting. Leaders have conviction and are tenacious. They do not compromise for the sake of social cohesion. Once a decision is determined, they commit wholly. —Jeff Bezos.

Path to CEO

How does one reach the top rungs of the corporate ladder? And why do some individuals seem to advance rapidly or even bypass others to reach the summit, while others face prolonged climbs or stagnation?

A recent study reveals that the average CEO attains their position after accumulating 24 years of work experience. Although only 24% hold elite MBAs, 97% have undergone at least one career "catapult" experience, with 50% having at least two. These catapult experiences appear crucial in shaping the behaviors that distinguish successful CEOs, such as decisiveness, reliability, adaptability, and the capacity to engage effectively for impact. Even individuals who never aimed for the CEO role ended up in such positions by following the catapult strategy.

Sprinters learn that their path to CEO is circuitous—some move in a lateral or even a perceived backward direction to gain valuable experience. For example, a temporary collateral role might allow you to launch a new product or division. Sometimes, smaller companies provide better opportunities to learn valuable leadership skills or assume responsibilities that escalate faster than what's available at large companies. People who build something from the ground up can make a substantial and recognizable impact. Running a section, a department, a division, or a new business unit within a larger organization, particularly when responsible for P&L, budgets, and strategic oversight, serves as essential groundwork for aspiring CEOs.

Over 30% of sprinters inherited and navigated their team through a "big mess." This might have involved a failed product introduction, an underperforming business unit, or bankruptcy. When faced with a crisis, an emerging leader has a unique opportunity to showcase their capacity to calmly assess an effective recovery path, make decisions under pressure, take calculated risks, rally others around them, and persevere amidst adversity. Such experiences serve as valuable preparation for assuming the role of CEO.

Over one-third of sprinters took a giant leap, often within the first decade of their career. They accepted an assignment that was a significant stretch from their previous roles, often feeling unprepared for the new challenges. This underscores the idea of "making your own luck" as you consider how to create or influence opportunities for significant advancement. Such endeavors may require leaving your comfort zone or even your current company, asking for more responsibility, or getting involved in alternative activities that provide better long-term potential. Embracing challenges and saying "yes" to new opportunities can pave the way forward, recognizing that the path ahead may not always be clear. Success requires a well-thought-out plan, unwavering commitment, energy, readiness to undertake new and challenging tasks, and a keen eye for identifying unique and career-enhancing opportunities.[10]

Some individuals may embark on a path to leadership from an early age, appearing destined for it, while others may stumble into leadership roles unexpectedly. Entrepreneurs who launch companies may initially be driven by a great idea or product invention, only to transition to executive roles within major corporations.

As you progress along the leadership path, it's helpful to regularly assess how your behavior is evolving with each role. Practice self-awareness frequently. Evaluate yourself for compassionate and empathetic leadership and your ability to remain composed amidst stressful challenges. Embrace making tough decisions instead of avoiding them. Trust and empower your team—that's why you hired them. Prioritize transparency and genuine honesty in your interactions. Keep your ego and arrogance in check, and actively acknowledge and celebrate the successes of others.[11]

> *Before you are a leader, success is all about growing yourself. When you become a leader, success is all about growing others.* —Jack Welch, American business executive, chemical engineer, and writer.

Engineering Executives

Can any non-technical business leader run an engineering organization? Do tech companies need a techie at the helm to thrive? MBAs and engineers may answer these questions quite differently. My entire career has been in tech, and I've worked at companies led by people with various business and technical backgrounds. My answer to these questions is: *It depends...*

I once worked at a tech startup where the CEO lacked any technical background. Given his history as a successful serial entrepreneur in non-tech business pursuits, he firmly believed that his prior achievements and experience practically guaranteed success in *any* future pursuit. He was confident that his business skills, intellect, and willpower were sufficient for any challenge. However, his tech startup failed because he persistently disregarded the advice and expertise of his technical team, choosing instead to develop strategies based on his intuition alone.

A common challenge in startups and tech companies is balancing business acumen and technical expertise in leadership. While a CEO's entrepreneurial success might be impressive, a lack of technical background can pose significant hurdles in navigating the complexities of a tech venture. Success in one domain doesn't always guarantee success in another, especially in highly specialized fields like technology.

Unsurprisingly, many successful tech leaders possess a solid engineering background, often complemented by an MBA. Even among Fortune 500 CEOs (of tech and non-tech companies), engineering has traditionally been the most prevalent undergraduate degree.[12]

While many experts suggest that CEOs must demonstrate expertise beyond operations and production, tech CEOs have proven that their grasp of technology is the most essential quality for success. STEM graduates are becoming some of the most successful and prosperous CEOs of technology companies.[13]

While 33% of S&P 500 CEOs hold undergraduate degrees in engineering, only 11% have degrees in business administration. Notably, 24 of the top 100 CEOs have engineering backgrounds. Engineers often excel as CEOs due to their systematic approach to problem-solving and the analytical skills honed during their education.

The following qualities highlight why engineers make exceptional leaders:

-   Attention to detail: Engineers are wired to pay attention to details. They understand the unique details of a problem and how they relate to the big picture.

-   Problem solvers: Engineers excel at deconstructing complex problems into their fundamental components, applying first principles to develop innovative and effective solutions. They also possess strong math, science, and analysis skills, which are valued in every business, whether the focus is on software, machines, bridges, or even non-technical pursuits.

- Networking: Engineers know and work with other engineers who "get it." Many are proficient at recruiting the exceptional talent required to perform complex tasks and innovate industry-leading products and solutions.

- Grasp of technology: In today's fast-paced global market, where technology touches almost everything, engineers are the people who design, build, and understand those technologies.

- Perseverance: Engineers routinely navigate complex challenges; perseverance is their superpower for overcoming obstacles and adversity. Building and leading great companies requires this same ability.[14]

Selecting the right leader to oversee a tech firm's engineering activities is essential. Success or failure hinges on their engineering prowess and innovative solutions. First and foremost, consider the requirements and expectations of your technical team carefully. You may already have team members with technical expertise who can handle certain aspects of the engineering leadership role. These individuals likely have a strong sense of ownership and valuable insights into the ideal candidate's skills and responsibilities. Consulting them for their opinions and insights can be invaluable.

Your ideal tech executive candidate should possess the following attributes:

- Ability to build and scale the engineering team while effectively managing various issues and activities related to customers, sales, finance, legal, and other cross-functional areas.

- Experience in leading tactical and strategic operations, with a keen understanding of the *big picture*. This combined ability enables the leader to develop compelling technology and product roadmaps.

- A track record of recruiting and managing cross-disciplinary teams and delivering compliant products or service releases on time, on performance, and with high quality and reliability.

- Experience in employing the necessary skills, behaviors, techniques, and maturity at each stage of a company's growth, from initial concept to volume production. Leading a team of 10 technologists at a startup substantially differs from leading hundreds at a large and established firm.

- Demonstrated breadth of experience spanning technology innovation and invention, new product introduction, volume manufacture, and end-of-life.

- Proven track record in developing a compelling intellectual property roadmap and patent strategy that aligns with the company's mission. This includes expertise in drafting and structuring patent claims, guiding patent attorneys, and establishing best practices in the laboratory for documenting and patenting inventions.

- Ability to collaborate effectively with other functional groups, including product and program management, go-to-market, policy, legal, HR, sourcing and procurement, and growth teams.

- Strong emotional intelligence and interpersonal skills, essential for building, developing, mentoring, and sustaining the technology team.

- Highly flexible and adaptable in thinking and behavior, able to deal with high levels of stress and ambiguity.

Technical founders often assume they're qualified to lead the engineering organization, but those assumptions can be unwarranted. Being a founder doesn't automatically qualify you as a leader; assigning yourself as the lead could harm your startup. It's important to bury your ego and prioritize what's best for your company. Avoid setting unreasonable expectations and follow a rigorous recruiting process to secure the best possible leadership candidate. If the technical founder emerges as the best candidate, then so be it, but don't cut corners for convenience.

Once the tech leader is selected and onboarded, focus on achieving quick wins to establish value early, build trust with the existing team, and cultivate a positive reputation. The new leader should allocate sufficient time to attend various executive and customer meetings and collaborate with their superior to develop a 30/60/90-day plan outlining achievable goals and metrics. This plan should be flexible and adaptable, allowing the leader to reinvent themself for the role and tailor their approach to the company's unique needs. Building a solid rapport with the engineering team and other cross-functional leads is essential, with active listening being the most critical behavior. Acting impulsively to demonstrate authority can backfire; showing respect and appreciation for the team's work and abilities is crucial. When a new leader is surrounded by more knowledgeable technologists, it creates opportunities for growth, collaboration, and mutual learning.[15]

It's not uncommon for the engineering VP to report to the CTO. Therefore, it's necessary to understand the distinct differences between these roles and ensure mutual support for success. Ambiguity in roles or responsibilities can ignite competition and divisiveness, ultimately harming the working dynamic. Clarifying expectations and promoting collaboration between the engineering lead and the CTO is essential for maintaining a productive and harmonious environment.

The VP of Engineering is primarily a people manager, blending engineering prowess with the ability to motivate and manage teams. In contrast, the CTO assumes a visionary role, shaping the organization's technological pursuits and staying abreast of market trends. While both are exceptional engineers who work together to drive the engineering culture, the CTO delves into technical intricacies, advancing the state of the art. At the same time, the VP focuses on team cohesion and strategic direction. The VP excels in management, team-building, recruiting, and issue mitigation, while the CTO embodies technical expertise, serving as the brand's technical face. The CTO is an architect, a thinker, a researcher, a tester, and a tinkerer. Given their distinct focuses, it's rare to find individuals excelling in both CTO and VPE roles.[16]

Technology leadership requires combining technical expertise, strategic vision, and interpersonal skills. It is essential to select these leaders carefully. They must align their technical skills with the company's needs while demonstrating strong communication and soft skills to motivate diverse teams. Successful tech leadership also hinges on skill matching, ensuring team roles align with individual strengths, and facilitating collaboration to drive innovation. Effective tech leaders create an environment where technology, people, and strategy align seamlessly to achieve shared goals.

> *Technology makes possibilities. Design makes solutions. Art makes questions. Leadership makes actions.* —John Maeda, American technologist, and designer.

CHAPTER 2

Mentoring and Coaching

A mentor is someone who sees more talent and ability within you than you see in yourself, and helps bring it out of you. —Bob Proctor, Canadian self-help author, and lecturer.

Mentoring is a powerful and transformative partnership built on sharing advice, expertise, and guidance that enriches long-term personal and professional growth. At its core, mentoring is more than providing answers—it involves empowering others to navigate challenges, seize opportunities, and develop their unique potential. Unlike coaches or bosses, mentors act as trusted advisors, focusing on holistic growth rather than performance metrics. While mentors may initially be colleagues, mentoring relationships often extend beyond specific work assignments, spanning years or even decades.

Mentors can provide many positive benefits. Through their mentees, they can influence virtually any aspect of a company's success. For example, mentors can improve how companies attract and retain employees. They can boost employee engagement, encourage healthy and productive risk-taking, create safe and inclusive work cultures and environments, enable robust succession planning and employee advancement, and inspire management and leadership development.

Mentorship is recognized as a critical leadership competency. It benefits the mentor by fueling personal growth and satisfaction as they contribute to the success of others. Mentoring often enhances the leadership capabilities of mentors themselves.[17]

Mentoring amplifies change, one relationship at a time. —
Unknown.

Research consistently shows that individuals with mentors tend to perform better, advance in their careers more quickly, and experience greater satisfaction with their work-life balance. However, despite the acknowledged impact of mentorship, over half of individuals lack such relationships in their working lives.[18] This gap often arises from reluctance or inertia. Some individuals may be unwilling or unable to seek mentors, while others may succumb to pride or arrogance. Additionally, many individuals become preoccupied with comparing their progress to others while failing to focus on their own growth and potential.

Mentoring and coaching are vital components of career development. They provide guidance, support, and inspiration to help individuals reach their full potential. By embracing mentorship and coaching, individuals and organizations can cultivate a more supportive, innovative, and resilient workforce.

We are all gifts to each other, and my own growth as a leader has shown me again and again that the most rewarding experiences come from my relationships. —Michael Dell, American businessman, innovator, and philanthropist.

Role Models

During our formative years, our parents, family members, neighbors, and teachers constitute a *village* of role models and mentors whose early influence can last a lifetime.

Role models were highly influential in my life. Growing up, my brother Bob and I saw our father only one day a month, leaving a noticeable absence in our lives. Thankfully, other influential male figures stepped in to fill that void. My oldest sister, Peggy, was in college when I attended elementary school. Her boyfriend, Jim, was adventurous, knowledgeable, and eager to share his passions with my brother and me. Jim's interest in science as a microbiology major sparked my curiosity as he introduced me to the wonders of microscopy and dissection. His gifts of surgical tools, preserved specimens, and a microscope fueled my fascination with biology and anatomy.

When they decided to build their own house, Bob and I spent many weekends helping them create the foundation, frame the walls and ceilings, and build the enormous fireplace in their living room. We also learned basic plumbing and wiring. While they benefited from our low-cost labor, we learned the nuts and bolts of home building, which has paid dividends over the years.

Mr. Sears, my neighbor and a retired airline pilot, was another influential role model. I spent countless hours in his garage, eagerly observing and helping as he worked on his cars and engaged in various mechanical projects. Under his guidance, I gained a comprehensive understanding of car systems and learned the basics of auto maintenance.

> *Everyone has dreams. Do what you can to help others achieve theirs.* —Stephen Schwarzman, American businessman, and investor.

My wife Elaine and I raised our children on a quiet cul-de-sac in Los Altos. Our neighborhood was tight-knit, and doors were always open. We looked out for one another. Children freely roamed between houses, playing and laughing, while parents socialized and offered mutual support. We organized occasional court parties and friendly cooking competitions with barbecues and games like ping-pong and badminton. Informal chats among neighbors were routine, and we collectively parented each other's children as we aspired to serve as positive role models.

While most mentors engage with their mentees personally, role models can serve as *virtual* mentors. We admire these luminaries and leaders close up and from a distance, learning from their actions and successes. Growing up, I found inspiration in figures like Willie Mays, Arnold Palmer, and Jack Nicklaus, aspiring to emulate their behaviors, attitudes, and values.

Professional role models demonstrate the traits and skills people strive to achieve in the workplace. They inspire others to perform better work, behave in ways that enable corporate success, and create supportive and nurturing cultures. Some common characteristics of influential role models include:

- Accountability: Role models accept responsibility for their actions and own their mistakes.

- Work ethic: Role models work hard to complete their tasks on time, on schedule, and on budget. They demonstrate a genuine eagerness to help others in every possible way.

- Positivity: Role models maintain a positive attitude even when the going gets tough. Their contagious positive attitude inspires others to display similar confidence and optimism.

- Persistence: Role models are experts in navigating adversity. They routinely overcome obstacles and inspire others to strive for excellence despite challenges.

- Integrity: Role models demonstrate honesty and integrity. They do the *right* things, even when nobody is watching. They lead by example and inspire others to uphold the same standards and values.

- Respect: Role models respect others in every situation. This creates a positive and respectful work environment.

Through their behavior and actions, role models improve morale, inspire healthy competition, motivate others, create a positive atmosphere, and communicate openly and transparently.[19] Great role models can fuel our learning and career advancement through their guidance, coaching, and encouragement. They can often provide access to challenging and stimulating work, and their networking can open doors to new opportunities that can shape our career trajectories.

Being a role model is the most powerful form of educating.
—John Wooden, American basketball coach and player.

Mentorship Impact

Mentors are available to offer guidance and counsel to individuals at all levels, regardless of their role or position. Even CEOs of industry-leading companies benefit from the wisdom and advice of experienced advisors.

There are many good reasons to seek out a mentor. The following list summarizes a few:

- Sounding board: Mentors offer qualified advice on work situations, challenges, worries, hopes, and insecurities. Ideally, mentors help mentees navigate challenges by sharing their experiences and offering valuable advice.

- Perspective: Great mentors offer valuable and unbiased advice, drawing from their viewpoints and experiences. Whether facing a new, complex problem or reinventing yourself, they provide a fresh, independent perspective that can be invaluable in tackling challenges effectively.

- Networking: Forging a deep relationship with a mentor offers the collateral benefit of the mentor's network. Whether seeking a career shift or a path to connect with others, a mentor's connections can be invaluable.[20]

- Skill development: Mentors help mentees refine existing skills and acquire new ones.

- Confidence building: Mentors encourage self-assurance through support and constructive feedback.

- Accountability: Mentors motivate mentees to stay consistently focused on critical goals and impactful progress.

- Inspiration: Mentors serve as role models, inspiring growth, ambition, and impact.

Successful leaders, including CEOs, benefit from mentors who offer wisdom and honest feedback, even at the highest rung of the corporate ladder. Executive mentors provide advice on running companies, building relationships, and transforming organizations. They also offer guidance on servant leadership, emphasizing the importance of empowering others to achieve corporate objectives by prioritizing their needs and inspiring their best efforts. Executive mentors should be chosen carefully to ensure they possess impeccable ethics, unwavering integrity, and other essential foundational traits.[21]

You have to reach back and lift up other folks who will one day step into your shoes. —Michelle Obama, American attorney, author, and first lady of the United States.

When I first joined Ford Aerospace as a newly minted antenna engineer, I was quickly befriended by a senior scientist within the antenna directorate, Terry Smith. Terry, known for his innovative brilliance and creativity, guided me through my challenging projects, providing growth opportunities and visibility within the organization. He offered steady support without being overbearing and was always available when needed. Terry's approachability, humor, and non-judgmental demeanor made him the perfect mentor. In difficult situations with customers, Terry defended me, and during yearly reviews, he provided glowing feedback on my performance and accomplishments. He was my advocate, cheerleader, and technical advisor.

As I ventured into consulting, I often sought Terry's technical advice. When I co-founded Endgate, Terry was among the first consultants we brought on board. After several other startups, I once again sought Terry's expertise. He gladly provided an internal referral to Space Systems Loral (formerly Ford Aerospace), which provided me with a path back to the satellite industry.

Mentors can have a remarkable and unpredictable impact on one's career and life. Their value cannot be overstated.

A mentor is someone who allows you to see the hope inside yourself. —Oprah Winfrey, American talk show host, television producer, actress, author, and media proprietor.

Attracting a Mentor

While you may actively seek out and engage potential mentors, the truth is that *you* don't choose your mentors—*they* choose you. Mentors are drawn to individuals who demonstrate exceptional effort, commitment, and passion in their work. When mentors observe something special in you, they see the value in donating their time and energy to support your career growth.

As you perform at your highest level, you hope to attract the attention of influential mentors who will take a personal interest in your success. Once a mentor begins to support you, it's crucial to prioritize their guidance and strive to make *them* successful to the best of your ability. This reciprocal relationship is what makes mentorship genuinely effective and rewarding.[22]

> *When the student is ready, the teacher will appear.* —Buddha, Indian religious teacher, ascetic, and founder of Buddhism.

When seeking a mentor, it's important to clarify the support you need—short-term guidance or a long-term relationship. Determine if you're seeking a mentor, career coach, sponsor, recruiter, or someone to establish connections for you. Once you've identified the type of mentor you need, carefully search for someone you respect, trust, and can relate to. Not every leader or specialist is necessarily an effective or willing mentor.

When approaching a potential mentor, take the time to develop a genuine connection before making your support request. Avoid putting them on the spot initially—offer them an easy out in case they're uninterested or unavailable. For instance, phrase your request: "I completely understand if you don't have time, but could you please...?" Remember that just because you have challenges doesn't mean a mentor is obligated to help. Conversely, don't expect to absorb advice from a mentor through proximity alone; explicitly engage them and request their mentorship.

When your mentor provides advice, take it seriously and act on it if you agree. Failing to do so can be discouraging for both parties. Show enthusiasm and appreciation for their insights and acknowledge their valuable time. Respect their support by being prepared, efficient, and responsive during meetings or discussions. Take an active role by offering suggestions, insights, and proposed solutions rather than passively listening to their advice.[23]

Sometimes, engaging multiple mentors is necessary to achieve your objectives. Each mentor can offer unique insights and support, depending on your needs. For instance, if you seek expertise in a specific field, find a mentor who is a master in that domain. For advocacy and networking, locate a mentor who connects and champions causes. A peer mentor can be helpful if you require guidance on project management or navigating organizational dynamics. If you are looking for psychological support and help in confidence-building, secure a mentor who can serve as a trusted sounding board, even if they are external to your workplace.[24]

While mentors can be invaluable, not all advice is helpful, meaningful, or correct. Some mentors may waste your time or even steal your ideas for their own benefit. Mark Cuban and other successful leaders argue that relying too heavily on mentors can hinder progress, as others cannot always be trusted to provide the correct answers or constructive advice. Ultimately, you are responsible for doing the groundwork and heavy lifting before seeking mentors to enhance your journey.[25]

Listen to your inner voice when receiving advice. Regardless of the mentor's credentials or experience, don't accept advice unquestioningly. When necessary, respectfully challenge their perspectives to identify errors or inconsistencies. Maintain your self-reliance and avoid becoming overly dependent on the wisdom or advice of others. Trust your instincts and judgment to guide you in evaluating and integrating advice into your decision-making process.

Mentoring, whether giving or receiving, is not a spectator sport. Monitor your mentor's responsiveness and value, and act swiftly to disengage if your expectations aren't being met.

> *The delicate balance of mentoring someone is not creating them in your own image, but giving them the opportunity to create themselves.* —Steven Spielberg, American director, writer, and producer.

Joy of Mentoring

Mentoring is one of the most rewarding experiences in both personal and professional life. It's a chance to guide, inspire, and empower others while nurturing meaningful connections. Beyond imparting knowledge, mentoring creates a ripple effect of growth, fulfillment, and shared success, reminding us of the joy of helping others reach their full potential.

> *Most people think of management as getting work done through people, but the best of managers develop people through work.* —Unknown.

For most, mentoring provides the following benefits that make the endeavor personally rewarding and worthwhile:

- Paying it forward: Mentoring is an excellent way to energize your karma and experience a sense of satisfaction, accomplishment, and pride that's hard to match. Observing how your influence continues to yield dividends through the people you mentor and seeing them mentor others creates deep and lasting personal gratification.

- Helping others succeed: Guiding and advising others without expecting anything in return provides a sense of fulfillment and purpose. It also embodies the essence of selflessness. Witnessing their eventual success can be a source of pride.

- Self-reflection: Mentoring others compels you to delve into topics you may not have considered otherwise. This self-reflection cultivates personal growth as you aid others in their development.[26]

- Personal growth: Mentoring helps mentors refine their communication, leadership, and interpersonal skills while gaining fresh perspectives from mentees.

- Professional development: Mentoring often strengthens a mentor's reputation as a leader, coach, and trusted advisor.

Managers mentor their employees by empowering them to think and act independently. Rather than micromanaging, they offer flexible assignments and encourage workers to devise solutions based on their strengths and abilities. This approach cultivates a sense of ownership and promotes self-motivation among employees. By granting freedom and minimizing oversight, effective managers inspire creativity and pride in the work produced by their subordinates.

> *CFO asks CEO: 'What happens if we invest in developing our people and then they leave us?' CEO: 'What happens if we don't, and they stay?'* —Peter Baeklund, strategic leadership consultant.

Exceptional mentors prioritize honing their own listening skills. Instead of providing solutions, they guide through questioning, encouraging mentees to think independently. Mentors promote critical thinking and self-reliance by challenging mentees to solve problems themselves while offering supportive guidance.

In my mentoring sessions, I ask probing questions. Regardless of the issue, I encourage thorough consideration of pros, cons, risks, opportunities, alternatives, and consequences. By asking "why," I push mentees to think deeply and critically about their challenges. Once they reach their decision or conclusion, I provide support and encouragement while requesting periodic updates to stay informed and involved. Maintaining availability and approachability ensures that mentees feel comfortable seeking guidance whenever necessary.[27]

Helping mentees evolve in their strategic thinking and problem-solving approaches is gratifying. Initially, mentoring can require significant energy and attention, but support gradually transitions into periodic check-ins or tune-ups. Even in retirement, I receive occasional calls from former employees or colleagues seeking advice on new challenges. However, these interactions are usually topical or reinforcing, which provides a source of validation that boosts their self-confidence.

The mediocre mentor tells. The good mentor explains. The superior mentor demonstrates. The greatest mentors inspire! —Lucia Ballas Traynor, Hispanic media executive, consultant, and entrepreneur.

Mentoring Responsibilities

Effective mentoring typically involves more than just casual or ad hoc interactions. While some mentors may prefer informal relationships, adding a bit of structure and defining responsibilities can enhance engagement. Here's an abbreviated list outlining the primary responsibilities of the mentor and the mentee:

Mentor:

- Accept and acknowledge that the mentee might initially be bashful, embarrassed, or apprehensive.

- Listen to the mentee's needs and expectations.

- Offer candid feedback and guidance to bolster their success and advance their career development—act as a devil's advocate and truth-teller, delivering the necessary feedback to help them progress. Encourage mentees to embrace calculated risks while considering the potential consequences of their decisions.

- Work with the mentee to develop realistic and achievable goals.

- Take a genuine interest in your mentee as a person. Understand that you will act as your mentee's role model, champion, cheerleader, and coach.

- Follow through on your commitments.

- Offer suggestions, feedback, and advice, but don't try to solve the mentee's problems for them.

- Refrain from molding the mentee into a version of yourself.

- Help facilitate self-reflection and self-development.

- Share some previous personal mistakes or failures and how you learned and grew from them. This demonstrates vulnerability and authenticity, which builds trust and helps mentees understand that growth often comes from overcoming setbacks.

- Celebrate your mentee's milestones and successes.

Mentee:

-   Understand your career goals, list the biggest obstacles to achieving them, and allow that to inform the type of mentor you should seek.

-   Search for mentors across your network. Candidates might first say no, but don't be shy about making big requests—you'll never get what you want if you don't ask for it.

-   Make your request, but take it slow. Ask questions to determine whether there is alignment and a willingness to engage. Face-to-face discussions are best.

-   Discuss your needs and expectations with your prospective mentor and understand their objectives for the relationship. During the conversation, focus on getting to know the mentor and encourage them to share their insights.

-   Start by requesting a small favor and express your gratitude. Strive to make it convenient for your mentor to offer the support you need and avoid becoming a burden on them.

-   Prepare for every session with your mentor.

-   Take an active role in your learning and help drive the process.

-   Be receptive to suggestions and feedback.

-   Respect the mentor's time, and arrive promptly for all sessions.

-   Follow through on commitments and take informed risks as you try new options and behaviors to support your career and development goals.

Mentee and Mentor (shared):

-   Respect confidences and trust each other.

-   Maintain a professional demeanor at all times.

- Resolve a mutually agreeable commitment and engagement process, including items such as where, when, and how often discussions will occur, whether in person or virtually, confidentiality, etc.

- Discuss and resolve mutual goals and accountability. How will each party be held accountable, and what do they want from the experience?

- Discover common ground and respect each other's differences.

- Be yourself, and be flexible. Don't forget to have fun and enjoy the experience.[28]

The roles and responsibilities of mentors and mentees are pivotal in cultivating a productive mentoring relationship. A balanced partnership ensures mutual development and the achievement of shared goals.

A mentor is not someone who walks ahead of you to show you how they did it. A mentor walks alongside you to show you what you can do. —Simon Sinek, British-American author, and inspirational speaker.

CHAPTER 3

Consulting and Partnerships

Difficulties mastered are opportunities won. —Winston Churchill, British Prime Minister, statesman, orator, and author.

Consulting can be an excellent career or an enriching supplement to your day job. It can be a great source of income, enable you to work on genuinely inspiring jobs, and provide you with the freedom to run and control your career.

Being your own boss can be enticing, especially if you're unsatisfied with your current job. Consulting offers control and flexibility, allowing you to set your work hours and choose your work. It can also be financially and professionally rewarding. Beyond these benefits, consulting can be a path to self-improvement. Many of us find ourselves caught in the corporate grind, working to enrich others while sacrificing time that could be applied to pursue our aspirations. Interestingly, statistics show that over 75% of consultants reach their previous income levels within two years of launching their consulting careers.

Consulting presents challenges that push you to operate and perform in new and exciting ways. For instance, you'll have the opportunity to sharpen your sales and marketing skills. Seeking diverse work assignments will require exploring new information and concepts and expanding your knowledge and skills. Networking and customer relations will be just as vital as your technical abilities. Consulting teaches self-reliance; as you overcome your deficiencies, your confidence will grow and drive further success.

> *Happiness lies not in the mere possession of money. It lies in the joy of achievement, in the thrill of creative effort.* — Franklin D. Roosevelt, politician, banker, attorney, and 32nd president of the United States.

Building a solid customer base that generates reliable income can take time. A strong network and recognized expertise can expedite this process. If you lack these advantages, consider saving reserves to cover lean periods or consulting part-time while maintaining your regular job.

> *You don't have to be great to get started, but you have to get started to be great.* —Unknown.

Part-Time Consulting

Consulting part-time offers a risk-averse approach to exploring this potential career path while maintaining income from your regular job. It allows gradual exposure to the consultant's life and helps you determine if you have the necessary skills and connections to succeed.

Statistics show that 65% of consultants began their consulting business while still employed, while 35% launched their consulting pursuit after quitting their jobs. Coaching or mentoring is common among consultants, with over 90% doing so to prepare for their new careers. Additionally, more than 50% of consultants secured their first client from a former employer, highlighting the value of existing and prior connections.[29]

If you're considering consulting part-time, you must avoid conflicts of interest with your current employer. Carefully review your existing employment contracts, including NDAs and non-compete agreements. Ideally, discuss your consulting intentions with your employer beforehand to seek approval. While many employers may not be keen on their employees consulting part-time, some may grant limited approvals, allowing you to proceed without the specter of secrecy.

Great leaders tend to be fair and open-minded when assessing whether to allow their employees to consult part-time, as long as they don't pose risks to their company's interests. They understand that consulting can be a valuable learning opportunity and skill-building experience that can ultimately benefit their organization. However, some managers may outright reject your request.

Proceed cautiously when asked to execute an NDA with a consulting client. Some NDAs can be overly restrictive, so it's often wise to consider engaging a lawyer to review and revise NDAs before signing them. Investing in legal guidance upfront can save you from potential complications downstream. If you can't find a reasonable compromise on the NDA, walk away. Remember, nothing is worth jeopardizing your ethics or integrity or encumbering other current or future engagements.

Avoid utilizing your current employer's equipment, supplies, or facilities in your consulting work unless approved. Likewise, you must refrain from consulting during your employer's regular working hours—your consulting work cannot impact your primary job, and you must avoid even the slightest perception of conflict of interest as a consultant.

While consulting offers you the freedom to pursue your passion and can be a lucrative source of income, it also adds to your workload as a parallel pursuit, which can lead to burnout. Care should be taken to continuously monitor your stress level to ensure a sustainable and healthy lifestyle.

I began my part-time antenna engineering consultancy while working at ARGOSystems, with the approval of my boss, Phil Metzen. Within a few short years, I built a thriving side business based on a diverse clientele. My engagements allowed me to apply my expertise to various market spaces outside ARGOS' purview, including GPS-based surveying, aircraft collision avoidance, spacecraft antennas, and cellular communications. However, when combined with my ARGOSystems commitments and concurrent graduate studies, my heightened stress level eventually led to health issues, forcing me to deal with the effects of burnout.

Once I reduced my school work, I found that I could sustain my part-time consulting, which provided financial security as I ventured into risky startups. Looking back, consulting played a deeply impactful role throughout my career. It expanded my knowledge, skills, and confidence, broadened my professional network, and led me to employment opportunities that would not have materialized otherwise.

Discipline is choosing between what you want now, and what you want most. —Abraham Lincoln, statesman, lawyer, and 16th president of the United States.

Full-Time Consulting

Before you leap into full-time consulting, make sure you can pay your bills until your practice reaches its stride. Be conservative in your planning, and remember that you'll no longer be able to enjoy employee perks such as employer-funded health insurance. You'll also need to procure whatever supplies and equipment required to perform your activities. Careful planning will ease the transition and mitigate potential financial challenges as you start your consulting career.

Initially, it's helpful to prioritize attracting new clients by treating your consulting business as a marketing endeavor. Develop your marketing and sales skills to attract paying clients confidently. While modesty and humility are admirable traits, they may not be advantageous in your client search or when setting your initial billing rate. Ensure your pricing is fair and reasonable, and avoid undercutting or inflating your rates. Aim to provide exceptional service at a reasonable price to establish trust and value with your clients.[30]

You might find opportunities to attract your first few clients through pro bono work, where you can convince them of your abilities by offering some upfront work for free. This is a reasonable early strategy, but avoid falling into the trap of continuously providing it. Your goal should be to seek fair compensation for your valuable offering.[31]

As a skilled consultant, your knowledge and expertise enable you to efficiently perform critical tasks that your customers value. It's essential to price your consulting efforts appropriately. Depending on the project, consider quoting a project deliverable with intermediate milestone progress payments instead of opting for an hourly engagement. This approach makes sense when you're confident in the scope of effort, and the fixed-price structure reduces risk for the customer. However, an hourly engagement may be less risky for the consultant and more suitable for long-term projects involving experimentation or iterations with unpredictable durations. Choose the payment structure that aligns best with the project's scope and demands, while compensating your expertise fairly.

Full-time consulting offers professionals the autonomy to shape their careers, the flexibility to work on diverse projects, and the opportunity to expand their expertise across industries. It also allows individuals to leverage their skills, pursue their passions, and achieve personal fulfillment and professional success in a dynamic and competitive marketplace.

A consultant is only as good as their last project. —Jon Taffer, American entrepreneur, and television personality.

Marketing Yourself

The best advice I ever received was to underpromise and overperform. Your goal as a consultant—or an employee, for that matter—is to exceed your customers' expectations every time. Repeat business and positive referrals are your path to independence. It takes time to develop a positive reputation and build customer trust, which you'll earn through consistently exceptional performance.

Remember, your clients must advocate for you when seeking internal funding for your services. A successful track record makes it easier for them to secure approvals. Rather than being seen as a risky or unfamiliar contractor, your clients can showcase your credentials through your work history and testimonials from previous clients. Building a solid reputation and track record enhances your client's ability to secure approval for your services.

While working on your existing projects, look for potential growth paths. These follow-on projects can expand your working engagements and provide continuity of funding. Take advantage of every opportunity to discuss possible next steps with your customers, further growing your value.

When you've concluded a project, remember to ask for a letter of recommendation or referrals to other possible clients. Referrals are the lifeblood of a consultant; cold-calling can be a long haul, but referrals put you directly in front of people who value your expertise. When you stay connected with past clients, you'll keep a pulse on their active and planned activities. Remaining front and center will remind them that you're interested in their pursuits and are willing to support them continuously.

Your prior employers are likewise potential clients. If you leave each employer on a positive note, you'll be welcomed back when they need your consulting expertise.

Marketing yourself as a consultant is essential for attracting clients, showcasing expertise, and staying competitive. By strategically defining your unique value proposition, utilizing effective communication channels, and consistently demonstrating thought leadership, you'll build your reputation, expand your client base, and achieve long-term success in your consulting endeavors.

Building Your Reputation

When building your reputation, leverage every opportunity to showcase your achievements as a consultant. Write articles, start a blog, or send outreach emails. Consider becoming a subject matter expert in court cases and presenting papers at conferences. Networking is critical—make connections and maintain them. Keep in touch with past clients to show you care about them personally and professionally.

Offer free support or advice to demonstrate that your willingness to support your clients transcends profit-taking.

When publishing or otherwise highlighting your consulting work, always seek prior permission from your client. For example, uploading images of your consulting project to your website may violate your signed NDA and breach your customer's trust.

Consider collaborating with your client on articles or papers. For example, I hired a consultant who regularly published our significant work. I often joined him in these pursuits, which proved mutually beneficial, highlighting his expertise and our company's capabilities. Presenting papers at symposiums expanded our network, leading to new opportunities with experts who eventually became consultants or clients.

As a client, I regularly offered recommendations and testimonials to ensure that each project provided compelling benefits to our consultants beyond compensation. I also showcased their contributions to leadership during project reviews and demonstrations. When consultants are rewarded by their clients in ways that further enhance their reputation, they're more likely to devote their valuable time to supporting *your* efforts rather than those of your competitors.

Reputation-building is vital for consultants, as it enhances credibility and trust, opens doors to new opportunities, and strengthens client relationships. Consultants can solidify their reputation as trusted advisors and leaders by consistently delivering high-quality work, demonstrating valuable expertise, and cultivating positive relationships within their professional networks.

> *If people like you, they'll listen to you. But if they trust you, they'll do business with you.* —Zig Ziglar, American author, salesman, and motivational speaker.

Respecting the Craft

Consultants can be worth their weight in gold or a waste of time, energy, and money. In the worst case, they can lead their clients down expensive rabbit holes. However, if chosen carefully, the best consultants can be game-changers.

As with any profession, some consultants are inept, incompetent, or imposters pretending to be skilled experts. Fraudsters exist everywhere, so research and interview your consultants as you would any other employment candidate.

Exceptional consultants typically demonstrate the following behaviors:

-   They care less about billing and more about providing extraordinary value.

-   They engage in ways that prioritize long-term customer impact and satisfaction over short-term personal gain.

-   When they need to research new concepts or learn new skills to perform on a project, they do so on their own time.

Consultants who fail to perform typically exhibit one or more of the following behaviors:

-   They complicate even the simplest of tasks, whether outwardly or surreptitiously, to prolong an engagement for greater pay.

-   They use technobabble, acronyms, and a complicated vocabulary to impress or exaggerate their knowledge, intellect, or expertise.

- They appear incapable of simplifying complex concepts. If they can't explain something in a way anyone can understand, they may not understand it as well as they think.

- They fail to commit to milestones and end dates, preferring to keep engagements open-ended and flexible. This implies a lack of commitment or accountability.

- They fail to communicate progress or work details promptly and transparently.

- They fail to provide honest judgments, assessments, or opinions by choosing instead to appease, ingratiate, or flatter.

- They exude arrogance or superiority. They may also annoy, ignore, or upset employees during their engagement.

- They bill for hours expended on learning knowledge or skills they should have already possessed.

- They fail to exhibit the skills or abilities for which they were hired.

- They refuse to offer advice or expertise, except when doing so results in billable hours.

Every consultant should realize that their conduct, demeanor, and proficiency reflect on their profession. It's crucial that you excel and consistently maintain a positive reputation. If you cannot meet or surpass expectations, refrain from charging for your services. Acknowledging limitations is more honorable than pretending competence. Understand your boundaries and operate within them to uphold professional integrity and trustworthiness.

> *Be generous with your knowledge. Clients return to the richest wells first, when they're thirsty for help.* —David A. Fields, American author, speaker, and consultant.

Consultant Management

While consultants can force-multiply your team's efforts substantially, they must be managed and led to maximize their impact while protecting your company's interests. The following is a list of essential management guidelines to consider:

- NDAs: Ensure your contract documents, especially NDAs, are reasonable. Overly restrictive agreements can deter potential consultants and lead to lengthy negotiations. Strive for fairness to cultivate positive relationships and streamline the engagement process.

- Balance: Consultants value guidance, but excessive micromanagement strains the relationship and hampers their contribution.

- Shared success: Every decision should prioritize mutual benefit, with both parties supporting each other throughout the consulting engagement. If the relationship becomes overly one-sided, both parties stand to lose.

- Goals: Consultants work best when their goals and objectives are clearly defined and communicated. For best results, follow the standard SMART goal approach (specific, measurable, achievable, relevant, and time-based).

- Roles and responsibilities: Discuss and clarify the consultant's role and ensure everyone on the team understands why the consultant has been hired. Provide the consultant with all relevant information and documents necessary to perform their job effectively, including mission and value statements, specifications, and other pertinent materials.

- Collaboration: While consultants can and do operate somewhat independently, the best consultant engagements occur when they're embedded within and regularly collaborating with the team, thus directly complementing their skills and abilities.

- Context: Provide your consultant with essential context, such as what they'll work on, its strategic importance, alignment with organizational objectives, established priorities, etc.

- Onboarding: Ensure the consultant has everything they need to deliver maximal impact. Introduce them to team members, provide equipment or access to labs, set expectations on work hours, clarify communication methods, etc.

- Feedback: Consultants require performance feedback to understand what they're doing well and what they need to improve.

- Control: Prevent scope creep to avoid incurring additional costs. Consultants aim to exceed expectations, but effective managers ensure that desired services are delivered within budget constraints.[32]

Effective management of consultants involves communicating expectations, maintaining regular feedback loops, and promoting a collaborative environment where both parties can leverage expertise for mutual benefit. By establishing transparent project goals, maintaining open lines of communication, and providing necessary support, organizations can maximize consultants' contributions, leading to successful project outcomes and strengthened partnerships.

Navigating Partnerships

A successful partnership can lead to a dynamic and fulfilling career. Collaborations often yield outcomes greater than individual efforts while nurturing cooperation and synergy. Partnering can also enhance relationships as individuals unite to pursue shared goals and passions.

Opportunities increase when you help others win. A little win for a partner is a little win for you. —Unknown.

Despite the best intentions, the world is littered with partnerships that failed for various reasons. A recent study found that 20% of small businesses typically fail in the first year, 30% by the second year, and 50% by the fifth year. Whether or not a business succeeds, friction between partners is almost inevitable. Partners may second-guess each other, argue, nitpick, or panic when the going gets tough. Partnerships can fail due to poor management, a lack of financial security, bad exit planning, misaligned values, ethics, or objectives, or even personal or family issues. As a business grows, the decisions become more complex and significant, placing greater pressure on the partners. While one may prioritize steady income and stability, the other may be more inclined towards risk-taking and business expansion. This discrepancy in strategy or objective can strain the partnership dynamic, leading to potential conflicts and challenges in decision-making.

A shared vision is vital in partnerships. Yet, many partners start their ventures without discussing long-term aspirations. When these discussions arise later, the business may face critical decisions where divergent visions threaten success. Without effective communication, minor disagreements can escalate. Transparency and open communication are essential values for partners to maintain a healthy partnership.[33]

> To build a successful partnership it needs to be mutually beneficial and closely managed with an emphasis on growing trust. —Unknown.

The following suggestions may help you to avoid partnership failure:

- Make it personal: Get to know the person behind the partner. What drives them? Why are they interested in partnering? What inspires them? What are their strengths and weaknesses? What are their personality traits, and how will those translate into business? Do you respect their opinions, ethics, and values?

- Avoid arguments: If disagreements persist, seek ways to resolve them without escalating into arguments. If necessary, step back or involve a neutral mediator to facilitate a resolution. Chronic arguing may indicate deeper issues.

- Me vs. you: It is easy to succumb to tunnel vision while losing sight of the bigger picture. When this happens, it may help to step back and climb out of the weeds. Consider what a neutral third party might say to inform your next step or possible resolution.

- Be creative: There's always another way to solve a problem. Don't get stuck on a singular solution, especially if the outcome is biased toward one partner. Figure out what you care *less* about, and go from there. Focus on fairness, which should be the overarching goal of any partnership.

- Relationship: Reflect on your initial reasons for partnering. If your feelings toward them have changed significantly and you no longer enjoy their company, it might be a sign that the partnership has reached its natural end.

- Common objectives: Partnerships thrive on shared objectives. Misaligned goals can lead to conflict and difficulty in making crucial decisions. Before entering into a partnership, ensure that you and your partner share similar objectives to avoid potential challenges downstream.

- Sequencing: Before diving into work or sharing your intellectual property, ensure your partnership contract is finalized and signed. Remember, it's okay to withdraw from a partnership if necessary—don't feel obligated to continue based on prior efforts.

- Contract: Invest the necessary resources to create a thorough, legally binding contract that addresses voting rights, valuation in buy-out scenarios, and unexpected circumstances like death. Consider various end states and negotiate in good faith. Ironing out these details beforehand is essential to avoid contentious negotiations during turbulent times.

- Business plan: Develop a detailed business plan and discuss your assumptions for success. Throughout this process, you will learn about your values, motives, and aspirations, which can facilitate partner alignment.

- Roles and responsibilities: Establishing clear roles and responsibilities among partners is essential for maximizing individual impact and avoiding redundancy. Identify any blind spots and determine how to address them effectively. Plan for growth opportunities to keep each partner engaged and motivated in the venture's success.

- Plan for changes: Business is never static, and the unexpected will often occur. Invest in nurturing a relationship that thrives during times of uncertainty and ambiguity. Successfully navigating difficult situations can become a partnership superpower, creating a competitive advantage for the business.

- Mediate: Work with a mediator to help resolve conflicts and settle disputes. The courtroom should be your last resort.

- Be kind: If you decide to dissolve your partnership, prioritize ending things amicably. Remember that maintaining friendships is more valuable than money. Avoid getting entangled in arguments and prioritizing winning minor battles. Emotions and biases can cloud judgment, leading to regrettable endings.

Strategic alliances and collaborative relationships, built on mutual trust, shared goals, and effective communication, can drive individual and organizational success. Enduring partnerships enhance career growth and professional fulfillment through practical strategies and proven methods.

You get what you give. —Unknown.

CHAPTER 4

Entrepreneurship

Great companies start because the founders want to change the world, not make a fast buck. —Guy Kawasaki, American marketing specialist, corporate evangelist, author, podcaster, and venture capitalist.

I'll never forget the saying, "Starting a company is like jumping off a cliff and building an airplane on the way down." For a corporate founder, success often demands everything you've got and feels just out of reach for extended periods.

Successful founders possess an abundance of courage, perseverance, and optimism. They tend to cultivate a mindset that views setbacks as opportunities for growth. Difficulty is reframed as a challenge, and failures are simply examples of *not yet*. Entrepreneurs also demonstrate ingenuity, exceptional creativity, and a thirst for risk. It's worthwhile to consider whether your skills, penchant for risk, and mindset align with the role of an entrepreneur.

If you're contemplating launching a new venture, you'll need the support and unique skills of others to build that *airplane*. You'll also need great agility to do things quickly, react, and adapt to rapid change. Founders succeed when they remain calm under intense pressure while treating the breathtaking plunge into entrepreneurship as exhilarating. Everyone is in it together, so we win or lose as a team.

The stakes of building a startup quickly are high, as slow-moving startups often fail. Entrepreneurs must wear many hats to succeed, but their greatest strength lies in their ability to identify and accomplish both immediate and long-term needs while swiftly and continuously refining their approach as necessary.[34]

> *I don't think that it's happenstance that people become successful. I think it's very intended, and you work toward that goal with every inch of your mind and body. The smartest thing you can invest in is yourself.* —Barbara Corcoran, American businesswoman, investor, syndicated columnist, and television personality.

Entrepreneurship is usually associated with founding a company. However, its true meaning is far broader. One can be an entrepreneur or an *intrapreneur* within an already existing company. An artist can be an entrepreneur without ever starting a company.

Tim Denning defines entrepreneurship as 'starting something from scratch and adopting a way of life that combines a novel idea with the necessary action to produce true innovation.' Many people come up with great ideas, and that's where it ends. Entrepreneurs, on the other hand, find opportunities to do new things, or the same things but in an improved or novel way. They take charge, execute, innovate, and inspire others through initiative and creativity. They routinely solve large and complex problems. Instead of *dreaming* about doing something, entrepreneurs *do* it![35]

> *In order to become the 1%, you must do what the other 99% won't.* —Unknown.

Launching your own company can be the thrill of a lifetime. It's an opportunity to chase a dream and experience incredible fulfillment while growing in ways that often exceed one's imagination. Startups provide a chance to be a *shit disturber*, to have some fun, to get into some trouble, and to be a disrupter when you feel like it. It's a way to make magic happen.[36]

However, for first-time founders, a dose of reality is advisable. An unsuccessful business pursuit can be emotionally draining and financially ruinous. Startup endeavors can be all-consuming, occupying thoughts from morning to night. They can demand late nights, weekend work, constant networking and nurturing of client relationships, and frequent travel.

Recent studies reveal that 49% of entrepreneurs face some form of mental health issue, with nearly a third reporting depression. Founders often experience higher stress levels due to their company's challenges, financial pressures, and investor expectations. These stressors can spill over into personal life, leading to higher rates of divorce and social isolation. Founding a company requires resilience and mental fortitude.[37]

> *As a startup CEO, I slept like a baby. I woke up every 2 hours and cried.* —Ben Horowitz, American businessman, investor, blogger, author, and technology entrepreneur.

As an entrepreneur, you should resist the temptation to listen to naysayers or succumb to stereotypes. For instance, many successful startups prove that a college degree is not a prerequisite for entrepreneurial success. Similarly, while an MBA can be beneficial in *managing* a business, it doesn't guarantee success in *starting* one. The most valuable lessons in entrepreneurship come from hands-on experience. It's never too late to pursue a dream, try something different, or begin anew. Refuse to let others limit your aspirations, and don't become paralyzed by the fear of failure.

Entrepreneur is not a job title. It is a state of mind of people who want to alter the future. —Guy Kawasaki.

Realism and Optimism

Before embarking on a new venture, consider the stark realities of startup success. The majority of startups either fail or struggle to survive. The National Association of Small Business' 2017 Economic Report indicates that statistically, only 56% of all U.S. startups make it past their fourth year in business. These figures underscore the importance of pausing and carefully evaluating whether you're adequately prepared for the challenges ahead.[38]

Studies on business unicorns (billion-dollar startups) reveal interesting insights. The number of co-founders isn't significantly correlated with startup success. Additionally, most unicorn founders lack prior experience in the startup's specific industry, and many face intense competition from established incumbents. However, the standout trait among billion-dollar startup founders is their history of entrepreneurship. Those who previously created ventures that generated value, even if deemed failures by VC standards, are more likely to launch successful subsequent companies. This suggests that VCs should encourage and fund serial founders to pursue follow-on startups, even after initial failures.[39]

Startups can disrupt even the most peaceful life. Startup success demands exceptional teams, strategy, and execution, but even then, success is not guaranteed. Additionally, "black swan" events, which represent unpredictable and highly improbable occurrences, can suddenly disrupt a thriving company, jeopardizing its gains and even its existence.

For those skeptical about the impact of black swan events, consider the several significant occurrences over the past century. For example, the dot-com bust significantly affected my first venture, resulting in my first layoff. Conversely, another black swan event, the 9/11 attacks, spurred the need, conditions, and urgency that led to my third startup venture (SafeView), where we innovated the full-body scanners that are easily identified at airport security checkpoints worldwide.

Another black swan event—the COVID-19 pandemic—devastated numerous startups, forcing many to close. During periods of rapid change and uncertainty, startup founders face difficult decisions, incomplete information, and challenges beyond their control, which critically test a leader's resilience and determination.

Don't be misled into thinking that entrepreneurship is exclusively for the young. Recent data reveals that in 2021, individuals aged 55-64 constituted 23% of new entrepreneurs in the U.S. This demographic has driven the most business startup activity globally over the past decade. Increasingly, people and investors recognize that new businesses founded by older, seasoned industry professionals, in collaboration with energetic young entrepreneurs, create a dynamic and impactful partnership.[40]

Business success is rarely achieved through shortcuts. It demands time, commitment, dedication, and resilience. Success comes from building trust and reputation and relying upon a customer base that evolves one client at a time.

Customers often hesitate to switch to new suppliers when they already have established ones. The timing of product introduction and the technology offered can significantly impact success. Even startups with exceptional offerings can falter if their technology is perceived as too early or too advanced. Many customers prefer proven, reliable technology at a reasonable cost, leveraging existing economies of scale.[41]

> *Running a startup is like being punched in the face repeatedly. But working for a large company is like being waterboarded.* —Paul Graham, English-born American computer scientist, essayist, entrepreneur, venture capitalist, and author.

Exhilaration and Opportunity

Reflecting on my own entrepreneurial journey, the time spent building and working at startup companies remains among my life's most enjoyable, stimulating, and rewarding work experiences. The impact and benefits derived from the startup environment are numerous and invaluable. Personally, starting a company was not a predetermined path but a natural progression from my early consulting endeavors.

> *The most noble thing you can do in your life, in my opinion, is to start a business and quit your job.* —Kevin O'Leary, Canadian businessman, investor, journalist, and television personality.

If pressed to recall the most exhilarating moment of my career, it was the day we took Endwave public on October 16, 2000. We gathered around our engineering bullpen, staring at a large wall monitor where our Nasdaq symbol (ENWV) was proudly displayed. The price per share was static, fixed at $14/share (our initial offering price). Electricity was in the air as we eagerly anticipated our CEO ringing the Nasdaq Stock Market opening bell, which would initiate the first public trading of ownership shares in the company I had co-founded roughly ten years earlier.

Doug Lockie, our founding partner, seemed to hover above the carpeted floor, his excitement palpable as we waited for the bell to ring. Always the optimistic and energetic corporate evangelist, Doug had poured his passion and expertise, cultivated across multiple startups, into reaching this pivotal moment. Transacting an IPO was a significant milestone, validating our team's hard work, commitment, and accomplishments. It signaled to investors that we were on a positive trajectory and offered our employees a path to reap the financial rewards they deserved for their hard work and dedication.

Later, as the closing bell rang, we felt relief seeing our share price hold steady, even rising slightly despite high market volatility. At the same time, I felt momentarily disappointed that the share price hadn't experienced a sizable jump on our first day, something that is never expected but occasionally occurs for the fortunate "rock star" companies. The rest of the day was spent enjoying a catered lunch on the front lawn with a steady supply of adult beverages. Our corporate *mascot*, Doug's old, red panel truck with its Johnny Walker label emblazoned on its side, proudly stood guard at the curb before our gathering. This significant milestone was a testament to our long, treacherous road to success.

Our IPO represented progress, accomplishment, and a hopeful future. It spoke to our having created a valuable company and our ability to secure substantial investment capital from a vast source of investors who were sufficiently confident in our abilities to gamble with their wallets. Our partners and spouses joined the celebration, sharing the joy of our achievements and the promising future ahead. It was a day filled with hope and excitement, one we'll never forget.

After my time at Endwave, I ventured to another startup—Protura Wireless—where we innovated creative cellphone antennas. I later joined another startup in Menlo Park, initially named Holographix, soon renamed SafeView. SafeView was a new startup focused on developing a holographic millimeter-wave imaging system to detect weapons and other threats concealed on people's bodies for use in military installations, airports, government buildings, and other places where people congregate. This was the period immediately following 9/11 when large amounts of capital were funneled into various homeland security pursuits, from which we benefited directly.

SafeView was founded by our CEO, Rick Rowe, a seasoned executive with a successful career at Honeywell and MCMS, a prominent contract manufacturer. Our journey began in a Menlo Park incubator led by Mir Imran, a serial entrepreneur, medical inventor, technologist, and venture capitalist. Dr. Imran, known for his inspiring work in the medical field, welcomed us warmly and provided invaluable support as we embarked on our venture.

I remember spotting Rick's ad for an engineering VP position, which aligned well with my background. After responding with my résumé, I had an informal face-to-face interview with Rick, which sparked my interest in his company. We agreed to a trial period where I joined his team of three in a consulting capacity to assess our compatibility. After a few months, I accepted the full-time job and began building a top-notch engineering team. Within three years, we had assembled a remarkable virtual team spanning five states, completed beta tests of our body scanner, and deployed dozens of units internationally at airports, government installations, and military checkpoints for critical field trials. Shortly thereafter, L-3 Communications made a lucrative offer to acquire SafeView, which our Board eagerly accepted.

Our body scanner disrupted the industry with superior imaging performance and privacy algorithms while eliminating the health risks associated with incumbent X-ray systems. Today, when I travel domestically or internationally, I'm proud to see our systems installed at nearly every airport, knowing our efforts have made the world safer.

> *If you want what you've never had, you'll have to do stuff you've never done.* —Anthony Moore, British experimental music composer, performer, and producer.

Beyond attesting to the excitement of working at startups, I've found they can also provide the best environments to learn and grow. At large companies, every employee is like a cog on one of many wheels of a vast machine; we perform our jobs within well-defined boundaries, beyond which other employees step in to do theirs. In contrast, startups offer the opportunity for employees to dramatically expand their roles, diversify their responsibilities, and enhance their learning opportunities. At startups, we learn different roles to complete every job despite our limited staff. Learning and performing in roles not customarily assigned can be fun and stimulating.

The following is an abbreviated list of some additional advantages of working at startups, which can lead to accelerated learning and professional growth:

- Independence: Startup employees enjoy autonomy and expanded decision-making authority, encouraging leadership, strategic thinking, and decision-making skills. Startup environments also encourage professional growth and adaptability.

- Experimentation: Startups usually lack the established protocols, rules, and structures of large companies. This enables startup employees to experiment with building their own unique processes, procedures, and operating frameworks.

- Engagement: Startup employees can develop much deeper connections with their smaller pool of co-workers, which leads to greater engagement and work satisfaction. Every employee has a critical role in contributing substantially to the venture's success.

- Mentoring: Startup employees often work directly with the company founders and executives. This can lead to enhanced mentorships.[42]

The fast-paced startup environment and the chance to innovate offer endless opportunities for growth and fulfillment. Entrepreneurship can be a pathway to discovering new passions and achieving one's aspirations in ways that traditional careers might not provide.

> *Being an entrepreneur is sexy...for those who haven't done it. In reality it's gritty, tough work where you will be filled with self doubt. Entrepreneurs are survivors.* —Mark Suster, American entrepreneur, and venture capitalist.

Clarify Your Motive

When launching a startup, having a meaningful purpose beyond personal gain is essential. While startups can offer the potential for remarkable personal wealth, it shouldn't overshadow the primary objective of creating value. To ensure alignment with your vision, prioritize long-term growth over short-term gains. The fulfillment derived from achieving your corporate goals and accomplishing something deeply worthwhile often surpasses monetary rewards.

Keep your priorities straight to align your decisions with long-term value creation, sustained growth, and profitability.[43]

> *Focus on making meaning, not money. If your vision for your company is to grow it just to flip it to a large company or to take it public and cash out, you're doomed.* —Guy Kawasaki.

Warren Buffett is an excellent example of someone who chose a career he was passionate about and experienced stratospheric financial rewards as a consequence. Warren's son Peter writes about his father's work ethic in his book *Life Is What You Make It*. He claims that Warren is so in love with his chosen work that his concentration while pouring over company performance analyses, borders on the mystical. His challenging work is joyful and perhaps even sacred. It is so satisfying that he receives the same rush of endorphins athletes get from extreme physical effort. While demanding and intense, his work makes him extremely happy.

Buffett advocates for following your passion, advising college students to pursue the job they'd choose if money were no object. He suggests this approach leads to genuine happiness and excellence in one's work. While some argue that passion may not always translate to financial gain, Buffett emphasizes the sustainability of pursuits that one loves deeply. Unlike careers chosen solely for salary potential, which may become burdensome routines, passionate pursuits offer enduring fulfillment.[44]

Businesses fail, people get laid off, and economies are cyclical. Financial rewards can be taken away, but the enjoyment of doing what you love cannot. To be truly happy, endeavor to emphasize passion, focus, and seriousness of purpose.

Every risk is worth taking as long as it's for a good cause, and contributes to a good life. —Richard Branson, British entrepreneur, adventurer, and business magnate.

Purpose and Profit

Some argue that profit is the core purpose of business. However, profit is not a purpose; it's a result. Purpose is the underlying reason for engaging in activities that ideally generate profit. It's important to remember why you started your business in the first place. When you stay closely connected to your purpose and achieve success in line with it, profits naturally ensue. Profit, therefore, serves as a measure of how effectively you're monetizing your pursuit of purpose.

> *A business without a path to profit isn't a business, it's a hobby.* —Jason Fried, software entrepreneur, and business executive.

Corporate leaders and venture capitalists often undergo cycles in which the metrics that are valued and monitored in a business continuously evolve. Not long ago, any software company led by a team of twenty-somethings was all the rage. Then, the emphasis shifted to market share and growth, leading to sky-high valuations for companies unable to generate profits. Several unicorns valued at $1 billion or more faced scrutiny from public market investors when they failed to become profitable after going public.[45]

Many leaders mistakenly equate business growth with revenue growth and profit, overlooking the importance of growing revenue *while maintaining* profitability. Pursuing business growth without regard to costs jeopardizes wealth-building and profitability. Tying performance metrics solely to business growth can lead to misplaced priorities.

Achieving substantial revenues and profits requires a genuine focus on profit-making. Expanding the business by acquiring more clients, contracts, employees, products, services, locations, and sales transactions can offset the benefits of growth with increased expenses, overhead, and management complexity.

Gross margin and profitability should be considered the primary metrics of any successful business. Entrepreneurs should maintain detailed financial models and steer product strategy toward sustained profitability. While growth is crucial for startups, failing to demonstrate sustained profit before an IPO can lead to a drop in stock price due to lackluster financial performance.

> *The idea that growth equals profitability is a misconception. If you can't afford the financial or qualitative side of growth, it can just as easily put you out of business.* —Mark Cuban.

Alternatively, many leaders adopt cost-cutting measures to improve their bottom lines, often resorting to penny-pinching tactics. However, this approach usually strains employee and vendor relationships. This approach to profitability can have long-lasting and damaging effects on organizational culture and workforce morale, often causing more problems than it solves.[46]

Furthermore, layoffs often fail to improve a company's fortunes. Some business experts view layoffs as a confession of poor management. Many companies have avoided layoffs for decades and have thrived. Those companies tend to avoid substantial hiring bursts or embarking on spending sprees during upturns. Layoffs also hamper the ability to restart when things improve. Not surprisingly, voluntary employee turnover increases significantly at companies conducting mass layoffs.

Focusing instead on revenue growth encourages companies to manage their costs and investments effectively while expanding their top line. The goal is to generate more revenue from every company asset, whether tangible or intangible. This approach requires everyone in the organization to evaluate the payoff, impact, and value of every effort and expenditure, whether in time or money. Key metrics to monitor include efficiency, productivity, impact, and quality, while also focusing on eliminating waste and inefficiency.

Smart investments, such as automation or rapid prototyping, can lead to higher revenue at lower costs. Financial incentives for vendors to work faster and with fewer iterations promote accelerated revenue growth while strengthening vendor relationships. Similarly, employee bonuses tied to innovative revenue growth and cost-containment processes align the workforce with a profit-focused mindset.

Achieving profitability signifies that your strategic efforts are paying off and providing genuine customer value. Profitability enables continued growth and the ability to serve customers and employees effectively. It demonstrates competitiveness in the market and validates your commitment to serving stakeholders. Further, when you prioritize profitability and integrate it into corporate decision-making, you align the company's interests with its employees. This creates a motivated and cohesive workforce working in partnership with leadership to serve customers effectively and create sustainable job opportunities.[47]

Profitability is the sovereign criterion of the enterprise. — Peter F. Drucker.

10X Thinking

Ideas are a dime a dozen. Everyone has them, but not all are worth pursuing. It's necessary to critically analyze each unique idea to ensure that the one you choose to move forward with carries deep meaning and has the potential to deliver lasting value.

It's as easy to do something big as it is to do something small, so reach for a fantasy worthy of your pursuit, with rewards commensurate to your effort. —Stephen Schwarzman.

Human nature often leads us to overestimate the novelty of our ideas and their potential impact. Therefore, it's usually worthwhile to solicit the opinions of others you trust. These people will assess your idea's true potential through a clear and unbiased lens.

Consider the following questions when selecting an idea to pursue:

- Does your idea meet a critical need?

- Does it solve a significant or widespread problem?

- Will it stimulate the emotions of your customers?

- Is it inventive, innovative, or revolutionary?

- Can it be patented and otherwise protected?

- Is it intuitive to use, or does it require complicated instructions or training?

- Is it elegant in its simplicity, or does it require a multitude of features?

Steve Jobs' approach to market analysis offers valuable insights for evaluating ideas. While experts and customers may provide helpful feedback, their opinions aren't infallible. *The Innovator's Dilemma* underscores how market-leading companies can lose their edge by relying solely on customer feedback or flawed market research.

Instead of focusing on direct customer opinions, it's worth considering the needs of the end-users or the customers' customers. Customers may not accurately articulate their needs, and their feedback may be limited to incremental improvements. By looking beyond direct customer feedback, entrepreneurs can uncover deeper insights that shape more impactful, forward-thinking solutions that reshape industries and exceed customer expectations.

> *If I'd have asked my customers what they wanted, they would have told me 'A faster horse.'* —Henry Ford, American industrialist, industry magnate, and founder of Ford Motor Company.

Jobs' statement, "It's not the consumers' job to figure out what they want," highlights a fundamental truth in innovation. Engineers and tech enthusiasts often possess insights into customer needs and market trends that surpass conventional wisdom. Trusting your intuition after seeking independent evaluation is essential, especially when considering revolutionary ideas. While feedback is valuable, groundbreaking innovations often challenge existing paradigms and require visionary leadership to navigate uncharted territory. In such cases, intuition can be the most reliable guide when deciding whether to pursue your idea.

Unfortunately, most of us lack Jobs' exceptional intuition. Therefore, we must engage with customers and their customers. Continuous questioning helps us understand their needs, desires, likes, and dissatisfactions. These conversations and surveys are invaluable as they can provide insights for enhancing our products and services. Embrace feedback, even the negative, as it stimulates learning and growth. Avoid siloing your thinking and remain open to constructive criticism.

Remember that nobody has a crystal ball when seeking feedback. Sometimes, we reach out to industry experts for strategic advice or commentaries on new markets or products. While specific individuals have earned our respect for their knowledge and accomplishments, predicting the future is beyond the ability of our greatest experts.

For example, Bill Gates has been routinely summoned for opinions ranging from software and consumer products to AI. While his knowledge and insights are remarkable, he doesn't always get things right. Let's recall his famous proclamations regarding three of Apple's most successful products:

> "As good as Apple may be, I don't believe the success of the iPod is sustainable in the long run." —This was Gates' comment on the iPod in 2001. Apple went on to sell millions of iPods over the next two decades.

> "It's a nice reader, but there's nothing on the iPad I look at and say 'Oh, I wish Microsoft had done it." —This was Gates' iPad comment in 2011, while adhering to his affection for traditional tablets. Apple has sold more than 500 million iPads since its release.

> "It's a nice little device, but it doesn't have a keyboard, which makes it not a very good email machine." —This was Gates' comment on the iPhone following its release in 2007. The iPhone now dominates the smartphone market, with billions of users worldwide.

Often, the best way to confirm whether you have a winning idea is to see it through to its logical conclusion. Move forward, test it out, adjust, and test it again. Think of how much progress you'll make by advancing your idea rather than spending more time and energy analyzing its merit or potential.

> *Everyone who has taken a shower has had an idea. But it's the people who have gotten out of the shower, towel off, and do something about it make the difference.* —Nolan Bushnell, American businessman, entrepreneur, and engineer.

It's also necessary to ensure that your idea is *durable*, meaning it has the potential to create a near-monopoly. If your offering is just an incremental improvement over the current state of the art, you will likely face substantial and well-funded competition. Robust competition tends to jeopardize durability and can squeeze your profits, driving your venture toward a low-margin endeavor.

Billionaire entrepreneur Peter Thiel suggests aspiring to greatness by targeting ideas that yield a unique and proprietary advantage, deemed at least ten times better than the closest substitute. According to Thiel, capturing a small percentage of a large market as a foundational startup objective is unwise. Instead, aim for something revolutionary and non-obvious and deliver an order-of-magnitude advancement. This can be achieved by inventing something entirely new or substantially improving an existing solution. Commanding a robust and growing market should be the target for every worthy pursuit.[48]

> *When 10X is your measuring stick, you immediately see how you can bypass what everyone else is doing.* —Dan Sullivan, entrepreneurial visionary, and strategic coach.

Guy Kawasaki reinforces this theme further. He suggests we continuously target the "Holy Grail" when spending our innovation, marketing, sales, evangelism, and other valuable resources. The goal is to do something extraordinary and be the only source for it. This is where you make money, margin, and history. Kawasaki uses the iPod as a great example of this form of thinking.[49]

It's important to direct your team's efforts toward outcomes that matter. Small teams often spread themselves too thin while attempting to accomplish simultaneous and competing objectives. Maintaining focus while avoiding interruptions and distractions is the key to success. While Steve Jobs was exceedingly talented in this regard and practiced it extensively while leading an enormous company, honing this skill is even more critical while leading a startup. Jobs' guiding wisdom is certainly worth considering:

People think focus means saying yes to the thing you've got to focus on. But that's not what it means at all. It means saying no to the hundred other good ideas that there are. You have to pick carefully. I'm actually as proud of the things we haven't done as the things I have done. —Steve Jobs.[50]

When seeking inspiration in marketing, Steve Jobs stands out as an unparalleled role model. His visionary mindset enabled him to anticipate customer needs before they arose, revolutionizing industries like personal computing and digital music. Jobs excelled in articulating his vision and assembling exceptional teams to bring it to fruition. His relentless focus on the customer experience propelled Apple's success and cemented his legacy as a marketing icon.[51]

Embracing 10x thinking as an entrepreneur challenges conventional limits and inspires innovative, transformative solutions, driving exponential growth. This mindset encourages bold, visionary strategies that unlock new opportunities and redefine success.

If you see a huge, transformative opportunity, don't worry that no one else is pursuing it. You might be seeing something others don't. The harder the problem is, the more limited the competition, and the greater the reward for whomever can solve it. —Stephen Schwarzman.

Protect Your Ideas

It's wise to be cautious when sharing your novel business idea—without protection, it's vulnerable to theft by opportunists and unscrupulous actors. Given your substantial investment of time, energy, and money, safeguarding your work product from unauthorized use is essential to protect its value and ensure the long-term success of your venture. History is rife with stolen ideas, highlighting the importance of taking the necessary steps to safeguard your intellectual property.

> *There is no greater fraud than a promise not kept.* —Scottish Proverb.

Once you've settled on your winning idea, safeguard it with a non-disclosure agreement (NDA) before discussing it with potential co-founders, investors, and experts. The NDA says, "I have confidential ideas and information that I want to share with you, and you agree not to use them or share them without my permission."[52]

More specifically, an NDA is a legally binding contract that prohibits individuals from disclosing confidential information about your company, including intellectual property, designs, business strategies, customer details, and financial data. It covers various parties, including employees, consultants, advisors, and interview candidates. Depending on the specific situation and parties involved, an NDA can be unilateral (one-way) or bilateral (two-way). It is a crucial tool for safeguarding sensitive information and protecting against unauthorized disclosure.

Engaging an attorney to assist in drafting appropriate NDA documents and developing an overall protection strategy can be a wise investment. NDAs should be treated seriously by leadership and employees alike and executed consistently. While locating boilerplate NDA templates online is straightforward, engaging professional legal help is often advisable. Don't compromise on an attorney's expertise; a poorly drafted NDA may leave you vulnerable. Look for a reputable attorney specializing in intellectual property, and seek recommendations for the best *outcome* rather than the best *bargain*.[53]

It's necessary to distinguish between an NDA and a "Confidentiality Agreement," as they each serve distinct purposes. While both are legally enforceable contracts preventing the unauthorized sharing of sensitive information, they have unique roles. Confidentiality agreements are often used in mergers and acquisitions to control the sharing of sensitive information during negotiations. NDAs, on the other hand, are employed in situations involving unilateral information flow, such as discussions with employees, clients, or investors, or when selling or licensing products. A confidentiality agreement binds all parties to keep information confidential, while an NDA establishes a confidential relationship between the signing parties.[54]

If you're seeking venture capital (VC) financing, requesting that potential investors sign your NDA before disclosing your business plan might seem prudent. However, it's important to understand that VCs don't typically sign NDAs. For VCs, the NDA represents an administrative burden and a business liability. While it's natural to feel apprehensive when pitching your plan to VC firms, you can rest assured that they aren't likely to steal your idea.

VCs typically don't sign NDAs for the following reasons:

- Reputation: VCs avoid NDAs to protect their reputation. If they sign your NDA and fund a similar deal with someone else, it could falsely imply idea theft. By steering clear of NDAs, VCs uphold their credibility and integrity in the investment community.

- Teams over ideas: VCs typically invest in *teams* rather than *ideas*. Ideas are relatively easy to come by, but successfully executing them requires an exceptional team with the right skills, experience, energy, and dedication. VCs are not in the business of stealing someone's idea and backing a different team to execute it.

- Overhead: VCs typically evaluate 20 potential deals weekly, totaling 1,000 or more annually. The administrative burden of negotiating an NDA for every deal would impede their ability to explore adequate investment opportunities, which is critical for their business success.

- Trust: VCs operate on trust within the investment market. Requesting a VC to sign an NDA suggests a lack of trust and understanding of the early-stage financing system. VCs value their reputation, knowing that breaching confidentiality could tarnish it. Their reputation outweighs any singular idea, making trust paramount in their dealings.

As an entrepreneur, your job is to attract well-aligned and positioned investors to support your venture. Look for investors who don't already have investments in similar companies, and refrain from overly divulging your *secret sauce*. It's often enough to share the *cake* without also sharing its *recipe*.[55]

Protecting your intellectual property with patents, trademarks, and copyrights is also critical. Ensure that every contract, including terms and conditions (Ts & Cs), is reviewed by a qualified attorney. Unscrupulous businesses may include clauses that benefit themselves, hidden in the fine print. Some customers or contractors seek to exploit loopholes for cheap market entry. A competent legal team shields you from such practices.

Protecting your inventions and know-how is crucial for your business and satisfies investor expectations. Investors typically require a solid patent strategy to safeguard their investment and future profit potential. A startup's value substantially relies on the robustness of its intellectual property protection. Patent applications and issued patents are also pivotal in valuing your business during funding rounds, and significant equity events like IPOs or mergers/acquisitions.

The U.S. patent system adds the fuel of interest to the fire of genius in the discovery and production of new and useful things. —Abraham Lincoln.

While patents can be a company's greatest asset, companies that patent their ideas also perform better financially. For example, between 2011 and 2020, pre-money companies *with* patents received 93.2% higher valuations than those without. When companies with patents were acquired, their median exit value was 154.9% higher than those without. During the same period, VC exits from companies with patents accounted for 78.6% of profits despite making up just 24.1% of the companies they invested in. Statistically, companies that pursue patents go public five times more often than those that don't.

Therefore, it's essential to avoid overlooking the patentability of ideas, products, and processes, even if they appear mundane. Engineers often overlook an idea's novelty when immersed in it.[56]

In summary, protecting startup inventions, ideas, designs, and know-how is essential to safeguarding innovation and ensuring long-term success. Entrepreneurs must navigate a complex landscape of intellectual property tools, including NDAs, patents, trademarks, and copyrights, each serving a specific purpose. NDAs help maintain confidentiality during discussions with partners, investors, and employees, preventing the premature exposure of ideas. Patents provide exclusive rights to inventions, protecting unique products, processes, or technologies from unauthorized use. Trademarks secure brand identity by safeguarding names, logos, and slogans, while copyrights protect creative works like written content, software, and designs. By leveraging these tools, startups can minimize the risk of idea theft, build trust with stakeholders, and establish a solid foundation for sustainable growth in competitive markets.

Competition and Disruption

Competition can often lead to a "race to the bottom," where the focus shifts to cutting costs rather than innovating and creating value. Thankfully, competition can also inspire innovation, offering something unique or focusing on a specific niche is preferred over engaging in a price war.

The value you provide to customers should far exceed its price; ideally, it should be something they can't find elsewhere and can't live without. Rather than fearing competitors, it's better to understand and meet your customers' needs, as they hold the keys to the revenue you seek.

> *All failed companies are the same: They failed to escape competition.* —Peter Thiel, German-American entrepreneur, businessman, venture capitalist, and political activist.

Disruption is an overused buzzword in the startup community. It involves solving existing problems in innovative ways while rendering old approaches obsolete. Disruptive companies change entire industries by offering what people don't realize they need.

To disrupt, you must anticipate and capitalize on emerging trends faster and more effectively than your competitors. For instance, Apple revolutionized the music and cellphone industries, showcasing the power of disruptive innovation.[57]

Focusing solely on disruption or being the first mover can sometimes lead to setbacks. Allowing others to move first provides opportunities to learn from their struggles and mistakes. Being the *last* mover with a superior offering can often result in higher profits. Strategic flexibility allows for leveraging competitors' experiences while aiming for long-term success.[58]

For example, in the early 1990s, we launched Endgate to design a revolutionary satellite payload for Calling Communications. Calling, later named Teledesic, aimed to provide low-cost internet globally through a constellation of advanced MEO satellites. However, they were ahead of their time by at least 30 years. Despite substantial funding and support from industry giants like Bill Gates and Craig McCaw, Teledesic faced insurmountable challenges, leading to its eventual demise. We're only now experiencing a global revolution in deploying expansive, low-cost satellite constellations that achieve what we set out to do 30 years ago.

SafeView, on the other hand, capitalized on impeccable timing when we developed our full-body security scanner. We rolled out our first beta product shortly after the 9/11 attacks, when there was a robust global demand for enhanced security measures at airports and government installations. At that time, existing body scanners relied on X-ray imagery, which raised serious health concerns due to their use of ionizing radiation. SafeView's solution utilizes millimeter-wave radiation, eliminating health risks while matching or surpassing the X-ray system's threat detection capabilities. Today, SafeView's body scanner, now under the stewardship of one of several acquiring companies, dominates the market, a testament to our foresight, innovative approach, and, perhaps most importantly, our market timing.

As an entrepreneur, your idea is everything. Maintain a laser focus on it. Despite the perception that small, agile companies move faster, anticipate a non-linear path filled with strategic shifts and unforeseen challenges. Be prepared for multiple course corrections and unexpected hurdles, honing adaptability as one of your key strengths.

If you're smart, you'll move slowly to move fast. Avoid haphazard approaches and prioritize thorough and realistic planning. Anticipate future needs to prevent costly rework. Implement strategies for

efficient execution, consider contingencies, and maintain adequate reserves in your budget and schedule.

> *Success comes down to rare moments of opportunity. Be*
> *open, alert, and ready to seize them. Gather the right people*
> *and resources; then commit. If you're not prepared to apply*
> *that kind of effort, either the opportunity isn't as compelling*
> *as you think or you are not the right person to pursue it.* —
> Stephen Schwarzman.

Business Plan

Entrepreneurs often initiate their business plans as drafts, refining
them collaboratively as their founding teams materialize. As you further develop your business plan, consider engaging mentors with direct experience in founding and building companies. They can offer
insights to help you avoid early pitfalls and guide you toward fruitful
paths as you prepare to engage investors. Remember, a business involves more than just making and selling products or providing services; it's a complex pursuit requiring strategic navigation.

Developing a detailed business plan forces you to think critically
about your future business. But don't allow the process to paralyze
you. Taking action matters more than perfecting your plan. Avoid
overcomplicating things or documenting every possible permutation.
For instance, our initial business plan for launching Endgate was relatively lean, probably fewer than 20 pages, excluding the appendix.
Founders can initially pitch to investors with abbreviated plans, but
expect those plans to expand as the business progresses and more information relating to strategy, roadmaps, progress, and projections
evolves.

When preparing your initial business plan, focus on a few essential items:

- Describe your product or service concisely to investors, focusing on brevity. Not everything can be known in advance, and investors don't need to see every detail. It is better to divulge only that which is required to secure funding.

- Identify your future customers, ensure your list is believable, and tailor your execution strategy accordingly.

- Describe what differentiates your product or service from the incumbents. What is your special sauce, and what is it about your solution that will attract paying customers?

- Describe how your offering will provide a durable advantage within the marketplace, capable of fending off the entrenched and better-funded competition.

- Describe how you will protect your intellectual property. Patent protection generally requires that your invention be new, original, novel, and non-obvious.

- Provide an assessment of your projected costs and profit margins. How will your money be spent, and how much will you need to execute successfully? If you're inexperienced in developing basic financials for your venture, find a qualified accountant who can provide the necessary expertise.

- Explain how you will manage your company's growth. If you are not an operations expert, contacting others for expert advice can be worthwhile. You'll need a solid plan for growing your business, including investments, sales, marketing, and strategic staffing.[59]

- Showcase your exceptional founding team. A list of co-founders and their brief bios will help your investors understand your initial team's skill and character makeup. Remember that they are investing in people, so provide them with this early introduction.

Business plans are essential roadmaps that outline a venture's vision, strategy, and objectives, providing a clear path to success. These plans guide decision-making, attract investors, and ensure a structured approach to achieving business goals.

> *Failing to plan is planning to fail.* —Unknown.

Laying the Foundation

Establishing a solid corporate foundation is crucial for a startup's eventual success. Without it, your venture will likely become more of a reaction-driven, ad hoc pursuit, which may succumb to the effects of chaos and stunted traction.

> *A startup messed up at its foundation cannot be fixed.* —Peter Thiel.

At a minimum, a solid startup foundation involves the following:

- Exceptional founding team: The earliest phase of any new venture depends almost entirely upon the founding team. It should consist of competent and experienced experts who work well together and possess relevant and complementary skills.

- Roles and responsibilities: Every team member should have clearly defined roles and responsibilities to avoid confusion, gaps, or redundancy. Hire only those who are critically necessary at each phase. Many of the skills found within mature companies are unnecessary during the earliest stages of a startup.

- Equity and compensation: Employment candidates should receive formal offers that clearly explain and delineate their compensation packages, including benefits and stock options.

- Controls: Clarify who controls what and to what level. Conflicts and overlaps should be identified and eliminated.

- Product or Service: Baseline a product or service that can (ideally) achieve an order of magnitude (10X) impact in a sizable and growing market.

- Business plan: Develop a compelling and believable business plan. The extent and details depend on the stage of the venture.

- Funding: Secure funding from reputable and compatible investors who will contribute relevant expertise and advice to your venture.

- Mission, Vision, and Purpose statements: These documents clarify, align the team's efforts, and inspire stakeholders by articulating the company's goals, values, and long-term aspirations.

A solid foundation is essential when launching a startup. It ensures a structured and strategic approach that significantly enhances the likelihood of long-term success. By adequately laying the groundwork, entrepreneurs can more effectively navigate challenges, attract investors, and build a sustainable business model.

Startup success is driven most by the product passion, quality, vision, team-work and persistence of the founding team and the talent that the team attracts. —Jim Breyer, American venture capitalist, entrepreneur, business executive, and philanthropist.

Assemble Your Team

Your startup team is essential to driving business success—qualifications and skills matter, but so does compatibility. If you naturally socialize outside of work, that's a positive sign. Founders shape the company's culture, so if there's a lack of personal connection among them, it will be evident to investors, employees, and customers.

Great teams operate as one and succeed together. They also create the collective energy and passion observable by others. Conversely, weak leadership leads to inferior teams, which produce low energy, poor performance, high turnover, and even chaos. A strong team won't necessarily guarantee success, but without it, the odds of success are rather slim.[60]

I've learned that engaging with others brings valuable perspectives and insights, even when I think I have all the answers. Surrounding yourself with experienced partners, mentors, coaches, and colleagues can dramatically accelerate progress and lead to far better solutions and outcomes. Singular thinking can lead to *average* thinking and underachievement. Networking with successful serial entrepreneurs can be beneficial—their valuable wisdom and strategies can help you avoid mistakes and accelerate your pursuits.

Entrepreneurs should prioritize hiring early employees who align well with the founding team to avoid underperformance or disruptive influences. Offering competitive salaries alongside compelling stock options promotes motivation and long-term commitment amongst the workforce. Equity ensures team alignment and a shared commitment to the company's goals. Candidates primarily interested in cash compensation rather than equity, the mission, or the ability to work with a fantastic team may not be the right fit for the company's culture and goals.[61]

Focus on your team's roles and responsibilities instead of titles—title inflation is common in startups. Ownership clarity and accountability are necessary to ensure everyone understands and accepts their responsibilities. Timelines will be short, and messaging throughout the organization needs to be crisp, direct, and uncluttered.[62]

A hierarchy in the organization will inhibit rapid progress, so creating a lean, tightly connected organization with the freedom to innovate and excel makes good sense. The reporting structure amongst the founding team and early hires is especially critical, so superior-subordinate assignments must be established by assessing and aligning compatible personalities.

Use consultants strategically and sparingly, with strict oversight, and engage them through reasonable NDAs. It is also prudent to identify a trustworthy legal expert. Many legal firms are willing to invest in startups, recognizing the long-term value of building relationships with emerging businesses that may become lucrative clients as they grow.

The business mantra "hire slow, fire fast" garners supporters and detractors. Some suggest that firing people quickly risks losing valued contributions through knee-jerk terminations. Adopting a more patient and empathetic approach towards adjusting an underperformer's role or relocating them to a job they are better suited to can be a more cost-effective and reasonable solution. Others argue that hiring slowly risks losing out on exceptional candidates, where a more aggressive or expedient approach to securing A-players is desirable. Ultimately, the best approach depends on the unique circumstances of each situation.

In my view, it's worthwhile to adopt a patient approach to hiring while prioritizing recruiting top talent and compatible personalities. Each employee plays a vital role in a small team, leaving no room for mis-hires. If securing a critical skill demands swift action, then accelerate the hiring process and prioritize excellence.[63] Those skills can often be temporarily retained through consultants while searching for permanent hires.

When you hire someone, you accept an obligation. In a real sense, you have a moral imperative to create a work environment that allows, encourages, and enables employees to thrive and innovate. Sometimes, that includes allowing them to stumble before they hit their stride.

Every startup is one hire away from greatness. —Unknown.

Funding

When you fund your venture through personal savings, loans, or support from friends and family, you'll maintain control of your business and avoid much of the inconvenience of seeking funding from other sources. However, suppose your venture involves the long-term development of a complex product or service requiring a team of well-compensated professionals, capital-intensive equipment and facilities, and many other expenses. In that case, you may need funding from more substantial sources.

> *Accessing capital to start a business can be a daunting process, especially for entrepreneurs who start out with a great idea, but have no familiarity with the business world.* — Gavin Newsom, American politician, and businessman.

Cash is the lifeblood of traditional startups—it fuels their operations and growth. Unfortunately, raising capital consumes significant time and effort from executives and founders. The *runway* (cash balance divided by burn rate) is critical in startups, so executives are often busy fundraising to ensure there's enough money in the bank to sustain the company's spending. After closing one round of funding, they'll begin preparing for the next, repeating the cycle.[64]

There are three primary types of investors:

- Transactional: Transactional investors seek short-term ROI.

- Relationship-oriented: Relationship-oriented investors prioritize long-term relationships and pursuits.

- Legacy: Legacy investors are focused on disrupting industries or changing the world.

Selecting investors whose objectives align with your company's mission is crucial. For example, we attracted legacy investors at Endgate to make a significant, long-term impact. Conversely, we intended to "flip" SafeView within three years of launch, so we engaged transactional investors. Regardless of the type of investor, it is necessary to thoroughly vet candidates to ensure alignment with your company's values, vision, and leadership philosophy, including the treatment of employees, shareholders, and customers. Additionally, compensation, equity grants, and corporate ethics alignment are essential.[65]

When seeking funding from venture capitalists, be aware that you'll exchange equity and autonomy for capital, legitimacy, and connections. Running a VC-backed company is akin to co-parenting your children, as substantial control may be relinquished. Before pursuing this path, explore all available alternatives, such as non-dilutive options like term loans, credit lines, or revenue-based financing. These options protect ownership, increase independence, and are often founder-friendly. Remember, VCs are only one of many possible sources of credibility or relationships. For example, strategic advisers can offer valuable guidance and connections without demanding substantial equity.[66]

When researching potential investors, narrow the list based on criteria like stage preference and investment philosophy. For example, are their deals primarily late-stage or seed? Do they typically look for fast returns or emphasize long-term growth plays? This process requires time, persistence, and thorough due diligence.

When you secure a pitch appointment, make the most of it. Arrive fully prepared to present your idea succinctly, efficiently, and persuasively. Understand the difference between what you *need* and *want* from the investment.

When pitching to investors, you must tell a story that paints your vision for the company. Your narrative, more than anything else, needs to be *nailed.*

As a minimum, you should be prepared to answer the following fundamental questions:

- What problem are you solving?

- Why are you and your team uniquely capable and positioned to solve it?

- Why is your offering revolutionary or substantially superior?

- Can your intellectual property be protected?

- Why should the investor want to avoid missing out on it? [67]

Investors invest in the founding team and their compelling plan. You'll use the pitch deck to tell the story behind your plan. Ideally, you should describe the world as it currently exists, what your company will do to change the status quo, and how it will ultimately change the world. Your story should be concise and include all the critical elements underpinning it. More than a presentation, your pitch should be a *conversation* as you guide your investment audience to believe that your company is unique, will be highly successful, and is something they'll want to be a part of. You won't get a second chance to make a solid first impression, so your pitch needs to be perfected by weeding out the unimportant from the critically impactful.[68]

The pitch deck is your tool to convey the essence and vision of your venture to those with investment funds. It must be prepared carefully and thoughtfully, following some basic rules to ensure success. Venture capitalist and tech guru Guy Kawasaki provides some excellent suggestions in this regard:

- You may win or lose in the first sixty seconds of your pitch. Don't delay your attention-grabbing highlights.

- Embrace storytelling with a captivating narrative. Engage your audience by offering a solution to a huge problem they can relate to and get excited about.

- Use metaphors to facilitate the audience's comprehension of your message.

- Observe the 10/20/30 slide rule: use a minimum font size of thirty points, restrict your pitch to ten slides, and present them within 20 minutes.

- Adopt clarity and specificity—don't waste their valuable time.

- Consider enhancing your pitch by utilizing demos, etc.

- Prepare for anything. Bring backup equipment in case your computer fails. Don't assume your wi-fi or internet connections will be perfect.

- Practice and project confidence.

- Actively listen when you're not talking. Take notes—you can learn a lot from brief encounters with VCs.

-   Follow up a day or two after your pitch. Ask if they need more information, and provide anything you promised in the meeting.

-   Expect *many* rejections. Funding is a numbers game. Some successful entrepreneurs have endured hundreds of rejections before eventually striking gold.[69]

When seeking venture capital financing, it's necessary to understand how VCs operate. They raise capital from limited partners to invest in new and existing ventures, aiming to increase their value rapidly and ultimately achieve an exit event like a merger, acquisition, or IPO. To pitch to VCs effectively, you must present a clear investment picture, including the use of funds and potential exit options. You should also convey why your venture is compelling and why your solution is superior to others in addressing the same problem. VCs assess whether your venture is significant and urgent enough for their appetite and whether your solution stands out among alternatives. This requires deep conviction in your pursuit, which evolves over time.[70]

Strong connections within the venture capital community and an understanding of financing practices can accelerate your fundraising efforts. However, newcomers can also succeed with the support of angel investors who offer guidance and introductions to VCs. Organizations like the National Venture Capital Association (NVCA) provide funding and advisory resources. Books and blogs offer valuable advice, but opinions vary, so caution is advised.

> *Most venture capitalists won't read a business plan unless the entrepreneur is introduced to them by a contact.* —Guy Kawasaki.

Seeking venture capital can be exhausting and humbling. Successful entrepreneurs are known for their persistence and willingness to persevere despite countless rejections.

For example, our lead investor at Endgate, Ed Tuck, recounted his experience seeking VC investment to pursue the world's first commercial-grade GPS device. He told me he spent a year being rejected and embarrassed by 85 potential investors, who said: "It'll never work," or, "It's too big an undertaking." Fortunately for Ed, those naysayers made him even more passionate and committed. The 86th investor thought his idea was genius, which led to the launch of Magellan, the maker of the world's first portable and affordable GPS device.

Be realistic about how long it takes to secure venture financing. Funding pursuits are marathons, not sprints. Your fundraising efforts will not end until you can sustain operations through cash flow and profits. Receiving a term sheet is a significant milestone that marks the *beginning* of the fundraising journey. Negotiations, legal procedures, and revisions demand further time, effort, and resources before financing is finalized, so plan accordingly.[71]

After securing your investment, consider investors integral to your extended team. Keep them engaged through consistent communication and updates, including key success metrics, team developments, monthly assessments, and upcoming goals. Investors are vested in your success and actively support your business endeavors.[72]

Top-tier investors prioritize building sustainable, socially responsible businesses and emphasize paying it forward. They go beyond monetary support, offering invaluable mentoring and coaching. At Endgate, Ed Tuck demonstrated this philosophy by encouraging a blend of work and play in our corporate endeavors. By creating a culture that embraced experimentation and fun, we learned to approach challenges with levity. We shared our experiences generously, understanding that time and expertise are always well-spent when shared with others.

Friends, Family, Angels, and CVCs

Statistically, over one-third of startup founders have raised money from friends and family. Startups receive more than $60 billion yearly from those investors, more than angel investors and venture capitalists combined. However, while raising money from friends and family may enable you to retain more leadership independence and business ownership, there are also certain downsides to consider.

It's not uncommon for entrepreneurs to offer friends or family members an overly generous equity stake in their company in exchange for their investment. However, early overvaluation can lead to downstream funding challenges when the founder eventually seeks angel or VC investment to fuel corporate growth.

For example, sophisticated and institutional investors are bound by fiduciary duty, securities regulations, and best practices to make prudent, well-researched investment decisions based on valuation and fair pricing. If previous share valuations were inflated beyond fair value, the company would need to be restructured, with previous equity shares reallocated among friends and family to align all investors to fair value. This can lead to bad feelings amongst the initial investors, whose equity stakes might require a downward adjustment. Additionally, the initial overvaluation can lead to costly legal and tax consequences. Bringing in all investors at fair value from day one is essential to avoid this issue.

Additionally, friends and family investments must comply with applicable securities regulations involving "blue sky laws," certain disclosures, SEC registration, etc. Before you ask for investments, hiring a lawyer to help you navigate your funding efforts is always a good idea.

Inexperienced investors often seek involvement in company leadership to safeguard their investment, potentially causing interference in daily operations. Remember, you're seeking their investment, not their leadership. Avoid soliciting investments from friends or family who can't afford losses; wealth only sometimes translates to suitability as an investor. Overpromising and underperforming can strain personal relationships and lead to legal disputes with those closest to you.[73]

> *The individual investor should act consistently as an investor and not as a speculator.* —Benjamin Graham, American economist, professor, and investor.

Angel investors, typically sophisticated, high-net-worth individuals, take calculated risks by investing substantial amounts in illiquid, high-risk ventures led by entrepreneurs aiming to build impactful companies and create job opportunities. With roots predating the emergence of VC firms, angel investing traces back to influential families like Rockefeller, Whitney, and Phipps, who laid the foundation for California's VC industry. Today, angels are vital in bridging the funding gap between personal and institutional investors. Quietly contributing to the economy, they often serve as seed round contributors in VC-funded ventures, with hundreds of thousands operating in the United States. Unlike VCs, angels primarily invest personal money rather than pooled funds from limited partners such as pension funds or endowments.

A typical entrepreneur might be able to raise tens of thousands of dollars from friends or family members. Angels, by comparison, typically fund up to a million dollars each, the typical lower-end threshold for VCs. The wise entrepreneur considers angel and VC investments complementary—there's usually room for both, and each has a different role.

The ROI objectives of angels differ from those of VCs. Angels might be satisfied with a $30 million return on their investment, whereas VCs usually look for much larger exits (because they need to impact bigger funds). VCs look for home runs or grand slams, where billion-dollar "unicorns" are considered the ultimate prize.[74]

> *Angels were behind Google, Apple and Facebook when they first started, and VCs were there when they swung for the fences.* —Bob Pavey, American venture capitalist and angel investor.

In addition to VCs, angels, and friends & family, Corporate Venture Capital (CVC) funds can support and enable next-level growth. Unlike traditional VCs, CVCs are backed by established companies, which means that strategic support, market insights, expertise, networks, customer pipelines, and potential partnerships can be readily tapped to benefit and scale your venture.

CVCs are unique in that they don't just invest for financial returns—they look to invest in ventures that complement or otherwise support their core business. Thus, CVCs can offer faster go-to-market paths and access to big-company resources. CVC partnerships often provide strategic advantages, such as mentoring, industry-specific guidance, and scaling pathways through co-development, distribution channels, or customer introductions. Additionally, aligning with a corporate investor can enhance credibility, attract further investment, and reduce barriers to market entry, making CVCs a powerful catalyst for growth in competitive industries.

When seeking funding for a startup, considering multiple sources—friends and family, angel investors, venture capitalists (VCs), and corporate venture capital (CVC)—can provide a well-rounded foundation for growth. Friends and family investors often offer accessible, relationship-based funding with minimal bureaucracy, while angel investors bring valuable experience, mentorship, and networks alongside their capital. With their larger investments, VCs provide funding, strategic support, deep industry knowledge, and a network of connections to accelerate growth. CVCs, on the other hand, provide not only funding but also strategic partnerships, market insights, and credibility through alignment with established corporations. By diversifying funding sources, startups can leverage the unique strengths of each, creating a balance of financial support, expertise, and opportunities that align with their immediate needs and long-term vision.

Advisors and Directors

As a founder, it's vital that you establish a transparent governance system that aligns with your company's vision and defines decision-making roles within it. Your Board of Directors (BOD) selections are crucial, regardless of your company's size or stage. As you navigate critical decisions with lasting implications, having an experienced board to provide unbiased advice will guide your strategy and decision-making process.

> *If you have been invited to the room, you belong in the room. If you are in the room then you have a seat at the table. If you have a seat at the table then you have a responsibility to speak.* —Carla A. Harris, investment banker, advisor, and business executive.

Incorporating individuals with capital raising and legal expertise can be crucial for your startup's success. Likewise, having someone with business experience in your market space can help to refine your execution strategy. Their insights may lead to personal introductions to potential customers and supporters, enhancing your venture's reach and impact.

Avoid the pitfall of surrounding yourself with like-minded individuals. A diverse board comprising varied backgrounds and experiences offers unique perspectives that enhance your strategies and decision-making quality. To resolve ties effectively, baseline an odd number of board members. For a small corporation, a board of 3 to 5 members is adequate. In general, having fewer board members than too many is advantageous.

Your board members must share a unified commitment to your company's success. They should carefully scrutinize and remove integrity concerns or conflicts of interest. Ethical decision-making and robust nominating and governance procedures are also essential. Experienced board members adeptly employ strategies to navigate tensions in the boardroom.

Board independence is critical to your company's success. Unfortunately, many boards are comprised of individuals handpicked by the CEO to merely endorse decisions, leading to a lack of critical discourse. When boards swear loyalty to the CEO, relations between the board and the CEO become friendly to a fault, confrontation and difficult conversations are avoided, and criticism of the CEO's performance is strictly forbidden. This practice is not in the company's best interest, even if the CEO wishes it to be.

Boards should be encouraged to speak truth to power, brainstorm and advise without reservation, and bring their *whole selves* to each meeting, having fully prepared beforehand. They should also be encouraged and empowered to meet independently from the CEO for "executive sessions," discussing high-level strategy, CEO performance, and compensation.

CEOs are more likely to look for a 'cocker spaniel' than 'pit bulls' for their board. —Warren Buffett, American investor, entrepreneur, and businessman.

As a CEO, navigating the dynamics of working and negotiating with your board requires time, patience, and persistence. While your focus may be on business growth and daily challenges, your board may prioritize different concerns. They might inquire about the pace of growth, customer retention rates, or customer acquisition costs. Each board member brings a unique focus and priority to the team, and their perspectives may vary widely. Understanding and managing these differences is critical to sustaining effective collaboration and decision-making within the boardroom.[75]

Corporate advisors can significantly enhance your Board of Directors. At SafeView, we enlisted a few seasoned industry and academic advisors who provided insightful support during major reviews, board meetings, and critical brainstorming sessions. Their advice was usually enlightening, insightful, and impactful. There's no fixed rule on the number of advisors; replacing them as necessary is straightforward. Continuously seeking valuable advisors aligned with your goals is worthwhile for organizational success.

Beyond selecting your founding team, a board of directors, and a collection of critical advisors, there are other early hires that you should attract for your exceptional team, who will help you to navigate the many urgent and complex challenges that your venture will encounter throughout its earliest stage. These first few hires will materially influence your internal culture, enabling you to attract even more impressive talent. They will also shape the external perception of your company, which is crucial for impressing investors, customers, and stakeholders.

Clients do not come first. Employees come first. If you take care of your employees, they will take care of your clients.
—Richard Branson.

Incentive Stock

Incentive stock options have been a part of Silicon Valley culture for decades. They are a critical recruitment and retention tool startups utilize to level the playing field. By their very nature, startups are usually cash-strapped—they can't always afford the competitive salaries or fringe benefits that are commonplace in larger, established firms. Incentive stock options enable startups to attract and retain exceptional talent by offering the enticing potential for substantial, sometimes life-changing financial rewards sometime in the future when the company meets its objectives and creates real value.

Stock options permit employees to buy a set number of company shares at a fixed price within a specific timeframe. If the company's stock price increases, the value of the options also rises. For instance, if employees receive options early in the company's history, each share might initially be valued at $1, as determined by investors. Each year, a portion of their option "vests." When the company goes public, employees can purchase their vested shares at the option price and then sell them in the open market at the prevailing market price, profiting on the difference.

During each sequential funding round (e.g., Series A, Series B), investors inject cash in exchange for increasing amounts of stock, which leads to the issuance of more shares. Consequently, an employee's percentage of ownership decreases relative to the expanded total—a phenomenon known as "dilution." To counteract this, many companies provide employees with new "refresher" stock options annually or during each funding round. These options renew work incentives and partially mitigate the dilutive impact of successive funding rounds.[76]

I've witnessed firsthand the impact stock options can have on a startup's ability to attract, retain, and energize top talent. For employees, the prospect of their shares potentially translating into significant wealth based on company success can motivate exceptional performance and deep corporate loyalty. Options align employee interests with those of other shareholders in a manner that salaries and bonuses alone cannot achieve.

A few years of grinding can produce a lifetime of freedom.
—Unknown.

Execute!

In the business world, ideas are abundant, but the ability to execute effectively and efficiently often determines success or failure. Many companies struggle, lingering for years without realizing their full potential or lofty goals. These stagnant entities are frequently dubbed "the living dead."

Ideas are a commodity. Execution of them is not. —Michael Dell.

To enhance your chances of success, begin with modest aspirations but maintain ambitious goals. Starting small mitigates initial risks, allowing for swift iteration and testing in the market. Focus on refining components or subsystems before scaling to the system level and expanding to a portfolio of products or services. Strive to avoid becoming irrelevant, aiming instead for significant impact. Even if you fall short of your grand vision, you'll achieve more than if you had settled for smaller objectives.

Even groundbreaking products won't sell themselves. The effort invested in sales, marketing, branding, and distribution is as critical as innovation, invention, and optimization.

Many business owners struggle to scale their companies because they centralize operations around themselves, inadvertently becoming the primary bottleneck. I observed this firsthand at a self-funded company, where the CEO routinely disregarded advice from the experts he hired. Relying solely on personal intuition and sheer willpower, he insisted on doing things his way. This led to the loss of valuable talent, a failure to execute successfully, and ultimately forced the company to close its doors.

Executing effectively in startups is essential. It transforms innovative ideas into tangible results and drives business growth. Focused execution ensures that plans are implemented efficiently, resources are optimized, and strategic goals are achieved, setting the stage for long-term success.

> *Vision without execution is delusion.* —Thomas Edison, American businessman, and prolific inventor.

Move Fast and Iterate

I've observed two distinct approaches to decision-making. The first emphasizes gathering extensive information before making critical decisions, as data forms the foundation for high-quality decisions.

The alternative approach advocates for swift decision-making, prioritizing action and rapid course corrections over waiting for additional information.

Many successful leaders embrace the second approach, driven by the concept of opportunity cost. They understand that delaying decisions means forfeiting time that could be used for experimentation, iteration, and learning. In today's fiercely competitive business landscape, allowing competitors an advantage due to inaction is risky. It's often wise to experiment, learn, and iterate continually rather than delay progress to gather more data.

Consider Guy Kawasaki's insightful guidance concerning iterating:

> "Don't worry; be crappy. Don't worry about shipping an innovative product with elements of crappiness. The first permutation of an innovation is seldom perfect—Macintosh, for example, didn't have software (thanks to me), a hard disk (it wouldn't matter with no software anyway), slots and color. If a company waits until everything is perfect, it will never ship, and the market will pass it by."

And...

> "Churn, baby, churn. I'm saying it's OK to ship with elements of crappiness—I'm not saying that it's OK to stay crappy. A company must improve version 1.0 and create versions 1.1, 1.2, ...2.0. This is a difficult lesson to learn because it's so hard to ship an innovation; therefore, the last thing employees want to deal with is complaints about their perfect baby. Innovation is a process, not an event."[77]

Hardware developments pose significant challenges, but technological advancements have made iterating hardware designs far more expedient. With computer design and analysis tools and 3-D printers, prototyping and experimentation now take hours and days instead of weeks and months. Empirical experimentation is invaluable, as it allows us to experience the device firsthand, evaluate its utility and impact, and observe human factors in its use and utility.

Leadership that promotes rapid iterating, fearless risk-taking, and encourages employees to experiment and learn from mistakes creates a culture of expedited innovation within the workforce. Prioritizing early and frequent prototyping while removing barriers such as slow procurement approvals or unreasonable budget constraints is essential. Celebrating experimentation, regardless of the outcome, encourages continued innovative behavior.

Mark Zuckerberg ingrained this philosophy into Facebook's DNA with his famous mantra, "Move fast and break things." I witnessed firsthand the power of this philosophy during my time there. While the wording of the mantra may have evolved slightly, the fundamental execution philosophy of rapid iteration and experimentation has remained a constant within the company.

It's important to involve leadership throughout the design iteration and optimization process, prototype early and frequently, and continuously seek input from marketing and leadership teams during each prototype evaluation. This approach prevents surprises and disappointments and ensures that key stakeholders contribute to the final product design, resulting in a better overall solution. Avoid siloing your developments, and remember that while computer modeling and simulation tools are impressive, nothing beats experiencing a physical prototype.

Failure serves as a profound teacher. The most effective way to improve is to overcome concerns and dive into action, even if initial attempts are less than stellar. Those who are prematurely fixated on quality and perfection often find themselves with nothing but lofty theories and abandoned ideas. It's through action and learning from mistakes that actual progress is made.

Above all, remember that prototyping enhances problem understanding, communicates use cases and potential solutions, and facilitates comprehensive design optimization. Prototyping shouldn't be viewed merely as a final deliverable but as an integral part of an ongoing iterative process. Iteration encourages us to set aside perfectionism in design, embrace experimentation, and learn from experience.

> *The design process is about designing and prototyping and making. When you separate those, I think the final result suffers.* —Jony Ive, British industrial and product designer, and business executive.

Customers and Customization

In cash—and personnel-constrained startups, it's important to prioritize a few key pursuits that align with your highest priorities. Steve Jobs was exceedingly successful and perhaps even obsessively focused on this. Persistent iteration, simplification, and refinement are essential until objectives are achieved. However, it's important to avoid tunnel vision.

When innovating a new product or service, consider your objectives holistically, recognizing that your creation can be rejected for any number of reasons, some logical and expected, others unanticipated, and even irrational. Assess every aspect of your product: its appearance, feel, smell, mass, aesthetics, color, and functionality. Do the moving parts provide pleasant tactile feedback? Do the buttons and knobs feel solid? Does it evoke a sense of quality? Is it intuitive, fun, and easy to use? If your offering is a service, the same process applies. Such considerations ensure a well-rounded development approach that leads to enhanced market acceptance.

> *Perfection is achieved, not when there is nothing more to add, but when there is nothing left to take away.* —Antoine de Saint-Exupery. French writer, poet, journalist, and pioneering aviator.

When racing to secure your first customers, there's a temptation to over-customize your product to meet their specific preferences or requirements. In my experience, our earliest customers often requested unique features tailored to their applications, which consumed significant time and effort and diverted resources from other essential tasks. We became inundated with special requests that were treated as prerequisites for order placement. If not managed effectively, customization can impede your ability to scale and mass-produce your products efficiently and cost-effectively.

Customization is increasingly becoming the norm, offering opportunities for differentiation and market advantage. How you handle it depends on your specific goals and pursuits. Transparency and close collaboration with potential customers enable you to understand and explain the positive and negative implications of each custom feature regarding cost, schedule, performance, quality, and manufacturability.

Consider advocating for phase-1 or beta contracts to generate incremental revenue while customizing your designs. Upon successful prototype demonstrations, follow-on orders can be drafted. This strategic approach helps manage customization while establishing a revenue stream and nurturing ongoing customer relationships.

By engaging your customers via early contracts during the design phase, customers will more carefully consider which features and customizations are worthwhile, given that they are at least partially funding those developments. It is easy to ask for the moon, but requests become more focused when you have to pay for them.

When contractually engaged with your customer, you may find that they can provide additional, helpful support or resources, such as access to their supplier base, manufacturing expertise, test equipment, raw materials, tech writers, and other vital support to accelerate your development or otherwise enhance your ability to accomplish your mutual objectives. Nothing incentivizes a customer more than having a *vested interest* in their supplier's success.

As you refine your product in collaboration with your customer, appoint someone in authority to ensure that all new products or features meet acceptable standards of quality, reliability, manufacturability, and production cost. These considerations should be integral to the design process from the outset.

> *Customers want to know what to expect. A consistent, predictable experience gives the customer confidence. That can lead to trust, which can develop into coveted customer loyalty.* —Shep Hyken, customer service and experience expert, and keynote speaker.

Ultimately, business is all about relationships built on honesty and integrity. When choosing your initial customers, prioritize those you trust, respect, and admire. Perform thorough due diligence by researching their history and checking references. Socialize with their principals to gauge compatibility, and trust your intuition—if something feels off, it probably is. Establish relationships based on communication, transparency, and mutual goodwill. Address issues promptly and base decisions on solid data. Demand integrity throughout the partnership.[78]

If a customer isn't a good fit for your company or working with them distracts from your product or mission focus, it's important to know when to walk away. Freeing up your team allows them to excel in other essential pursuits. Trust that another customer, more aligned, collaborative, and appreciative of your offering, will emerge soon.[79]

Selecting the right customers is crucial for startups, as it enables sustainable growth and aligns pursuits with the company's core strengths. Excessive customization can strain resources and dilute the brand's focus. Balancing customer needs with strategic objectives ensures long-term viability and success.

> *Make every detail perfect and limit the number of details to perfect.* —Jack Dorsey, American entrepreneur, programmer, and business executive.

Focus and Flexibility

Entrepreneurs are often plagued by the "shiny object syndrome," a persistent challenge to maintain focus and stick to their plans. There always seems to be something better worth pursuing, often emerging from the next conversation with a potential customer. This tendency can lead to a lack of focus and hinder progress on the core pursuit. When employees are continuously redirected to explore new avenues, it detracts from the primary mission.

One way to stay on track is to confine your attention to what is critically aligned with your objectives. In a sense, this is applying *blinders* to ensure focus. Acknowledging the limitations of your team's work capacity is essential for success.

However, while maintaining focus is critical, assigning one team member, such as your marketing expert, to monitor market trends and explore alternative possibilities can be beneficial. This individual can uncover opportunities that may enhance your offering with minimal interference to the core focus. However, this person must refrain from directing the team's daily activities and priorities, allowing them to remain focused on their primary objectives.[80]

Flexibility and adaptability are key in the fast-paced startup environment. Sun Tzu, the philosopher and General of the Zhou Dynasty, emphasized the importance of adapting to each new situation, like water shaping its course according to the ground it flows over. This principle underscores the value of agility in responding to changing circumstances and seizing opportunities in the startup landscape.[81]

> *It's not the strongest of the species that survives, nor the most intelligent, but the one most responsive to change.* —Charles Darwin, English naturalist, geologist, and biologist.

When you change your company's direction, avoiding the knee-jerk reaction of assembling a tiger team or launching an all-hands-on-deck recovery effort is often prudent. Instead, take the time to process critical information and carefully formulate a plan that will lead to positive transformation. Consider focusing initially on the *who* and the *how* before determining the *what*. Ensure you have the right people and advisors to inform your strategy and plan, as they will contribute to the best outcome.[82]

Each entrepreneurial journey is shaped by chance, adaptation, and risk. Instead of dwelling on factors beyond your control, focus on dealing with what you can influence. Prioritize efficient and judicious spending, execute plans effectively, and take calculated risks when the potential rewards are significant. Seek creative solutions to conserve cash flow, leverage opportunities for favors, and take proactive steps to shape your future rather than merely reacting to circumstances as they arise.

I can't change the direction of the wind, but I can adjust my sails to always reach my destination. —Jimmy Dean, American country singer, television host, actor, and businessman.

Sales and Marketing

Ideally, everyone within a startup organization acts as a salesperson and marketer. During the earliest phase of a new company, virtually every employee can be customer-facing. However, hiring an expert sales and marketing team (at the right time) is critical to every company's success.

Marketing is not a function, it is your whole business seen from the customer's point of view. —Peter F. Drucker, Austrian-American management consultant, educator, and author.

Salespeople who go the extra mile are usually rewarded with orders when selling their products or services. Quite simply, salespeople need to do other people's work for them. They must thoroughly understand their customers' needs, interests, and desires, sometimes even before they do. They need to know precisely what their customers are looking for, and then they need to deliver their products and services in a way that's at least *perceived* as being customized to them. Customers need to be led to the point of quickly understanding why they're being offered something unique, compelling, and even revolutionary—something they can't possibly do without. It's a lot of work—perseverance is a salesperson's superpower.[83]

Care enough to create value for customers. If you get that part right, selling is easy. —Anthony Lannarino, author, speaker, sales expert, and entrepreneur.

Significant time and effort are dedicated to determining the prices for your products and services. As Warren Buffett emphasizes, price reflects the actual and perceived value of the offering. Customers often compare prices with those of competitors and make judgments accordingly. They tend to associate higher prices with higher value, though this isn't always rational. Sales and marketing professionals are experts in pricing strategies and effectively communicate the value proposition of products and services to drive sales.[84]

Successful salespeople are characterized by their unwavering persistence and relentless pursuit of opportunities. They understand that the timing of a sale can be unpredictable and recognize the importance of seizing the moment when a potential customer is receptive. Continuously pushing forward with energy and creativity, they remain vigilant in their efforts to close deals. They know that hesitation or passivity can result in missed opportunities, as competitors quickly step in when a salesperson lets down their guard. Therefore, successful sales professionals maintain a sense of urgency, are always ready to ask for orders and guide customers in purchasing decisions. They understand that a gentle nudge is sometimes all it takes to encourage customers to take the plunge and commit to a purchase.

I recall a time at Endwave when we were on the cusp of closing a critical funding round. We had been courting our first important international customer, but our sales manager had been reluctant to press them to place an order, fearing that appearing overly eager or anxious might weaken our negotiating leverage. As our board meeting turned to funding discussions, Doug Lockie, our founder and evangelist, observed uneasiness amongst our board members. He quietly left the room and called our prospective customer's CEO. Within minutes, Doug had asked for a preliminary order, which the CEO agreed to on the spot. Feeling empowered and energized, he requested a commitment to partially fund the effort to customize our product to their specific requirements, which the CEO likewise accepted. With this information, Doug returned to the board meeting and silently slipped his handwritten note to our CEO, Ed Keible, who read it and winked at Doug. When Ed announced our crucial new order to the board, our investors enthusiastically committed to funding our next round. By the end of the meeting, our next funding round was over-subscribed at a share price that exceeded our expectations. The lesson here was: when in doubt, ask for the order!

Beyond sales and marketing, continuous innovation is essential for sustaining success in a competitive marketplace. Complacency can quickly lead to obsolescence, even when your product or service is revolutionary. Competitors are always looking for ways to outshine or undercut you, so it's critical to remain proactive in refining and enhancing your offerings. Even while purchase orders flow in, de-signing and creating your next breakthrough is essential. You main-tain your competitive edge by continuously innovating and ensuring a steady stream of appealing enhancements for existing and prospec-tive customers.

> *Many companies forget what it means to make great prod-ucts. After initial success, sales and marketing people take over and the product people eventually make their way out.*
> —Steve Jobs.

Branding and MarCom

Branding is a strategic framework that guides a business toward its objectives by shaping its identity, including elements like logos and messaging. While companies may introduce numerous products over time, a brand remains distinct from its products and persists independently.

Marketing involves understanding customers' desired products or services and determining the optimal pricing strategy. It also entails monitoring competitors to anticipate their actions and adjusting strategies to secure and retain customers. Branding utilizes Marketing Communications (MarCom) to communicate its offerings to the target audience through advertising and other promotional activities.[85]

> *A product can be quickly outdated, but a successful brand is timeless.* —Stephen King, American novelist. and short-story writer.

Branding is a startup cornerstone. It requires a long-term strategy and a narrative-driven approach. Initiating branding efforts early in a new company's journey ensures alignment between the product and brand as they evolve. However, it's essential to remember that the brand and the product hold value only if they generate profit.[86]

Branding becomes essential as your startup matures and the first product begins to gel so your customers will quickly identify and experience your company's offering optimally and holistically. Your company's brand should accurately symbolize who and what you are as a business. It should also represent how you want potential customers to perceive and think about you as a company. An effective brand helps everyone distinguish a business's products, which helps them connect to the company and mission and ultimately select your product over your competitor's. The brand story should guide the product, and the product and brand should never be allowed to separate.

Statistically, ninety-five percent of customer purchasing decisions are subconscious. That means customer decisions or product selections aren't limited to rational factors. Their choices are often substantially influenced by a company's brand and how they *feel* about a company. Startups can't always compete with the large incumbent competitors on a feature-by-feature basis, so they must prioritize creating a brand that effectively communicates their mission and values. This promotes a deep connection with customers, enhancing their likelihood of choosing the startup's offerings.[87]

> *If people believe they share values with a company, they will stay loyal to the brand.* —Howard Schultz, American businessman, and author.

Selecting a company name is a crucial aspect of branding. Ideally, the name should be easy to spell, memorable, available for use and registration, and broad enough to accommodate future pursuits. For instance, Jeff Bezos wisely chose "Amazon" over a narrower name like "BooksOnline." When considering a name, envision your company's future growth and expansion. Investing in professional graphic designers specializing in branding can also lead to exceptional outcomes. At Endgate, we designed our first logo, which lasted for a few years. Eventually, we hired experts to take our branding to the next level, learning that while engineers excel in many areas, graphic design isn't necessarily one of them.

The most successful companies prioritize branding over direct selling. Take Apple, for instance. Rather than pushing specific products, Apple focuses on cultivating lasting customer relationships. Its advertisements emphasize the transformative experience of using its products, highlighting simplicity and ease of use. This approach builds a strong bond with consumers. Similarly, Nike's marketing revolves around its brand values of promoting active lifestyles and achieving physical goals. Instead of just selling shoes, Nike inspires and empowers athletes through its brand messaging.

Whether running a small business or a large corporation, your company should emphasize long-term relationships over singular transactions. When you bring real value to your customers, you can collect clients and build a legacy. If you create the best and most impactful products or services that bring meaningful change to people's lives, your business will thrive in the long run. Investing in building a solid brand presence allows you to consistently outperform traditional sales tactics and establish enduring connections with your customers.[88]

> *Your advertising, social media, content, PR—all of this informs. Your brand convinces.* —Unknown.

Money and Crisis Management

Startups survive only as long as their cash reserves last. If your company is venture-funded, you must continually perform and advance to secure each successive infusion of investment capital until it is no longer required to grow and sustain operations.

Surviving the pre-revenue phase of your business is extraordinarily challenging. You will have multiple demands on capital, both monetary and human, as well as conflicting guidance and opinions from your board, employees, and advisors. Even with high profitability, failure is possible without adequate cash flow management. Embracing "absolute austerity" means spending exclusively on items directly related to generating sales and reinvesting earnings to attract more prospects.

> *Time and the unknown are the enemy, while capital is the only ally.* —Unknown.

During a crisis, such as a market downturn or a viral pandemic, sustaining operations while preserving your business base and employee skills is critical for future success. Prioritize paying vendors and suppliers and servicing debt. Assess your supply base for vulnerability by reviewing their financial health and operational capacity. Establish contingency plans to ensure the continuity of critical supplies or services. You must ensure your company's survival so that it's positioned to thrive downstream. If your cash and capital reserves become depleted, the outcome is predictable.

Startups often face financial challenges because their leaders tend to be overly optimistic in planning and estimating the funding required for each growth phase. The most successful leaders find nuggets of opportunity within every crisis to weather the storm and accomplish things that their competitors are too timid or frugal to attempt.

> *You never let a serious crisis go to waste. And what I mean by that it's an opportunity to do things you think you could not do before.* —Rahm Emanuel, American politician, and diplomat.

As you grow and scale, your gross margin and profit projections should be realistic. To sustain your growth, you'll continue to need more people, equipment, and general and administrative staff. You may also outgrow your existing office space. Remember that your net profit margins can *decrease* if you scale your company without controlling your expenses.[89]

When pricing your products as you begin to scale to multiple customers, remember to avoid the trap of pricing early products based on what they might *eventually* cost at high volume. High volume may never come, and the cost benefits at scale might not materialize to the degree anticipated.

Instead, you might benefit from pricing your products based on known costs to ensure profitability at each stage. Add a profit margin when in doubt. Avoid assuming that keeping costs down will naturally drive higher volume. While larger companies may sustain such strategies, they can be disastrous for startups. It's essential to base management decisions on concrete factors rather than hope or luck.[90]

Be conservative when recruiting high-priced personnel such as CIOs, CMOs, and CFOs. They should only be hired when their expertise is critical to success or advancing your corporate evolution. Depending on your company's stage of development, hiring them too early can drain cash and limit their effectiveness.

In a startup, it's important to be realistic about what you can spend on activities like marketing. You might have experience working at a large company with an enormous marketing budget. In a startup, you'll need to embrace a different mindset. Challenge yourself to find inexpensive, creative, and impactful solutions to your marketing needs. Break the mold and do things *your* way. Leverage social media and become an expert in manipulating its levers. Twitter and Facebook, for example, are incredibly effective ways to get your message out to many people. They're more cost-effective than traditional advertising, so use them to your advantage.

Social media is an excellent way to communicate with customers and supporters and generate chatter, energy, and excitement. Pay attention to the feedback you receive, and use that information to further refine your campaigns.[91]

When you maintain a sense of frugality in your personal life and spending habits, that same behavior can also transfer to your business tendencies, which can influence co-worker behaviors. Conversely, suppose you begin to reward yourself extravagantly as your business takes off. In that case, co-workers might emulate your spendthrift behavior as they make purchasing and investment recommendations and decisions.

Don't allow early success to go to your head. Instead, maintain the same fiscal control and restraint that underpinned your early corporate success. Make it a habit rather than an exception.

> *Most people, when they start scaling their business, also end up scaling their lifestyle. They want to get back to the normal or average standard of living they had before. However, you always want to live below your means, or you'll end up there quicker than you'd like.* —Austin Godsey, American entrepreneur, youth marketeer, speaker, and investor.

Celebrate Often

Maintaining a positive and supportive work environment pays dividends. It fuels passion, loyalty, and success. As startups strive to innovate and secure their first major customer before funding runs out, stress levels can spike. During these challenging times, remember to step back, breathe, and decompress.

Celebrating small and incremental successes, especially during peak workloads, was an enduring practice at Endgate. We established a tradition to commemorate breakthroughs, Aha! Moments, successful risk-taking, major achievements, and other significant events. Failures were also celebrated, as they led to valuable learning experiences. When success struck, we gathered in our office hallway, retrieved a bottle of champagne, and one person (or a team member in case of group efforts) fired the cork down the hallway in an attempt to beat the previous record-holder. The final cork location was marked on the wall with a brief note of the accomplishment, followed by the team's eager enjoyment of the champagne. These impromptu celebrations included customers, investors, advisors, and board members whenever convenient.

When an employment offer was accepted, we all signed a congratulations card and mailed it to the new hire to share our happiness and excitement. Promotions, marriages, and baby arrivals were publicly celebrated, creating a sense of family and unity.

On those rare occasions when employees chose to leave the company, we didn't treat them like traitors or sweep their departure under the rug. We hosted informal farewell parties, encouraged them on their new journey, and ensured they knew they were always welcome back. On several occasions, employees returned to the fold, which triggered further celebrations.

Events like these are fun, inspiring, and remarkably effective in building team camaraderie, pride, and loyalty. They also serve as excuses to lower the pressure during sprints. Work can be stressful but enjoyable with the right kind of leadership and corporate traditions.

> *Don't be afraid to celebrate your accomplishments. Just celebrate those of others more.* —Nina Vaca, Ecuadorian-born American entrepreneur, inspirationalist, philanthropist, and business executive.

Ed's Rules

When we launched Endgate, our seed investor, Ed Tuck, was a veteran venture capitalist and angel investor. We all came to know and love Ed not just as an investor and sage counselor but also as a friend and member of our corporate family. Ed was the epitome of an understated, humble, and inspiring advisor. The room became silent whenever he spoke as we focused intently on hearing his every word.

Ed provided each of the founders with a framed picture of what he had coined "Ed's Rules" for startups. These are his distilled recommendations on how to behave when launching and building a company, gleaned from his decades of experience:

ED'S RULES

"This above all, to thine own self be true:
And it must follow as the night the day
Thou canst not then be false to any Man."
—Hamlet, Act 1 Scene 3

- Describe the product honestly, and give your customer what you described; if the product doesn't meet your description, don't ship it until it does (or change the description).

- There are three equal participants in a company: its customers, its employees, and its shareholders. The best companies are those in which each third of the triad receives equal consideration.

- In a modern company, the line between management and workers is very fuzzy. All employees have some management responsibility, and all managers are employees. Each person's job is as important as another's; if this isn't true, the organization needs fixing.

- Work should be enjoyed. That doesn't mean that every moment is fun, or that a lot of it isn't unpleasant; but if it isn't enjoyable or rewarding on the average, you should try to change your job.

- Incompetent people destroy organizations, friendships and companies. To tolerate incompetence in an employee or associate injures you, him and your co-workers. Find work for him that he can accomplish, or get him out of the company.

- Treat everybody the same: young, old, high or low rank. This habit is a mark of good breeding.

- Everyone in a business must exercise not only his intellect and his skills, but his moral and ethical values. Everyone in a company is responsible for its performance and its reputation.

- Follow your instincts and your hunches; to ignore them is to deny your humanity.

It goes without saying that "man," "he," "him," and "his" include "woman," "she," "her," and "hers."

CHAPTER 5

Work Culture

Culture eats Strategy for Breakfast, operation excellence for lunch, and everything else for dinner. —Peter F. Drucker.

Every company cultivates a culture shaped by its leaders. The culture is an organization's operating system, encompassing values, behaviors, and processes that shape people's motivation and engagement. Culture isn't an intangible mystery; it's the outcome of intentional and sustained effort. Corporate culture profoundly influences organizational performance.[92]

Culture can be defined as a shared set of values (what we care about), beliefs (what we believe to be true), and behavioral norms (how we do things) within an organization. It aligns efforts, creates a sense of shared purpose and values, enhances predictability, and encodes organizational lessons about effective practices.[93]

Leaders who prioritize hiring a diverse workforce with shared common values nurture the best work cultures. These leaders actively prevent unethical and incompetent individuals from rising to influential positions. Building healthy work cultures requires exceptional skill in assessing employees and leadership candidates to ensure alignment with the culture while actively opposing those who under-mine it.[94]

> *Customers will never love a company until the employees love it first.* —Simon Sinek.

Some describe the work culture as the *glue* that binds us in good times and bad and the *grease* that facilitates innovation, fresh thinking, and resiliency. However, in unhealthy cultures, the glue can keep us stuck in the past, unable to evolve to a better state. The grease that keeps a work culture running smoothly can quickly become slippery, causing us to stumble when leadership falters or priorities drift astray.

Having a *strong* corporate culture isn't enough—having a *healthy* one is far more essential. When assessing whether a work culture is healthy, it's necessary to transcend what the leaders have to *say*. Most leaders will boast about how purpose-driven, customer-focused, in-novative, or collaborative their cultures are. But what are the employ-ees and customers saying? Are there discrepancies between leaders' claims and employees' perceptions? Are employees aligned with the organization's goals and leadership mindset, or do they feel that the culture is unhealthy and needs repair?[95]

Studies have shown that *why* we work influences *how well* we work. When people feel that their work has meaning, their work qual-ity, performance, and motivation levels are consistently higher.

Research conducted at the University of Rochester in the 1980s identified six primary reasons people work: play, purpose, potential, emotional pressure, economic pressure, and inertia. The first three motives generally enhance performance, while the latter hinder it. Successful companies strive to amplify positive motives like purpose and potential while mitigating negative ones like economic pressure and inertia.

A healthy culture creates tangible value and increases customer and employee satisfaction. This, in turn, produces better customer outcomes, which fuels corporate growth, profitability, and success. Establishing a clearly defined organizational identity allows workers to see how their work makes a difference. Culture shouldn't be left to chance. It requires sustained priority, attention, commitment, and nurturing.[96]

> *Work at your culture or it will build itself, and you won't like the results.* —Norman Murray, business and leadership consultant.

As a leader, whether your company is well-established or a startup, you should constantly ask yourself: What do we want our company to become? What is our company's vision? Whom do we recruit or reject? Will we prioritize corporate citizenship, such as sustainability and environmental responsibility? The founders, CEO, and executive team set the precedent. The leader at the helm sets the tone, and others follow suit. Leaders bear the ultimate responsibility for shaping and upholding the company culture.

As the saying goes, "The people are the greatest asset of any company." Therefore, investing in their continuous growth and well-being is essential for future success. Encouraging employees to be their authentic selves inspires their best work. Diverse teams are more innovative, reflective, and aligned with their varied customer base. Exceptional leaders are dedicated to cultivating vibrant, inclusive cultures that embody the core values of their workforce and the customers they serve. Culture, purpose, and people drive employee engagement and corporate success.

The corporate landscape is littered with failures traced back to unhealthy cultures. Alternatively, many companies that have existed for decades and those who've consistently led their industries have established and maintained positive and nurturing cultures. Their cultures benefit from top-notch leadership methods and sound policies and frameworks that underpin their foundations.

The organizational culture is essentially the sum of its parts. If you take care of your employees, they will care for your business and customers.[97]

> *Ultimately, it's on the company leaders to set the tone, not only the CEO, but the leaders across the company. If you select them so carefully that they then hire the right people, it's a nice self-fulfilling prophecy.* —Tim Cook, American business executive.

Some leaders prioritize profit over culture. Many of those leaders will, through inattention or misdirection, create toxic cultures. This can lead to stagnation, where visions are ignored, and missions go unfulfilled. However, healthy cultures go beyond employee and customer satisfaction. Many customers are now showing a preference for culture-driven companies.

A recent study by Northwestern University found that customers of companies with more engaged employees used the company's products and services more often and were more satisfied than those with less engaged employees. Your company values reflect your brand identity, and customers can perceive when your culture is weak or compromised.[98]

Culture-building demands time, conversations, and relationships. It requires prioritization and investment and should be part of management performance reviews. Many experts believe that a diverse workforce necessitates family-friendly leave policies to support employees as they start families. Leaders should also examine their policies to ensure that promotions, opportunities for horizontal movement, and other learning and growth opportunities are fair and available to the entire workforce.

A people-centric culture prioritizes giving back to communities by reinvesting a portion of profits into local initiatives. This might include providing an underserved community with education and creative tools, investing in future talent with training, resources, and mentorship, or applying its technology to solve local challenges. People-centric cultures prioritize employee well-being by monitoring engagement and mental health, offering time off to recharge, and providing resources for mental health support. Leaders in these organizations model healthy behaviors by promoting reasonable work hours and discouraging an "always connected" mindset.

Corporate culture plays a critical role in shaping an organization's identity, guiding its actions, and influencing the success of its people. It forms the foundation for decision-making, collaboration, and innovation, impacting employee morale, customer relationships, and overall performance. A well-crafted culture aligns values with goals, creating an environment where individuals and teams can thrive. If you enjoy the corporate culture where you work, do your part to support, protect, and reinforce it, and ensure you don't refer or hire those who would destroy it.

The culture of any organization is shaped by the worst behavior that leaders are willing to tolerate. —Unknown.

Mission, Vision, and Values Statements

A company's culture is more than how employees interact—it embodies its core identity. At the heart of this identity are mission, value, and vision statements, which serve as guiding principles for decision-making, behavior, and long-term goals. These statements define the company's purpose, the ethical standards it upholds, and the aspirations it strives toward, creating a framework that shapes daily operations and employee mindsets. When thoughtfully crafted and authentically modeled, they provide a strong cultural foundation that promotes alignment, stimulates engagement, and drives success. Mission, Vision, and Values statements are essential for every company, especially for startups.

The mission statement defines a company's purpose and values and outlines its commitments to shareholders, employees, stakeholders, and customers. It serves as a unifying guide, aligning everyone with the company's brand and objectives.[99]

Creating a mission statement demands considerable thought and reflection. As startups progress, it's natural for their mission statements to evolve. The CEO doesn't draft the most effective mission statements—they're the byproduct of team collaboration. For example, at Endgate, we continuously honed our mission and vision statements during annual off-site leadership gatherings.

A mission statement is not something you write overnight... But fundamentally, your mission statement becomes your constitution, the solid expression of your vision and values. It becomes the criterion by which you measure everything else in your life. —Stephen Covey.

When crafting your mission statement, be sure to articulate your corporate purpose clearly—describe *what* your business does and *how* it achieves its goals. Clarify *why* your company is pursuing its objectives. Values, credibility, inspiration, and specificity characterize an effective mission statement. By delineating your corporate purpose, you also articulate your core values.

The mission and vision statements are uniquely separate. While a mission statement focuses on the present, a vision statement looks ahead to the future. The mission statement defines what the business currently does, while a vision statement outlines what the company aspires to become.

> *Vision is a destination—a fixed point to which we focus all effort. Strategy is a route—an adaptable path to get us where we want to go.* —Simon Sinek.

A third important document is the *values* statement, which describes *why* the business exists in overarching terms. Before launching your company, contemplating its values is critical, as they form the backbone of your business decisions. Values bind your company's core components together, defining its essence. They must be established proactively, setting the tone from the outset. Revisiting these values is necessary during growth or transformation phases. Building a values-based company involves assembling and guiding a team that will follow and embody them. Your values should resonate with *all* your team members, regardless of position or seniority.[100]

Aligning values with profitability is a delicate dance in the business world. Leaders constantly face the challenge of harmonizing corporate values with business growth demands. Those who excel at this balancing act prioritize doing what's right on par with—or even above—maximizing profits. Their fundamental belief is that long-term profitability stems from ethical conduct and doing the *right thing* consistently.

Leaders should prioritize value-based ideas, practices, and behaviors to achieve this. They should embed their values into every aspect of the organization and empower employees to embody them. Company decisions and actions should consistently and transparently reflect these core values, and leaders must hold themselves and others accountable.

Culture stems from strategy and principles, so hiring individuals who resonate with the company's values is essential. Empowering employees who share these values to make hiring decisions creates a positive feedback loop, reinforcing the organization's culture. A principles-driven business maintains clarity about its beliefs, what it stands for, and the actions it is willing to take or avoid.[101]

When crafting your vision statement, avoid absolutes. Ensure your words are comprehensible, inclusive, and flexible to accommodate diverse expectations and perspectives. Avoid alienating anyone, especially your employees.

Likewise, your Mission statement should be realistic and attainable. If your words are perceived as impossible to achieve, your customers or employees might lose faith in the mission. Establishing overly aggressive or optimistic goals can also be a recipe for failure. Instead, ask yourself what to target *today* to make a real, material impact. This will fuel immediate and tangible actions that move the needle.[102]

Purpose Statement

As employees increasingly scrutinize their organization's impact on communities and the planet, corporate leaders are crafting purpose statements to reshape how people operate within the organization. Purpose represents a profound commitment shared throughout the organization, which drives motivation and action.

Purpose inspires workers by clarifying organizational priorities that fundamentally flow from its identity. It connects people's work with their values and feelings so that they'll act from the heart. When the corporate purpose is authentic in its alignment with what employees feel is important and is consistent with the work that the organization performs daily, employees are far more likely to exceed expectations by going the extra mile for their customers, colleagues, and the organization.

The purpose statement should be regularly reviewed to ensure the company consistently aligns with and upholds its purpose. Championing purpose requires the total commitment of top management, who must embrace and model it consistently. Further, the purpose statement should align with the company's strategy.[103]

While the mission statement includes discussions of purpose, the purpose statement serves a distinct but complementary role:

- Clarity and focus: While a mission statement addresses the broader "what" and "how" of an organization's goals and operations, a purpose statement pinpoints the "why." It distills the organization's reason for existing into a simple, motivational idea, ensuring clarity for stakeholders.

- Motivational impact: A purpose statement resonates personally, inspiring employees, customers, and partners by highlighting the more profound meaning and value the organization aims to create beyond profit or operational goals.

- Strategic alignment: The purpose statement acts as a guiding principle, helping to evaluate whether initiatives, decisions, and strategies align with the organization's core reason for existence. This deeper alignment isn't always achieved through a broader mission statement.

- Cultural reinforcement: A well-defined purpose cultivates a sense of identity and shared values within the organization, providing employees with a consistent narrative to guide their work.

The most purpose-driven organizations create impact and strategically define, measure, and manage their financial, social, and environmental objectives end-to-end. Tracking inputs (e.g., contributions to worthy causes) is not enough; measuring the outcomes and outputs is essential to confirm that the inputs effectively meet the stated objectives.[104]

> *The most powerful purpose statements are crystal clear and single minded in their focus.* —Roy Spence, business executive, entrepreneur, and author.

Authenticity

Teams thrive on the collective contribution and impact of individuals. When each team member feels valued, supported, and respected, they're more likely to contribute positively to the group dynamic. Encouraging authenticity, embracing diversity, and facilitating inclusivity create an environment where everyone can fully engage and perform at their best.

> *The authentic self is the soul made visible.* —Sarah Ban Breathnach, author, philanthropist, and public speaker.

Maintaining a strict separation between work and personal life may seem like a workplace safeguard, but it can lead to feelings of isolation and loneliness. Building friendships at work is natural and can create a stronger sense of community. When we allow ourselves to show our personalities and connect on a human level, we build deeper relationships with colleagues and gain respect and influence within our teams. Embracing our humanity in the workplace can make us more relatable and approachable and ultimately enhance our success.

When we're not being authentic, it requires energy to regulate those facets of our identity that we keep private. On the other hand, when we're encouraged to express ourselves freely in the workplace without experiencing fear or embarrassment, we experience relief and well-being.[105]

When we're encouraged to be ourselves at work, we can shed the noise associated with worrying about how we're being perceived or whether our work assignments, promotions, and advancement opportunities will be affected. Only then can we channel our presence toward remarkable performance, achievement, and impact.

> *The core of authenticity is the courage to be imperfect, vulnerable, and to set boundaries.* —Brené Brown, American professor, social worker, author, and podcast host.

Embracing authenticity in the workplace requires bravery, courage, and a degree of boldness. It flourishes when a company creates an environment that supports authenticity through its policies, leadership style, and culture. Authenticity means having the courage to voice your opinions, even when they challenge the status quo.

However, being authentic at work doesn't give us the license to impose our views on others or silence opposing voices simply because we've been permitted to speak up without reservation. Authenticity involves courageously expressing our best selves without fear of judgment. It's about being true to our unique personalities, speaking our minds respectfully, and letting our individuality shine.[106]

> *I don't think anybody could be Steve Jobs. I think he was a once-in-a-hundred-years kind of individual, an original by any stretch of the imagination. And so what I had to do was to be the best version of myself.* —Tim Cook.

Leaders who prioritize authenticity recognize its potential to drive innovation and success. Sheryl Sandberg's famous question, "What would you do if you weren't afraid?" exemplifies this ethos, encouraging employees to embrace authenticity and boldness. This mindset inspires workers to tackle big problems and deliver meaningful results, enhancing their organizational impact.

While authenticity is often encouraged, there are exceptions to this principle. Firmly and staunchly displaying one's true self may not be appropriate or advantageous in every situation. Some researchers have produced compelling counterarguments to workplace authenticity, including a phenomenon known as "mind-body dissonance" (MBD), in which people can gain a creative edge when they assume physical expressions that contradict their actual state of mind.[107]

I recall several situations where it paid to conceal my thoughts or feelings, particularly as a leader. Sometimes, we need to role-play for a desired effect. Other times, we might need to present an outward calm to our team when we're freaking out internally. Further, some workplaces are not well-suited for intimate rapport. Oversharing personal information with individuals not ready for it can have dire consequences. It can put a strain on working relationships, which can be harmful to everyone involved.

Being authentic at work can also make us feel vulnerable. Many are cautious about revealing their true selves in professional settings, fearing potential consequences. Raw authenticity can create a fear of being judged, criticized, or ridiculed. Some of us are naturally more private than others. Others may exhibit personalities perceived as unprofessional or unsuitable for advancement by supervisors. Additionally, natural quirks or awkward tendencies are often suppressed to maintain a neutral demeanor in workplace interactions. Sometimes, it's prudent to conceal certain aspects of ourselves to navigate professional environments successfully.

Embracing authenticity at work can present different challenges depending on an individual's background and experiences. Societal norms and attitudes, especially regarding topics like gender identity, may influence a person's comfort level when sharing more about themselves. Navigating authenticity in the workplace requires a nuanced approach involving self-awareness, emotional intelligence, and sensitivity to others' perspectives. Remember to consider the context and timing of conversations, exercise discretion, and avoid inappropriate oversharing.

When encouraging authenticity, management must create a culture of safety. People must feel comfortable speaking their minds or making mistakes without fear of reprimand. Creating psychological safety takes time and perseverance, but it's well worth the effort when we observe the payback that authenticity brings to the workforce.[108]

> *Be who you are and say what you feel, cause those who mind don't matter, and those who matter don't mind.* —Dr. Seuss, American children's author and cartoonist.

Working at Facebook helped me grasp the essence of being authentic in the workplace. From top to bottom, the company sustained an environment where being oneself was accepted and encouraged, enabling us to excel in our roles. Instead of fixating on how others perceived us, we were empowered to focus on making meaningful contributions by embracing our individuality. This approach allowed us to bring our whole selves to work, reinforcing a culture prioritizing personal choice and freedom without the fear of judgment.

Encouraging authenticity in the workforce allows individuals to bring their diverse backgrounds, cultures, traditions, and experiences to every problem and project. This diversity of perspectives stimulates creativity and innovation, ultimately leading to our best work and highest impact. Embracing authenticity in the workplace is a winning attitude that promotes inclusivity and drives success.

Bringing your whole self to work is about showing up with more of your humanity. Allowing yourself to be authentic and vulnerable, and also free to choose what you reveal about yourself. —Mike Robbins, American author, management consultant, executive coach, and speaker.

Bias and Inequality

Bias and inequality in the workplace don't just impact individuals—they shape the very culture of an organization, influencing how teams function, decisions are made, and opportunities are distributed. By understanding and addressing these systemic issues, businesses can create a more inclusive and equitable environment where everyone has the chance to thrive.

Gender and racial bias, as well as other forms of discrimination, exist in corporate America despite significant strides in recent years. Investments in unconscious bias training, revamped recruitment systems, and prioritization of diverse executive-level hires are promising signs of progress. However, there is still much work to be done.

Our inequality materializes our upper class, vulgarizes our middle class, brutalizes our lower class. —Matthew Arnold, English poet, and literary and social critic.

Systemic bias continues to persist in subtle yet pervasive ways. While this reality is well-documented, many deniers argue—without evidence—that systemic bias is a relic of the past. This stance often ignores or deliberately overlooks expansive data and lived experiences that reveal enduring inequities. These inequities manifest in hiring decisions, pay disparities, workplace treatment, and opportunities for advancement.

Instead of acknowledging these challenges, critics resist anti-bias initiatives, advocating for a "colorblind" approach that inadvertently perpetuates the very inequality that anti-bias initiatives seek to address. Critics also argue that "the playing field is equal now," but the data overwhelmingly shows otherwise. Addressing these inequities isn't about favoring one group over another but ensuring fair treatment, opportunity, and access for all. Systemic problems require comprehensive and durable solutions.

Corporate expenditures to eliminate bias and inequality often yield mixed results, with little tangible impact at the team level. There are questions about whether work cultures genuinely shift in the desired direction or if investments are merely superficial, ticking boxes without substantial progress. It's important to assess whether people are collaborating authentically or being coerced, if individuality is respected or conformity demanded, and if effective tools to address bias are provided and implemented across the organization. Continuous prioritization is necessary to sustain a work culture that aligns with company values.

Like systemic racism, gender bias continues unabated throughout society. Working mothers, in particular, face persistent challenges, including wage disparities and disproportionate responsibilities for childcare. The pandemic exacerbated these issues, with many women experiencing heightened levels of anxiety, depression, and loneliness while juggling work and family duties from home. The resulting exodus of women from the workforce has led to a loss of talent and innovation for many companies. The conflicting expectations placed on American workers and parents lie at the core of this issue.

Mothers face heightened expectations to be deeply involved caregivers, dedicating significant time and effort to their children's upbringing. Compared to predecessors from decades ago, the modern mother spends far more time with their children now, ushering and overseeing the many activities that constitute a child's life today. Despite women's advancements in education, taking time off for caregiving further widens the gender pay gap, perpetuating inequality in the workforce.

Ensuring equal pay for women and improving access to affordable childcare are critical needs in the American workplace. The high cost of childcare often prevents women from returning to work, highlighting the necessity for more accessible and affordable childcare options. Flexible work schedules, which enable women to duck out occasionally in the middle of the day to deal with their children, can help them balance their conflicting demands without feeling guilty.[109]

While some attribute societal decay to a decline in religion, the general acceptance of homosexuality, or the feminist movement, perhaps the proper solution lies in improving conditions that ease the challenges of raising children, strengthening economic stability for lower- and middle-class families, and eradicating bias and inequality in all its forms. This would promote happier, healthier families and pave the way for a more unified and thriving America.

Leadership plays an essential role in reducing, if not eliminating, bias in the workplace. The following are some general guidelines for leaders to follow:

- Persistence: Advocate for genuine diversity by implementing inclusive hiring practices and policies. Ensure a broad candidate pipeline includes qualified candidates from underrepresented groups for every role.

- Resistance: Combat homogeneity by establishing clear and objective hiring criteria for each position. Ensure consistency in evaluating all candidates to resist bias and promote diversity.

- Referrals: Be cautious of homogeneous referrals, where managers populate their teams with individuals of the same ethnicity, often through referrals from team members of similar backgrounds. If a team becomes too uniform in appearance and makeup, it signals a deficiency in diversity and inclusion efforts.

- Objectivity: Structure your interview questions around skills, knowledge, and experience, and use a standard rubric to evaluate candidates consistently. This helps avoid bias and ensures all candidates are assessed objectively based on their qualifications.

- Observance: Be aware of and mindful of bias, and look for it when it occurs randomly. For example, observe whether male colleagues talk over or interrupt women in meetings.

- Representation: Ensure that everyone is equally represented in meetings and corporate events. Consider the timing of meetings and whether they disadvantage certain groups, such as scheduling them late in the day, which may conflict with childcare responsibilities.

- Recognition: Avoid bias when assigning low-impact, low-visibility tasks to people. Appropriately recognize and appreciate their contributions and actively support their advancement opportunities.

- Access: Ensure everyone on your team experiences equal access to your time and attention. Make sure that your impromptu check-ins and walking meetings involve everyone uniformly.

- Fairness: Ensure fairness in performance reviews, raises, promotions, bonuses, and high-potential assignments for your team.

- Consistency: Differentiate between performance and potential, focusing on skills rather than personality to avoid double standards. Consistently apply processes and oversight to interrupt bias and stimulate change.[110]

We must never lose sight of our principles—eliminating discrimination, bias, and inequality remains a cornerstone of progress in business and society. Equal treatment of all individuals—regardless of gender, race, ethnicity, or background—is a moral imperative and a fundamental human right. Achieving fairness requires persistent effort to dismantle systemic barriers and cultivate environments where everyone can thrive. These workplace and community principles should guide our collective actions, ensuring that inclusivity and equality remain central to building a better, more just society. As modern society evolves, this commitment must continue to shape policies, practices, and cultural norms, reinforcing the shared belief that equity strengthens individuals and institutions alike.

Encouraging collaboration, lifting others, and embracing an abundance mindset where everyone can thrive together are the keys to enduring and impactful success. By prioritizing equity, empathy, and mutual respect, we can create environments that inspire innovation, cultivate trust, and achieve shared goals without perpetuating bias or inequality.

> *As long as poverty, injustice, and gross inequality persist in our world, none of us can truly rest.* —Nelson Mandela, South African anti-apartheid activist, politician, statesman, and philanthropist.

Mental Health

Mental health in the workplace has become a crisis in America. In a recent study, more than 40% of respondents claimed that their mental health had declined since the COVID-19 outbreak. Even these troubling statistics likely understate the actual magnitude of the problem.

Your mental health is more important than the test, the interview, the lunch date, the meeting, the family dinner, the football game, the appointment, and the shop-run. Take care of yourself. —Unknown.

Fortunately, many companies have responded to the call for better mental health support by strengthening their internal efforts and expanding long-term wellness strategies. They're actively working to reduce the stigma surrounding mental health discussions, which is crucial for promoting wellness treatments. Some create mental health information hubs to offer stress and burnout management techniques. Additionally, they're organizing guest speaker events to address the intersection of mental health, well-being, and race, helping employees navigate challenging situations effectively. Forward-thinking companies encourage open dialogue, promote healthier workplace norms, and prioritize increasing awareness of mental health issues.

Implementing executive team training sessions is another approach to aligning leadership on the importance of mental health in the workplace. This enhances their commitment to expanding and normalizing mental health discussions. Leading by example empowers employees to request accommodations and embrace new work norms, which creates a culture of support and understanding. Continuous leadership commitment remains essential for sustaining lasting cultural change in this regard.[111]

Just as great leaders prioritize diversity and inclusion within their organizations, they also recognize the importance of addressing mental health as a related factor. We understand that values, race, language, culture, and experiences influence how individuals perceive and manage mental health. Employees from underrepresented or marginalized groups may encounter workplace stressors ranging from microaggressions to systemic discrimination.

For instance, societal unrest is particularly taxing on BIPOC (black, indigenous, and people of color) communities, who were disproportionately affected by the COVID-19 pandemic. Additionally, Asian-American and Pacific Islander communities faced heightened xenophobia and hate crimes, which resulted from the pandemic. Leaders must ensure inclusive and accessible mental health resources to support their employees' well-being.[112]

Men's mental health is another area that is receiving much-needed attention. Suicide is the second most common cause of death for men under 39. Men die of suicide at a rate that's 3.5 times higher than women. Certain groups, like the veteran and LGBTQ+ communities, face even higher rates. Fortunately, the COVID-19 pandemic has prompted many organizations to step up and support those in need.

While leaders must prioritize their teams, customers, and companies, even small steps can significantly impact the broader community. Companies dedicating resources to mental health initiatives can provide crucial support and strengthen their brand.[113]

We should all recognize the power of a work culture that celebrates diversity, embraces inclusion, and amplifies belonging. This is good for the bottom line and the *right thing* to do. We desperately need more leaders who exemplify a strong moral compass, especially when many today tend to reinforce negative behaviors.

The workplace is often the most stressful place a person finds themselves in, employees and managers need to keep an eye out for signs of deteriorating mental health in fellow colleagues. —Paul Farmer, American medical anthropologist, physician, and educator.

CHAPTER 6

Work-Life Balancing Act

Never get so busy making a living that you forget to make a life. —Unknown.

In today's fast-paced world, people struggle to keep up with their exhausting, stressful, and often unproductive work grind. We're constantly inundated with emails, texts, instant messages, social posts, and the unrelenting beeps and chimes of the smart devices that seek to own us. We wake up, check our emails, sit in meetings, and switch between multiple apps all day, but we feel we're getting less and less of the more impactful work done, given all the noise and distractions.

Studies show that despite the many remarkable benefits of today's powerful technology, productivity growth has failed to accelerate. Every new tool or service we add to our daily lives creates more overhead, notifications, and complexity. These tools demand attention and response, making it increasingly difficult to focus on challenging, stimulating, and impactful work that requires sustained concentration. As a result, we've resorted to working evenings and weekends to catch up on our *real* work.[114]

The pandemic worsened the work-life balance dilemma, especially with the widespread shift to remote or hybrid work arrangements. Boundaries between work and home life have blurred, as work often extends into the evenings without clear limits. A recent study found that 67% of employees felt more stressed due to the pandemic, while another survey found that 29% considered themselves depressed. Yet another poll found that 58% of the U.S. workforce felt burned out—an increase of 13% in less than a year.

Post-pandemic, the transition to remote work has caused depression and loneliness due to limited social interaction and increased anxiety relating to mental health and money worries. As we navigate this new work landscape, striking a healthy balance and preserving sanity amidst these challenges becomes essential.[115]

Work-life balance (WLB) has become a critical focus area in corporate America. The detrimental effects of work-related stress are significant, contributing to approximately 85% of severe illnesses and costing businesses an estimated $200-300 billion annually in lost productivity.[116]

A recent study by the World Health Organization revealed that working 55 hours or more per week is associated with a 35% higher risk of stroke and a 17% higher risk of dying from ischemic heart disease. The COVID-19 pandemic has underscored the importance of managing work hours, especially as telecommuting has become widespread. It's clear: prolonged and excessive working hours can lead to dire health consequences, including premature death.[117]

Startups have gained notoriety for imposing intolerable and unsustainable work hours on their employees. For example, during my tenure at one such startup, my boss expected me to be available around the clock. I felt tethered to work, unable to enjoy guilt-free downtime with family and friends, even on vacation. The culture demanded long hours and consistent weekend work, leaving little room for personal time. I vividly recall a 2 a.m. call from my boss to confirm my availability if needed—an implicit reminder that my personal time was no longer my own. That incident sapped my motivation and prompted thoughts of seeking a change.

At another startup, the CEO didn't explicitly demand chronic weekend work, but his workaholic habits implied it. He would arrive at work on any given weekend and proceed to re-direct my team members unless I was present to resist his meddling influence.

Modern workers increasingly seek companies that offer the flexibility to integrate work and personal life during the workday. Fortunately, progressive employers recognize the business benefits of this approach. Studies indicate that incorporating short, frequent breaks into the workday boosts energy levels, sharpens focus, and uplifts mood.[118]

Setting boundaries is crucial in maintaining a healthy work-life balance. While employers have the right to expect dedication and commitment, they shouldn't demand *constant* accessibility or immediate email responses from employees at all hours of the day. Remember, your employer doesn't *own* you. It's perfectly acceptable to request time off without explaining every detail. Make your request and prioritize your well-being.

Your boss won't feel responsible for your failing health when you work yourself raw to meet their demands. I learned this lesson early in my career when I nearly ruined my health by working chronic overtime under extreme pressure to meet aggressive deadlines. After that experience, I always put my health and family first and work second. Although my bosses didn't necessarily appreciate that ordering of priorities, I always worked to meet or exceed performance expectations without resorting to persistent overtime, preventing any negative repercussions.

Balancing work and life can be especially challenging in competitive industries where rivals operate around the clock, creating pressure to match their pace. Striving for balance doesn't always mean equal time—it often requires thoughtful compromise, setting boundaries, and defining success on your own terms without sacrificing well-being or values.[119]

> *Balance is not better time management, but better boundary management. Balance means making choices, and enjoying those choices.* —Betsy Jacobson, Sociologist, and author.

WLB Alternatives

Not everyone supports or embraces the notion of pursuing a healthy work-life balance. Of course, there are business leaders who are hellbent on squeezing every last ounce of productivity from workers, personal lives be damned. While that philosophy isn't considered healthy or sustainable in the long term, it's unlikely that we'll all align our beliefs around WLB in the near term.

> *If the expectation is, 'Hey, we can live and not work hard and not strain extremely to a great degree,' this is false. That is not true. In order for us to succeed, in order for us to live, we must work very hard.* —Elon Musk, South African-born American entrepreneur, and businessman.

As an alternative to WLB, some embrace the notion that work and personal lives are wholly intertwined, overlapping in a fuzzy gray area that's impossible to parse. Some people are satisfied with and even energized by allowing their work activities to consume most of their waking hours.

For individuals in this category, the challenge is prioritizing what's most impactful so that their lifestyle is satisfying and sustainable. For example, sleeping and nurturing a family life require planning, time, and commitment. Those activities should be deliberately scheduled into a seven-day workweek. Scheduling time for meditation can help with stress and calm the mind when work becomes overwhelming. Exercise can be scheduled to sustain the body physically. Scheduling time for a spa treatment can clear the mind and soothe the body.[120]

Jeff Bezos offers another alternative. He believes personal and professional pursuits are better described as a "circle" rather than some form of balancing act. He explains that balancing our time and effort implies a strict trade-off between work and personal pursuits. Rather than compartmentalizing, he advocates acknowledging that the two are interrelated. For example, being happy at home can translate to better energy at work and vice versa.[121]

"Work-life harmony," a term gaining traction, offers an alternative perspective to the traditional concept of balance. Instead of aiming for an equal time division between work and personal life, achieving such a balance may be impractical. Instead, the focus shifts towards integrating elements of personal fulfillment and enjoyment into work demands. This approach encourages individuals to find happiness and satisfaction in both spheres without rigidly adhering to a predetermined split, creating a more holistic and integrated lifestyle.[122]

The evolving landscape of work-life balance continues to yield new perspectives and interpretations, with recent renditions like "Work-Life-Blend" emerging as part of the discourse. Yet, regardless of the terminology or framework employed, the ultimate goal remains the pursuit of a fulfilling and harmonious life overall. The overarching objective is striving for a quality of life where work and personal passions coexist, bringing joy and satisfaction.

Rather than fixating on a rigid 50/50 split, it's worthwhile to embrace the interplay between professional demands and personal fulfillment. As we shift from work to retirement, it's not unusual to transition from *all work and no play* to *no work and all play*. Our priorities naturally adjust alongside our evolving responsibilities and financial needs.

Achieving work-life balance or harmony is essential for well-being, productivity, and job satisfaction. Prioritizing this effort helps prevent burnout, supports mental health, and allows individuals to thrive personally and professionally.

> *Work-life balance is not an entitlement or benefit. Your company cannot give it to you. You have to create it for yourself.*
> —Matthew Kelly, Australian author, speaker, thought leader, and business consultant.

Workaholics

A clear distinction can be made between a workaholic and someone who works long hours because they're excited about and love what they do.

> *Workaholics are addicted to activity; super achievers are committed to results.* —Charles Garfield, psychologist, professor, lecturer, and author.

Workaholics often exhibit a compulsive need to work, driven by a deep-seated desire to prove their worth through productivity or achievement. Their emotional state at work is frequently characterized by hostility, tension, and irritability, stemming from anxiety and a relentless pursuit of perfection. Workaholics often intertwine their self-esteem with their professional achievements, leading to guilt and inadequacy when not working. This addiction to work can strain familial relationships and compromise personal well-being, which highlights the importance of recognizing and addressing workaholic tendencies for a healthier balance in life.

Workaholics can recover by employing their emotional intelligence. First, they should connect with their emotions to identify why they're working so hard. Figuring out what motivates them is the first step toward improvement. Are they trying to impress someone? Are they trying to prove something? Answering these questions is a necessary first step.

Sometimes, talking about their struggles with someone they trust can be helpful. That might be a coworker, a family member, or a counselor. Look for someone who is happy and enjoys healthy relationships—commiserating with another workaholic is unlikely to bear fruit.

Therapy is a valuable resource for individuals seeking insight into their work habits—it can help the patient better understand societal norms and establish healthy boundaries. Rediscovering or nurturing outside passions can help disrupt entrenched work patterns and alleviate the guilt associated with taking breaks. Disconnecting from work for extended periods is essential for overall well-being; it promotes mental, physical, and emotional renewal. Embracing vacations and unplugging during these times can enhance productivity and effectiveness upon return to work.[123]

Workaholism is often mistaken for dedication, but it's a self-destructive cycle that can lead to burnout, strained relationships, and diminished productivity. Unlike those with a strong work ethic, workaholics struggle to disengage, tying their self-worth to constant busyness. This obsession with work often stems from deeper issues—

perfectionism, fear of failure, or external pressures—rather than genuine passion. Breaking free requires setting boundaries, prioritizing well-being, and recognizing that sustainable success comes from balance, not exhaustion.

> *For workaholics, all the eggs of self-esteem are in the basket of work.* —Judith M. Bardwick, psychologist, author, speaker, business consultant, and academic.

Workload

Energetic and highly motivated employees are often eager to please and tend to accept too much work. When we spread ourselves too thin, we risk delivering critical work late, compromising our work quality, and suffering from frustration, stress, and burnout. While it's easy to fall into this trap, it's also straightforward to avoid it.

Research finds that highly competent and skilled employees often carry heavier workloads due to their efficiency and reliability. They excel at turning around assignments quickly and stepping up during emergencies, making them indispensable assets to the team. Unfortunately, these people suffer from the heaviest workloads and bear the stress and burden of accomplishing emergency tasks. Their reluctance to voice workload concerns may perpetuate the cycle of overwork, leading to potential burnout and dissatisfaction in the long run.

Bosses and co-workers should acknowledge the stress they impose on high performers when consistently assigning them extra work. Failing to recognize this burden risks driving these valuable employees away by neglecting their personal and psychological well-being. If someone regularly does more than their fair share, they should be appropriately compensated, rewarded, and recognized. Just because our competent employees *can* do more than others doesn't mean we should let them.[124]

The willing horse is always overworked. —Charles Darwin.

It's often difficult to say "no" when asked to accept another assignment, even when fully loaded. There's often a fear that saying no could harm your career prospects or brand you as someone unwilling to go the extra mile. However, when we weigh the risks of overcommitting against the benefits of managing a balanced workload, it becomes clear that finding equilibrium is a worthy endeavor.

A practical approach I've found effective is to initially lead with a "yes" while highlighting the potential impact of taking on additional tasks. For instance, if your boss requests you to handle a critical new project while your plate is full, you might respond, "Certainly, but what existing task should I de-prioritize to accommodate this?" This approach prompts a constructive dialogue with your manager to reassess priorities, ensure the right tasks are tackled in the proper sequence, and distribute the workload evenly to prevent excessive overtime.

When the person requesting your assistance fails to consider the impact on your existing workload, handling the situation respectfully and diplomatically is essential. While initially agreeing to the assignment, it's wise to outline the need to coordinate with your boss or other stakeholders to determine its place among your current tasks. Assure them you'll provide a timeline for starting and completing their assignment after consulting with relevant parties. This approach demonstrates your willingness to help while responsibly managing your other commitments. Usually, clear communication helps requesters understand the need for balanced prioritization among tasks.

You'll be accountable to multiple stakeholders in a matrixed organization, including your functional team, boss, and other supported organizations. Conflicts in assignment prioritizations can naturally occur when one hand doesn't know what the other hand is doing. This requires candid communication with your stakeholders to assess relative priorities. It can also be helpful to develop and maintain a comprehensive priority matrix. Sometimes, you can set this priority list independently if you understand your work assignments' relative impacts and priorities.

Considerate managers initiate work requests by acknowledging that accommodating new tasks may necessitate adjustments elsewhere. For instance, they might inquire, "If you take on X, what must you drop or postpone to maintain a manageable workload?" This approach reflects genuine concern for the employee's stress and well-being and showcases a commitment to reasonableness when assigning additional responsibilities. These managers foster a supportive and collaborative work environment by proactively addressing workload management.

These days, remote workers face a heightened risk of overwork compared to their in-office counterparts. Without clear boundaries, work hours can quickly expand, leading to burnout. Additionally, assessing workload and stress levels becomes more challenging in remote settings where face-to-face interactions are limited. Therefore, it's even more critical to deliberately discuss any new assignment and its prioritization in the context of existing work to avoid overloading the remote employee.[125]

Maintaining a reasonable workload is essential for sustaining high performance, preventing burnout, and ensuring employees remain motivated and engaged. Organizations can cultivate a healthier work culture that promotes long-term success and employee well-being by effectively balancing tasks.

Everyone has the right to rest and leisure, including reasonable limitation of working hours and periodic holidays with pay. —Eleanor Roosevelt, American diplomat, humanitarian, and first lady of the United States.

Managing Stress

Stress arises from how we react to situations, not the events themselves. Some people stress over strict deadlines or high workloads, while others face the same challenges and remain unaffected.

Stress transforms into pressure when we constantly dwell on past or future events, attaching negative emotions to those thoughts. Chronic worriers may experience severe health issues and emotional distress. However, those adept at managing stress have learned to break free from the cycle of worry.

Consider the following approaches to managing stress:

- Boundaries: Clearly define work and personal life boundaries to maintain well-being and prevent burnout.

- Communication: Embracing open and honest communication with your boss and colleagues can help address concerns and alleviate stress.

- Time management: To reduce stress, prioritize tasks, set achievable goals, and break large projects into smaller, manageable tasks. Completing the first step on a task or project can be liberating.

- Self-care without guilt: Exercise, meditation, and hobbies can relieve stress and promote mental health. Avoid guilt by realizing that these activities improve more than just your happiness—they also improve your work performance and productivity.

- Seek support: Securing help through employee assistance programs or counseling services can provide valuable professional guidance and support.

- Conflict resolution: Addressing conflicts directly and constructively can prevent lingering tensions contributing to stress.

- Request feedback: Regular feedback and recognition can boost morale and provide a sense of accomplishment while reducing stress.

- Transition: When you ruminate, transitioning to something physical, like standing or sitting up, can interrupt your negative thoughts.

- Mindfulness: Connecting with your senses, even momentarily, can break a sour mood and redirect your attention. While you can acknowledge and care about external factors or forces you cannot control, you can deliberately choose not to worry about them.

- Be reasonable: Don't catastrophize or exaggerate the negative issues or possibilities you commonly worry about. Don't overload your schedule, obsess over mistakes, or push for perfection.

- Sleep: Prioritize sleep to recharge your mind and body, enhance resilience to stress, and improve your overall mental clarity and decision-making abilities.

- Digital detox: Allocate time throughout the day to avoid screen time, especially in the evening and before bed. This practice improves sleep quality, reduces stress, and creates mental space for relaxation and reflection.

- Release: Accept and let go of the stressful concern or situation. This last step is usually the most difficult.[126]

As a manager, it's important to understand that you play an essential role in minimizing stress at work. Workplace stress can stem from various sources, such as toxic environments, demanding bosses, or unrealistic deadlines. Consider the following strategies to reduce workplace stressors:

- Exercise fairness: A leader who practices fairness learns about their team members' strengths and talents and finds creative ways to engage them effectively. Stress levels naturally reduce when workers believe they are treated fairly and equitably.

- Practice empathy and compassion: While excessive empathy may burden leaders emotionally, the right amount creates a sense of support among workers facing personal challenges. Compassionate leaders actively alleviate employee suffering, demonstrating genuine care and understanding.

- Set a positive example: Do not assign overtime to your workers while enjoying time off yourself. When your workers are occasionally required to work evenings and weekends, join them and share their burden.

- Set reasonable goals and expectations: Practice assigning "SMART" goals. Collaborate with workers when setting goals to enhance commitment and buy-in.

- Remove uncertainty: Clarity and transparency can reduce stress at work. Even when faced with ambiguity, effective leaders demonstrate patience and mindfulness, encouraging their team members to adopt similar attitudes.

- Reprioritize: Focus on achieving results and outcomes rather than maximizing hours worked. Encourage employees to prioritize personal and family time, as it revitalizes them and enhances their performance. Embrace a mindset that values work-life balance over prioritizing work above all else.

- Recognize and reward: Workers deserve recognition for their achievements. Place them in the spotlight and help them celebrate their wins. When their efforts are appreciated, they'll feel better about themselves.

- Recharge: Long-term projects resemble marathons, yet a sustainable work pace also includes occasional sprints. These sprints should be short-term, transparently managed, and followed by downtime for workers to recharge.[127]

Effective stress management is crucial for employees and managers. It enhances productivity, facilitates a positive work environment, and promotes overall well-being, ultimately contributing to sustained organizational success.

> *Nothing is permanent. Don't stress yourself too much, because no matter how bad the situation is... it will change.* — Unknown.

Declutter and Organize

As we consider ways to reduce stress, organizing our belongings and decluttering our offices and workspaces can have remarkable effects.

Recent research suggests that clutter is the most accurate predictor of procrastination, interferes with a high quality of life, and increases stress. Studies also reveal that individuals who perceive their living spaces as cluttered tend to experience elevated levels of depression. Additionally, cluttered environments create negative emotions that hinder progress.

Tidying up can positively influence your thoughts, emotions, and decision-making. Eliminating every obstacle helps you think more clearly, which leads to emotional well-being. The effort and accomplishment experienced in cleaning up provide you with the self-confidence and motivation to move forward.

Positive change often starts with small steps. You can progress by organizing your space at the beginning or end of each day. Start with your desktop and then move on to your office or cubicle, focusing on the most used areas. Commit just 5 minutes initially and stop when you feel like it. The key is to *get started*. Over time, consider scheduling regular maintenance time to ensure that your organizing efforts become a sustained habit.

Many organizations have embraced scheduling periodic "spring cleaning" days for their areas. This approach can rejuvenate teams and provide a common goal that everyone can rally behind. I've implemented this technique at multiple companies, which has had a consistently positive effect. If you struggle to motivate your team to support and commit to cleaning up, a well-timed customer tour can provide the necessary stimulus to inspire commitment.[128]

Decluttering and organizing boost efficiency and productivity and create a more pleasant and focused environment, empowering individuals and teams to achieve their best work. Employees can reduce stress and distractions by maintaining a tidy and orderly workspace, paving the way for greater creativity and collaboration, and ultimately enhancing overall job satisfaction and performance.

> *Letting go of physical clutter also declutters the mind and soul.* —April Williams, life coach, podcaster, and motivational speaker.

Mindfulness

Mindfulness involves being fully present and aware of what's happening in the present moment. It's about observing our experiences without judgment and with openness and curiosity. When practicing mindfulness, we pay attention to our thoughts, feelings, and sensations without getting overwhelmed by them. It helps reduce worrying and rumination by allowing us to acknowledge our emotions, such as anger or frustration, without harsh self-judgment and then letting them naturally fade away.

Practicing mindfulness allows us to observe our experiences and cultivate acceptance, especially for things beyond our control. We develop greater compassion for ourselves and others when we accept our thoughts and feelings without ruminating. This allows us to adopt a more balanced perspective in challenging situations and adjust our behavior accordingly. By releasing attachment to our feelings, we prevent them from defining or controlling our future actions.[129]

> *Mindfulness is the intentional, accepting, and non-judgmental focus of one's attention on the emotions, thoughts and sensations occurring in the present moment...* —Unknown.

The modern workplace presents unprecedented challenges and complexities. Constant distractions, competing priorities, and relentless deadlines can lead to frustration, disappointment, and other negative emotions. This environment can fuel employees' discouragement, outrage, irritation, and anxiety, highlighting the need for effective stress management strategies.

If you're constantly looking for a better job regardless of how many times you've moved, consider that the challenges you face at work can be opportunities for personal transformation. Mindfulness, which encompasses emotional intelligence, encourages us to observe and understand our reactions to stimuli and stressors, ultimately transforming our work experience and enhancing job satisfaction.

Engaging in the following mindfulness practices can significantly improve our overall work experience:

- Embodiment: The ability to maintain body awareness throughout the day. We can increase awareness of our emotions and identify the first signs of what can lead to stress and pain.

- Metacognition: The ability to observe our thoughts and actions when they occur. This enables us to acknowledge what we're feeling and accept those feelings with empathy and without judgment, as we allow them to pass gradually. The same holds true for the words and actions of others.

- Focus: The ability to focus our attention where we want it. For example, when we recognize that we're being distracted, we can intentionally return to the object of our focus. With practice, we can improve our understanding of how we become distracted, enabling us to predict and ultimately avoid it.[130]

Incorporating mindfulness at work promotes greater focus, emotional resilience, and improved interpersonal relationships, leading to a more harmonious and productive work environment. By cultivating a mindful approach, employees and managers can navigate challenges with clarity and maintain a balanced, positive outlook.

> *Peace of mind arrives the moment you come to peace with the contents of your mind.* —Rasheed Ogunlaru, English life and business coach, motivational speaker, and author.

Downtime

In my experience, workplaces that embrace and encourage periodic distractions throughout the day create healthier environments and help employees avoid overload.

Feeling guilty for taking breaks during work hours can contribute to burnout. Intentional pauses allow our minds to relax, explore new ideas, reduce stress, and enhance creativity. By incorporating such breaks, employees can maintain focus and productivity while caring for their mental well-being.

The *type* of break that you take is crucial. Checking your email inbox, scrolling through social media, or watching random videos online may *seem* like breaks, but they don't refresh you. They keep you tethered to your computer and drain your energy. These are considered unhealthy breaks as they contribute to cognitive overload and mental fatigue. Instead, choose activities that offer a genuine change from work and don't add to your cognitive load.[131]

Science has shown that periods of uninterrupted quiet time can profoundly impact our thinking and creativity. Downtime, or non-time, allows us to relax and see the big picture, enabling innovative ideas to surface in our minds.

Many creative individuals have intuitively understood this principle. Albert Einstein, for instance, credited his best ideas to moments spent idly on his sailboat. Steve Jobs routinely put things off, noodling instead on more divergent and creative ideas. He experienced long stretches of aimless contemplation fairly regularly. His walks with other creative geniuses like Jony Ive are legendary. This doesn't diminish the importance of hard work and attending to daily tasks, but embracing regular downtime can enhance creativity and productivity in unexpected ways.[132]

At Facebook, I experienced a workplace culture that embraced daily distractions and promoted a healthy work environment. They included leisurely walks around the campus, grabbing snacks or drinks at various cafeterias, taking fitness breaks, or simply meditating or relaxing in the many social spaces. I frequently indulged in walks outdoors as a small reward for completing a significant task or after a period of intense focus. I often visited the on-site woodshop to work on a project or acquire new skills. I viewed these brief diversions as mini-rewards for my hard work, which helped refresh and reenergize me for my next important task. Management actively encouraged socializing, exploration, and collaboration across different organizations, reinforcing a culture of passion and curiosity.

Experts claim that when we go for a walk, we improve our performance on tests of memory and attention. Our brain cells build new connections, which counters the natural progression of brain tissue loss with age. When we walk casually, our minds are left to wander and observe, which helps us to generate new ideas and think more creatively. Walking can also improve our sleep, thinking, and learning and reduce feelings of anxiety. Studies have shown that just five minutes of exposure to nature can improve our self-esteem and mood. It also allows us to recover from mental fatigue, which can be caused by prolonged, focused thought. If your mobility is impaired, spending short, idle periods outside can provide much of the same benefit.[133]

Breathing fresh air, especially amidst trees, plants, and soil, can substantially impact our health. It reduces blood pressure, heart rate, and stress hormones while alleviating anxiety, depression, and fatigue. It also diminishes inflammation. Scientists attribute these benefits to natural substances, such as organic compounds, pollen, fungi, and bacteria, which enrich a diverse microbiome essential for disease protection. Simply inhaling fresh outdoor air may bolster our immune systems.[134]

It's healthy to break free from the belief that you must be productive around the clock. While this may seem odd to some, it's important to realize that every moment doesn't need to be optimized. Instead, allocate some of your precious time to meaningful activities and connections. Resist the urge to stay busy constantly—life is too short. Setting aside time for yourself isn't laziness—it's essential. Ditch the guilt and refrain from apologizing for taking moments for self-care.[135]

We need to build downtime into our lives, so that we can have solitude without feeling overcome with guilt. —Melody Beattie, American author, and self-help expert.

Rest Your Brain

In today's world, our attachment to smart devices is undeniable. I've observed how we instinctively reach for our phones during a lull in conversation, even when socializing with friends. Interestingly, once someone reaches for their phone, it signals permission for others to do the same, leading to a uniform disengagement from face-to-face interaction.

Experts have uncovered the profound impact of prolonged smartphone use on our brains, altering both structure and function. It affects our ability to think deeply, focus, form new memories, and retain information. Heavy smartphone usage negatively affects neuroticism, self-esteem, impulsivity, empathy, self-identity, and self-image. Additionally, it contributes to sleep disturbances, anxiety, stress, and depression. These findings highlight the importance of providing our brains a break by disconnecting from smart devices, which can enhance our work and personal lives.[136]

Neuroscience research highlights the importance of mental breaks, which stimulate the brain to engage in vital "cleanup" processes. Even short pauses reinforce long-term learning and productivity. Engaging in mindless activities is the most effective way to leverage these breaks. Options include relaxing in a hot tub, sauna, or steam bath, bird-watching, or playing a simple non-scoring game on your smartphone. Taking a quiet solo walk in nature without focusing on step counts offers numerous physical and mental benefits. Cooking a simple meal can also encourage a wandering mind. Alternatively, you'll likely benefit from curling up in a comfortable chair to take a short nap.[137]

Over the years, I observed that many of my colleagues rarely took breaks. They always talked about work-related topics, whether walking around, at lunch, at dinner, or during business trips. It's as if they had nothing else interesting or amusing to discuss.

Not surprisingly, experts claim that engaging in casual discussions about non-work interests demonstrates genuine interest in the other person, not just their work. Learning about a colleague's hobbies or interests can enhance engagement and personal growth. Sharing details about personal passions and life outside work makes you more relatable. Non-work conversations also allow for injecting humor, easing stress and tension.

Learn to relax. Your body is precious, as it houses your mind and spirit. Inner peace begins with a relaxed body. —Norman Vincent Peale, American author, and minister.

Vacations and Unplugging

Work stress can build up and eventually lead to burnout, so experts suggest we all need to unplug and decompress occasionally. However, many people accumulate unused vacation days and cash them in instead of taking time off. Some consider that practice as an abuse of a vital company benefit intended to encourage workers to temporarily step away from their workplace, rejuvenate their souls, and experience a renewal that fuels creativity and energy.

Employees should be disincentivized from accumulating excessive, unused paid time off. Maintaining reasonable work hours and taking earned vacations should be integrated into performance metrics during employee reviews, influencing salary adjustments and bonuses.

Many workers mistakenly believe that taking time off risks sending a negative message to their manager, potentially slowing their career advancement. Americans are taking less vacation time than at any other period in the last four decades. Consequently, they're diminishing their happiness and success while eliminating an essential means of stress relief.

Recent research suggests that vacationing actually *increases* your chances of receiving a raise or promotion. Those who use all their vacation time have a nearly 7% higher chance of getting promoted than those who leave 11 or more days of paid time off unused or cashed in.

Enlightened managers recognize that encouraging vacations leads to better employee performance. Breaks from work stimulate higher engagement, offer a refreshed perspective, and boost brain energy, resulting in increased productivity and creativity. However, not all vacations yield the same benefits.[138]

According to experts, the benefits of short vacations may fade quickly. The stress of preparing for a vacation, followed by a backlog of work upon return, can diminish post-vacation positivity within a few days. One solution is to opt for more *extended* vacations, which can provide lasting benefits. Additionally, experts recommend incorporating 5 to 10 minutes of downtime for every 90 to 120 minutes of work to facilitate regular relaxation.[139]

Overworking is the black plague of the 21st century. Take a vacation. You deserve it. —Unknown.

If you feel you have too much work to take an occasional day off, it may be time to reassess your perspective. Is your dedication to work causing an imbalance in your personal life? Are you overestimating your indispensability at work? Could you be underestimating the ability of your colleagues or subordinates to carry on while you're away? Is your reluctance to step away from work, even briefly, indicative of tendencies towards micromanagement or workaholism?

When you take a day off, plan to *fully disconnect* from work and resist the urge to check texts and voicemails or answer work-related calls. Set clear expectations before you leave, informing colleagues of your unavailability during your absence. Arrange for a capable colleague to cover for you in your absence and trust them to handle their responsibilities. Use your time away to shift your focus and engage in activities that rejuvenate and bring you joy.

As a manager, establishing a culture where employees feel empowered to fully disconnect during their vacations is beneficial. Encourage them to unplug and enjoy their time off without worrying about work. Assure them that everything will be taken care of in their absence. This level of support creates a sense of trust and enables employees to return to work feeling refreshed and energized.

> *The time you enjoy wasting is not wasted time.* —Bertrand Russell, British philosopher, and logician.

People often spend more time at work than necessary, adding stress and exhaustion. A recent survey revealed that nearly seven in ten Americans extend their workweeks by a full day at least once a month. Two-thirds of respondents felt pressured to work weekends, and 61% struggled to avoid work-related tasks during their time off. Setting a realistic end time for work each day can significantly reduce stress and prevent workday creep. Sticking to this schedule consistently throughout the week is conducive to maintaining a healthy work-life balance.[140]

Many workers today are embracing the practice of postponing work-related email transmissions or text messaging to other employees after a specific time each day, typically around 6 pm. While some may find it challenging to avoid working into the evening, delaying non-critical communications until the following morning can help reduce stress for both senders and recipients. This practice requires support and modeling from managers and leaders to empower workers to unplug in the evenings and postpone messaging until the next day. I found adopting this behavior to be liberating and energizing. It eliminates the guilt of ignoring work messages after hours, especially in fast-paced or demanding work environments.

To succeed with this initiative, leaders must create a culture that prioritizes wellness, productivity, and efficiency over constant, around-the-clock busyness. Overtime and overwork should be portrayed as *negative* traits, which helps workers understand the detrimental impacts of continuing to work after hours. They should be encouraged to disconnect, tune out, and avoid arriving early or leaving late for their health and the company's long-term success. Additionally, leaders should commit to retraining micromanagers who habitually monitor workers' arrivals and departures to mitigate the adoption of toxic leadership practices. Encouraging and mandating a healthier work style among employees requires sustained effort and commitment from leadership. Corporate policies, employee handbooks, and executive directives should reflect these values consistently.[141]

Some countries have embedded downtime into their cultural norms. For instance, the Danes embrace "Hygge," which embodies extreme coziness and special moments like sitting by an open fire or playing board games with loved ones. The Spanish have

"Sobremesa," where family and friends linger at the dinner table, chatting leisurely. "Tech Sabbaths" within the Jewish faith involve stowing away screens and technology for 24 hours weekly to foster a sense of calm. Croatia celebrates "Fjaka," the joy of doing nothing at all. Initiatives like the "National Day of Unplugging" highlight the importance of achieving tranquility. These practices contribute to work-life balance and cultivate happy and productive employees.[142]

Many companies nationwide, from Fortune 500 giants to boutique firms and nonprofits, acknowledged the persistent risk of burnout post-pandemic as employees transitioned back to the office. To counter this threat, Bumble announced an unscheduled week off, while LinkedIn shut down for a week. Shopify implemented "Rest & Refuel Fridays" globally, and Fidelity granted U.S. employees five additional paid "Relief Days," among other innovative benefits for parents. Marriott International introduced three paid "TakeCare Days Off" before certain holidays and encouraged avoiding meetings on Fridays.

These creative health and stress-reduction policies yielded significant benefits, including better meeting attendance, increased job satisfaction, reduced health issues, lower stress levels, and improved morale. Investing in strategies to combat burnout proves effective and underscores employers' commitment to employee well-being.[143]

Unfortunately, some leaders argue that these practices discourage the behavior they seek in a committed workforce. They claim that crushing competition and the never-ending need to move fast require everyone to remain flexible—sometimes, we need to jump into action after hours. Elon Musk, for example, is known to send out emails late at night. He habitually works 80-100 hours weekly and expects others to model similar behavior. He has been quoted as saying: "There are way easier places to work, but nobody ever changed the world on 40 hours a week."

However, while *occasional* overtime may be necessary to meet deadlines, expecting perpetual work sprints isn't sustainable. Instead, it often leads to higher turnover, cultural stress, and a joyless workplace. Chronic overtime can also result in health issues and, in extreme cases, worker fatalities. Moreover, a culture that encourages constant overtime may struggle to attract and retain a committed, diverse workforce, which can hinder long-term success.

Instead, prioritizing work-life balance respects employees' lives outside of work, boosts productivity, and stimulates productivity, laying the foundation for long-term success.[144]

Evolving Trends

Many corporate leaders increasingly recognize the heightened levels of work stress and the necessity of addressing work-life balance through strategic initiatives and committed leadership. Research has revealed that burnout affects disengaged employees as well as deeply engaged and highly productive workers. Despite their dedication to their roles, engaged individuals may experience chronic exhaustion, overwork, and feelings of annoyance and underappreciation.[145]

Mental illness, depression, and anxiety are escalating globally, contributing to approximately $1 trillion in lost productivity annually, as reported by the World Health Organization. Among millennials (ages 24-39 in 2020), depression is the fastest-growing health concern. Employees now expect support from their employers in navigating these challenges. Unfortunately, when this assistance is lacking, many leave their positions. A study of 1,500 U.S. workers revealed that half of millennials and 75% of Gen Z employees departed from jobs in 2019, citing mental health reasons as a significant factor.[146]

At the most progressive companies, employees are encouraged and supported in seeking the professional medical care they require for their mental health. They are also urged to prioritize stress-reducing activities such as gym workouts, walking or running, or other wellness practices. Increasingly, employees are also taking sick leave to address mental health needs. Offering the option to work from home part-time can also reduce stress. Some companies even incorporate stress management and wellness as part of the management skills evaluated during annual performance reviews. The commitment of corporate leaders to acknowledging and addressing mental health challenges in the workplace is becoming a critical factor in attracting and retaining young talent.

The pandemic has ushered in challenges for working parents, compounding issues like the high cost of child care and limited paid family leave. While companies can't solve these challenges alone, they can offer empathetic leadership that supports parents throughout their struggles and commits to keeping them in their jobs while supporting their personal needs.

Leaders can also adjust employee benefits to lessen the load. For instance, parents can significantly benefit from laundry assistance, grocery delivery, virtual fitness classes, or subsidies for after-school care. Offering a stipend that parents can use according to their needs could significantly alleviate stress, especially during increased work pressure. Further, every company could implement some form of family leave policy. The fact that the U.S. is one of only seven countries without national paid maternity leave underscores the urgent need for improvement in supporting working parents and parents-to-be.[147]

Managers and leaders have faced an unprecedented increase in responsibility, especially during the pandemic. In a remote work environment, they've been expected to make quick decisions while demonstrating empathy, transparency, and compassion. This has required them to take on multiple roles simultaneously, from decision-makers to mentors and counselors. While they attend to their teams' stress and mental health, we must also acknowledge that *they* need support as well.

Many companies have had to resort to layoffs or furloughs during challenging times, placing an immense emotional burden on the managers implementing these decisions. Layoffs affect both those directly impacted *and* the managers themselves.

To address management burnout, managers must first assess the number of roles they're juggling and categorize them into those that fall within their comfort zone and those that stretch their capabilities. Stretch roles demand more preparation, attention, and support, which can increase the risk of burnout if not managed effectively. Managers should conduct a personal audit of their energy reserves and adjust their workloads or priorities accordingly. Just like on an airplane, they must prioritize their own well-being before assisting others.[148]

Embracing an evolving work culture is necessary for organizations to stay competitive and innovative. It encourages adaptability and creates an inclusive environment where diverse perspectives thrive. By continuously refining workplace practices and values, companies can better meet the changing needs of their workforce and drive sustainable growth.

> *For people, character is destiny. For organizations, culture is destiny.* —Tony Hsieh, American internet entrepreneur, and venture capitalist.

Work Flexibility

For millions of workers, punching the clock each workday has been a rite of passage. In the early 1900s, Henry Ford introduced the eight-hour workday to attract autoworkers from 12-hour shifts, and it became the standard. However, putting in one's time often became a proxy for performance, impact, and work ethic. While the 40-hour workweek became the norm, there's nothing inherently magical about the number 40.

Several studies and experiments on reduced workweeks have been conducted, with many more ongoing. In a recent survey, 29% of college students considered remote work with a flexible schedule a *right* rather than a *privilege*. Additionally, 66% of millennials cite a lack of support for flexible schedules as a significant factor in deciding whether to leave their job. Conversely, 72% of working parents believe that individuals with flexible hours have fewer opportunities for pay or promotion. Millennials are spearheading the push for flexible work hours, with their stance gradually becoming the norm across all generations. Technology is the enabler that makes working from anywhere possible.[149]

Another recent study revealed that productivity typically declines after 35 hours per week. Perpetual Garden, a financial firm in New Zealand, asserts that it boosted corporate productivity by transitioning 240 employees to a four-day workweek. Likewise, other companies featured in the Guardian Report reported gains of up to 30% in productivity when they instituted the four-day workweek.[150]

Microsoft experimented with a four-day workweek in its "Work-Life Choice Challenge." After closing its Japanese subsidiary every Friday for one month, they found that adopting a four-day workweek led to a 40% boost in productivity. They also reduced the time spent in meetings by implementing a 30-minute limit and encouraging remote communication.

There is also a significant international demand for a shorter workweek. In a study of nearly 3,000 workers in eight countries, the Workforce Institute at Kronos and Future Workplace found that the ideal workweek would be four days or less.[151]

Work flexibility is critical to enhancing employee satisfaction and productivity. It allows individuals to balance their personal and professional lives more effectively. Organizations that offer flexible work arrangements can attract and retain top talent, creating a more dynamic and resilient workforce. Implementing a shorter workweek while maintaining the same salaries should also benefit employees by reducing stress and absenteeism, increasing engagement and job satisfaction, and enhancing overall mental health.

> *Don't confuse having a career with having a life.* —Hillary Clinton, American politician, diplomat, and first lady of the United States.

Loosening the Work Shackles

The traditional notion of working hard has been deeply ingrained in our culture for decades. However, in today's fast-paced world, many of us work excessive hours while struggling to balance competing demands. Our understanding of "hard work" often stems from outdated agrarian or industrial ideals, which persist even as the nature of work evolves.

Despite our efforts, we feel perpetually behind, comparing ourselves to the seemingly relentless work ethic of others, including our workaholic bosses. We seek meaning and recognition in our daily grind, yet often question the value or impact of our efforts. Meanwhile, economic disparities persist, with the wealthy seemingly benefiting at the expense of the middle and lower classes. This work cycle can be frustrating, particularly for those who allow their work to define their sense of self-worth.

> *My boss arrived at work in a brand new Ferrari. I said: 'Wow, that's an amazing car!' He replied: 'If you work hard, put all your hours in, and strive for excellence, I'll get another one next year!'* —Unknown.

The pandemic has prompted a widespread reevaluation of priorities and career aspirations. For many, the shift to flexible work arrangements has proven transformative, leading to increased happiness and improved mental and physical health. Flexible work has also enhanced our private lives and reduced pollution from daily commutes. In many ways, the pandemic has offered a glimpse into the potential for a more fulfilling way of life.

The pandemic has also offered us a glimpse of a life in which we prioritize spending time with loved ones and attending to our well-being rather than enduring daily commutes to cramped offices. By reclaiming our former commuting time as leisure time, we've discovered renewed energy and rekindled passions. We've rediscovered the joy of socializing and the tranquility of solitude, allowing us to relax, enjoy music, or engage in simple tasks simply because we want to and find pleasure in doing so.

Many are reassessing their career goals and taking concrete steps to realign their professional paths. Some prioritize work flexibility and more leisure time, actively seeking new opportunities supporting these priorities. Others are choosing to retire in their search for fulfillment through personal pursuits. Across these diverse paths, a common theme emerges: Workers are seizing control of their lives and futures. In doing so, they're reconnecting with their true selves and rediscovering how they want to spend their precious time.[152]

Years ago, as my family life took flight, my priorities naturally shifted, prompting a reevaluation of how I allocated my time. While I remained passionate about my work, its significance began to take a backseat to my family. Rather than diminishing my dedication to work, this shift compelled me to work more effectively and efficiently, ensuring that every hour of every workday was maximized. Doing so reduced my overtime, creating more time for my family and our interests.

I took more active control of my schedule, prioritizing tasks and leaving nothing to chance. Gradually, I shed the guilt associated with leaving work before some of my colleagues who regularly stayed late.

In my early thirties, work defined much of my identity, but as time progressed, I viewed it more as a means to an end. I shifted away from equating success with wealth accumulation, recognizing instead its role in financing family activities, supporting my children, and securing savings for early retirement.

> *Statistics indicate that, as a result of overwork, modern executives are dropping like flies on the nation's golf courses.*
> —Ira Wallach, American businessman, and philanthropist.

If your CEO shows no inclination to improve work-life balance at your company, others must initiate the conversation and plant the seed for change. One executive can inspire others to join by starting the discussion, creating a critical mass that nurtures behavioral change. While initial resistance may arise, patience and persistence can pave the way for eventual transformation. In the worst-case scenario, if the current leadership opposes change, individuals may seek opportunities at companies better aligned with their WLB goals and values.

Many success stories illustrate how executives have championed and cultivated work cultures prioritizing work-life balance. It begins with a commitment, followed by courageous action and experimentation. As these stories become more publicized, initiating a conversation about WLB within your organization becomes easier. Discussing it is no longer taboo; it demonstrates enlightenment regarding its benefits to the organization and its employees. Failing to acknowledge or discuss WLB can now be perceived as a fiduciary failure. In today's corporate landscape, success increasingly hinges on prioritizing WLB, as many modern workers view it as a fundamental requirement. The more executives experience WLB firsthand or hear about positive experiences from others, the more likely the pursuit of work-life balance will become the norm.

Wise are those who learn that the bottom line doesn't always have to be their top priority. —William Arthur Ward, American motivational author, speaker, and college administrator.

CHAPTER 7

Tackling Toxicity

To deal with toxic people effectively, you need an approach that enables you to control what you can, and eliminate what you can't. —Travis Bradbury, author, influencer, and EQ expert.

Even the best job isn't perfect. While challenges are inevitable, a toxic work environment can drive employees away—often more than any other factor. Studies show that many workers leave their jobs not because of pay or workload but because of toxic bosses who create hostile, unsupportive, or unethical workplaces. When leaders weaponize fear, display favoritism, or cause dysfunction, even the most talented employees have little choice but to walk away.

A recent study found that 56% of American workers reported having a mildly or highly toxic boss, while 75% felt their boss was the most stressful part of their job. Despite these statistics, data suggests that workers tend to work longer for toxic bosses than non-toxic bosses, which is rather extraordinary. Some toxic people are entirely unaware of the adverse effect they're having on those around them, and others seem to derive pleasure from controlling others and creating chaos.[153]

Other research has found that toxic employees are the most destructive force in the workplace. A study of nearly 60,000 workers across several industries found that one toxic employee more than wiped out the gain from two superstars.[154]

In the most toxic work cultures, fear, intimidation, and the willingness to sacrifice colleagues to appease bosses prevail. Creativity dwindles as new ideas are stifled, and integrity takes a backseat to power-hungry, egotistical, and bullying leaders. Gossiping social cliques form, favoritism, and office politics become the time-consuming norm, and aggressive or bullying behavior at the top of the organization permeates throughout the organization as the rank and file begin to emulate the behavior of their superiors to seek favor.[155] Eventually, workplace misery jeopardizes health and happiness, and high-performing individuals leave to seek better opportunities elsewhere. This marks the demise of a company.

> *Culture and chemistry are critical to success. A team can have one knucklehead, you can't have two. One knucklehead adapts, two hang out together.* —Mark Cuban.

A clear distinction can be made between toxic behavior and simply being *different.* Diversity is valuable as it brings various perspectives and approaches to problem-solving and innovation. However, diverse teams also face challenges when individuals inadvertently frustrate or annoy others. Rather than labeling someone difficult or annoying, it's helpful to assume positive intent and refrain from negative judgments.

For example, someone who appears dominating may be simply influential or commanding. Approaching others with positivity often elicits a desirable response, which creates a reinforcing cycle. It's usually helpful to focus on a person's value to the work and seek common ground or shared objectives. As a leader, setting a positive example can inspire difficult colleagues to emulate positive behaviors, contributing to a more constructive work environment.[156]

Dealing with personnel issues requires patience and persistence. Many managers ignore such matters or lack the training, skills, or motivation to address toxic behavior. An all too common strategy is ignoring or dismissing feedback from colleagues and subordinates, allowing the problem to fester and escalate.

> *Nothing will kill a great employee faster than watching you tolerate a bad one.* —Unknown.

Effective managers in thriving work cultures act as coaches, intervening when necessary to effectively deal with toxic personalities and assist challenged employees in finding roles where they can excel. They avoid complaining or criticizing underperformers and refrain from mistreating them. Helping challenged employees become productive team members inspires loyalty among those who have received support.

Bullies and Jerks

It's helpful to differentiate between bullies and jerks, as each requires a different approach to handling their behavior. Bullies deliberately act with cruelty and contempt, targeting those who are weaker or have less power. They intimidate without regard for the impact on their victims, often scheming to mentally or verbally undermine others. Jerks, on the other hand, tend to behave thoughtlessly, often lacking intent in their actions or words. While anyone can display jerk-like behavior, especially under stress, bullies intentionally act with entitlement, believing they can misbehave without consequences. They often possess special privileges and maintain an aggressive or offensive attitude towards others.

Executives, in particular, may feel exempt from treating others with respect and empathy due to their position and the belief they'll be shielded from consequences. Similarly, individuals with advanced education sometimes mistakenly believe they are immune to workplace norms, given their perceived value to the organization. Regardless of their status, bullies create toxic work environments, leading to high turnover and damaged relationships. Their behavior can even incite violence, posing legal risks for the company and its leaders.

I've noticed that intellectual bullies enjoy correcting others. They tend to be argumentative and nit-picky, often losing their cool and picking fights with others. They can be impulsive and easily sidetracked. Rarely do they respect or appreciate the opinions of others. Instead, they strive to be the center of attention and often resent the success and recognition of others.[157]

When employees face mistreatment from co-workers or superiors, bosses occasionally excuse the perpetrators' behavior, especially if they are top performers or considered critical talent. Bullies who are closely aligned with their bosses are often shielded or protected from consequences. How bullies are handled depends mainly on the company culture, as leadership sets the policy and tone. Exceptional leaders recognize the implications of their response to workplace bullying on employee retention and job satisfaction. When reporting a bully's misbehavior results in retaliation, it reflects poorly on the company's leadership and culture.

Recently, bullies have become increasingly vocal and prominent in America and beyond. Almost daily, we witness the normalization of bullying behavior as political leaders, celebrities, and extremist talk show hosts verbally attack or silence their detractors and opponents. They often resort to character assassination in their pursuit of headlines, power, influence, and online engagement. This trend is evident in government institutions, school board meetings, colleges, and even live TV awards shows. What was once whispered in small circles is now openly expressed with confidence by bullies who wield support and encouragement from a growing number of enablers, followers, and sycophants.[158]

To combat bullying, it's helpful to follow these steps:

- Avoid providing opportunity or cover to those who would normalize or explain away toxic behavior.

- As soon as bullies attempt to deflect away from their bad behavior by invoking a "whataboutism" argument, stop them in their tracks. Force or encourage them to take responsibility for their actions.

- Set firm boundaries by clearly communicating what behavior is unacceptable, and stand your ground.

- Document everything. Keep records of incidents, including dates, details, and witnesses.

- Stay professional. Avoid emotional reactions—respond with calm, assertive confidence.

- Confront the misbehavior strategically. Address the behavior directly when safe, using facts and professionalism.

- Return the conversation to rational, fact-based content and observations.

- Escalate when necessary, especially if the situation or behavior persists.

If others attempt to provide a pass to a bully by citing that they're too valuable to hold accountable, remember that tolerating mistreatment by anyone is a recipe for ultimate failure. By condoning toxic behavior, leaders are messaging that it's acceptable for the culture to adjust accordingly.[159]

You never look good by making someone else look bad. You look good when you raise others up, and make a positive difference in someone else's life. —Unknown.

Incompetence

People can be pleasant, respectful, and considerate, but they can also be toxic to an organization if they act and behave in ways that negatively affect its success. This negative behavior is usually due to insecurity or incompetence.

When faced with an incompetent worker (or leader), it is important to assess whether they're willing and able to accept critical and constructive feedback on a path to improvement. The most problematic incompetents are utterly incapable of honest and thoughtful introspection and self-assessment.

No amount of evidence will ever persuade an idiot. —Mark Twain, American author, humorist, entrepreneur, publisher, and lecturer.

Psychologists have studied this cognitive bias phenomenon and named it the "Dunning-Kruger Effect (D-K)," wherein the subject is incapable of self-awareness. The skills required to *produce* the correct answer are those needed to *recognize* it. In other words, if you're incompetent, you're incapable of recognizing or acknowledging that you're incompetent. These otherwise capable individuals persistently overestimate their performance and abilities while disregarding, denying, or rejecting constructive feedback. Those affected by D-K may arrogantly tout their superior intellect while belittling others.[160]

Wisdom is, among other things, the ability to admit that there's a lot that you don't know. Wise people embrace continuous learning and the pursuit of knowledge and truth rather than focusing on being *right*. Wisdom also involves admitting when you're wrong, acknowledging your error or misunderstanding, and backing down amiably. Wise people aren't afraid of being wrong or admitting that they don't have all the answers.

> *The smartest people are constantly revising their understanding, reconsidering a problem they thought they'd already solved. They're open to new points of view, new information, new ideas, contradictions, and challenges to their own way of thinking.* —Jeff Bezos.

Narcissists

The Greek myth behind the term narcissist involves the hunter Narcissus, who was so utterly self-absorbed that he starved to death while gazing at his reflection in the river. Narcissists believe they're superior to everyone around them, leading to challenges in interpersonal relationships. Perhaps not surprisingly, some malignant narcissists rise to the highest levels of the corporate or political ladder.

Narcissists often justify building themselves up by tearing others down, failing to realize the negative impact on future collaboration and company dynamics. They frequently engage in office politics to advance personal objectives, especially in large companies where such dynamics are common. Believing they're adept at detecting hidden agendas, narcissists often justify their selfish behavior as a response to perceived exploitation by others.[161]

Hate is the complement of fear and narcissists like being feared. It imbues them with an intoxicating sensation of omnipotence. —Sam Vaknin, Israeli writer, and professor of psychology.

According to recent research, narcissists often secure more promotions at work, fueled by their strong egos and their desire for status and power. They also tend to seek job posts at the top of the corporate ladder where they can exert influence over others, and rate higher in self-promotion and sense of power than others. Self-promoting narcissists who exude power are more likely to be noticed by hiring teams and supervisors with promotion authority. Unfortunately, studies suggest that being *seen* as a leader equates to behaving like one.[162]

But while narcissists may tend to rise faster within organizations than others, they tend to fare worse in leadership positions in the long run. When they focus on their selfish pursuits of gaining power, prestige, influence, and money, it usually comes at the organization's expense—this despite their belief that their personal goals are aligned with those of the organization. For instance, a political candidate may resort to unethical or illegal tactics to win an election, convinced that victory at any cost will benefit constituents, especially when they perceive their opponent as inferior. However, such behavior ultimately undermines trust and integrity and diminishes long-term success.

In the workplace, narcissists can disrupt team dynamics, hinder collaboration, and create a toxic environment driven by their self-centered agenda. Recognizing and addressing narcissistic behaviors early can help mitigate their negative impact, create healthier work relationships, and promote a more positive and productive organizational culture overall.

You will never get the truth out of a Narcissist. The closest you will ever come is a story that either makes them the victim or the hero, but never the villain. —Shannon L. Alder, life coach, therapist, and inspirational author.

Passive-Aggressives

People who demonstrate passive-aggressive behaviors can be particularly frustrating to deal with. They often exhibit contradictory behavior, saying one thing to you and the opposite to others, or offering support while undermining behind the scenes. They may subtly copy higher-ups on emails to assert power and use seemingly polite phrases to convey irritation. Despite thinking they're clever, their actions come across as conniving. Some resort to manipulation tactics like the silent treatment or playing the victim to control situations. Typically, these behaviors stem from a fear of expressing anger outwardly, leading them to avoid direct conflict and operate covertly. Their behavior is inherently aggressive and detrimental to relationships and environments.

When a coworker copies your boss on a communication meant for you, they either act like a whistle-blower or instill a lack of trust in your ability to handle the matter independently. They also seek to align themselves with your boss to influence your response. In such situations, avoid including your boss in subsequent emails, which perpetuates the dynamic. Instead, forward the original email to your boss and inquire if they wish to be involved in follow-up correspondence. If your boss advises you to handle it independently, you can resume direct communication with the sender without copying others, reassured that your boss supports your approach. This approach establishes a new power dynamic, safeguards your position with your superior, and addresses passive-aggressive behavior effectively.[163]

In my experience, effectively dealing with passive-aggressive individuals involves assertive yet respectful communication. I typically address their behavior directly in a private meeting, shedding light on their actions and intentions. By confronting them professionally, I've found that this approach often yields positive results. Passive-aggressive individuals thrive on implicit communication, so bringing their behavior into the open leaves them with nowhere to hide.

> *It's a sign of your wisdom and growth when you choose to respond calmly to the negative behavior of others.* —Bernadette Logue, life coach, and author.

Micro-aggressions are sneaky *hit-and-run* attempts to hijack one's attention and self-confidence. This covert behavior subtly marginalizes others, such as privately showing support while publicly berating someone, or refusing to shake one person's hand while graciously greeting others. Those who engage in micro-aggressions employ subtlety to maintain plausible deniability and protect themselves from exposure or accusation.

Dealing with micro-aggressors requires practicing "emotional agility." Rather than reacting impulsively or dwelling silently on the incident, acknowledge your emotional response and assess the situation calmly. Formulate a deliberate plan for addressing it, ensuring your response is proportionate and balanced. Sometimes, maintaining composure and reflecting on the incident later is beneficial when you can analyze it calmly. It may also help to seek feedback or advice from someone you trust before responding.

Alternatively, an appropriate response is often no response at all. Ignoring an offender might be just enough to diffuse the situation. Responding with humor can also acknowledge an assault, but care should be taken to avoid minimizing or normalizing bad behavior. For cases that warrant escalation, your management and HR teams should ideally rally to your support to effectively resolve misbehaviors of this kind.

Always forgive your enemies; nothing annoys them so much.
—Oscar Wilde, Irish poet, and playwright.

Toxic Leaders

Adult bullies, particularly those who are intelligent and wield power, are proficient at hiding what they do. Their actions are subtle, as they poke and prod others without bringing undue attention to themselves. Their power fuels their bullying at work, as they believe their weaker subordinates are powerless to do anything. Some bullying bosses may ignore others, refuse requests for help, cut people off when talking, or even freeze certain workers out of team-building or social events. They often disrespect other people's time by intentionally arriving late to meetings, failing to meet deadlines, or subordinating requests from some while prioritizing others. They might sabotage specific ideas or projects, deny worthy contributors the praise and recognition they deserve, take credit for the work of others, and even target certain people as scapegoats for other people's problems.

> *If someone treats you bad, just remember that there is something wrong with them, not you. Normal people don't go around destroying other people.* —Unknown.

While managers demand excellence from their workers, it's not uncommon for them to fail to hold themselves accountable to the same standard, particularly regarding behavior and character—many seek immunity from accountability or judgment themselves.

Toxic bosses often display one or more of the following behavioral traits:

- They exhibit narcissistic personality disorder. They attempt to raise themselves at the expense of others. They criticize, undermine, belittle, ridicule, and even threaten their co-workers or subordinates.

- They fail to recognize and praise their workers.

- They fail to demonstrate or display compassion or empathy.

- They don't value or respect their workers and may treat them as easily replaceable commodities.

- They become control freaks, micromanagers, or dictators.

- They exhibit a "my way or the wrong way" attitude, objecting to and outwardly rejecting the ideas and decisions of others.

- They fail to connect deeply with their people, inspire their employees to do their best work, or provide the necessary tools for success.[164]

- They fixate on their own interests at the expense of their teams and direct reports.

- They get frustrated when they're expected to coach and mentor others.

- They resent their employees' superior skills and abilities, compounded by the annoying realization that they depend on those same workers for their own success.[165]

- They distrust the concept of working remotely, believing that it lowers productivity and promotes laziness. They fail to understand that allowing employees to work from home can *strengthen* their workforce through improved retention, resulting in heightened employee loyalty and commitment.

- They distrust entrepreneurs, fearing that those independent and creative individuals may leave the company armed with corporate secrets and know-how that the competition can leverage.

Many toxic managers fixate on clock-watching as a measure of productivity, failing to recognize that time-tracking is often irrelevant to actual performance in most roles. They view overworking as a symbol of dedication and loyalty, and expect their employees to work excessive overtime. Those who resist are often labeled as lacking commitment and may face ridicule, disciplinary action, or even termination.

Fortunately, we're experiencing an evolving workforce that has become far less tolerant of bullying bosses. Temper tantrums, power plays, and shouting laced with expletives are no longer deemed acceptable methods for motivating employees. That notwithstanding, HR and executives often side with the toxic manager, making it challenging, if not impossible, to address complaints or blow the whistle on such behavior.

Toxic leaders can profoundly undermine morale, productivity, and organizational success by creating fear, mistrust, and a hostile work environment. Addressing and mitigating the influence of toxic leadership through transparent communication, accountability, and the promotion of positive leadership qualities can help cultivate a healthier and more supportive workplace culture conducive to sustained growth and employee well-being.

> *If leaders are watching the clock, you have a problem. ...People in the wrong roles can be some of the best staff you have in your business if you can be compassionate enough to give them a second chance in a different role.* —Tim Denning, Australian entrepreneur, blogger, author, and coach.

Dealing with Toxicity

Working in a toxic environment can exact a toll many people fail to recognize or acknowledge. Over time, it can distort our perception of acceptable behavior, causing us to tolerate actions that should never be normalized, such as being yelled at. It's crucial not to lose sight of what's right and wrong. If your workplace condones yelling or other forms of bullying, listen to your inner voice urging you to seek a new job. Trust your instincts and prioritize your well-being above all else.[166]

> *Letting go means to come to the realization that some people are a part of your history, but not a part of your destiny.* — Steve Maraboli, behavioral scientist, speaker, business consultant, author, and philanthropist.

Toxic individuals often seek validation for their negative attitudes or conspiracy theories, hoping others will join in their behavior. It's wise to set boundaries and distance yourself from these individuals. The more irrational they become, the easier it is to disengage. While showing empathy is noble, be mindful not to get drawn into their negativity. Remember, you're responsible for how you respond and for protecting your well-being. Stay positive, but don't feed into someone else's toxic behavior.[167]

The solution to a toxic work culture begins with leadership. Leaders should consistently exhibit respect, empathy, trust, appreciation, and integrity. Addressing toxicity may involve removing toxic bosses or employees and promoting an atmosphere of appreciation, accountability, and a positive, healthy work environment.[168]

To address toxic behavior, managers should regularly assess employee engagement and satisfaction through meetings or surveys while encouraging honest feedback. Managers should act on this feedback, setting aside ego and implementing all necessary changes. Failure to do so may discourage employees and undermine future efforts to address toxic behavior effectively.

Remember, you can't control others' behavior, but you can control your reaction to their attempts to provoke you. Don't let their negativity consume you. Have a plan, and leverage your emotional intelligence to keep toxic influences at bay.

> *Never let anyone—any person or any force—dampen, dim or diminish your light.* —John Lewis, American politician, and civil rights activist.

Research suggests that, to a significant degree, our happiness is within our control, meaning we can change our circumstances and outlook on life. While it's common to experience setbacks and periods of unhappiness, it's important to prevent negativity from overwhelming us. We all face difficulties and setbacks, but what matters most is how we choose to handle them.

For example, even the worst bosses and workplace experiences can teach you significant life lessons when you search for the silver lining in difficult situations. Difficult bosses teach us what to avoid. They can even become unexpected mentors. Learning how *not* to behave is powerful, and every setback can be an opportunity for a comeback. Experiencing challenges and adversity can shape your leadership skills when these experiences are treated as opportunities for personal growth.

People who exercise positive habits and take proactive steps to address challenges are happier than those who struggle with chronic negativity. Rather than dwelling on problems or succumbing to toxic behavior, focusing on solutions and maintaining a positive mindset can help us navigate challenging situations, build resistance, and emerge even stronger.[169]

The following are some additional ways of combating toxicity:

-   Focus on trusting your team members to deliver results and evaluate their performance based on outcomes rather than the time they spend at their desks.

-   Cultivate a sense of gratitude by acknowledging the positive aspects of your life. Recognize that not everything is bleak, and some situations could be worse. Work to embrace a balanced perspective that allows the good and the not-so-good to coexist.

-   Do something you enjoy, even if only for a short while. Engage in projects or hobbies that ignite confidence and pride in your abilities. Sometimes, breaking a train of dreaded thought is necessary to gain a fresh perspective on your current situation.

-   Embrace self-compassion and humor when navigating a mistake or embarrassment. Accept your humanity and commit to improvement without seeking external validation.

-   Avoid negativity and toxic gossip. Seek out friends who uplift and support you, and distance yourself from those who bring negativity into your life. Step back from codependent relationships and focus on self-care and rejuvenation.

-   Avoid comparing yourself to others. Comparisons usually lead to disappointment.

-   Stop making excuses and take action. Nothing will change as long as you remain neutral. Take the first step to a happier life, for nothing ever comes from skipping the first step.[170]

Overcoming toxicity in the workplace is essential for maintaining a healthy and productive environment. It requires a combination of awareness, strategic action, and emotional resilience. While it's not always possible to change a toxic environment, recognizing when to walk away is just as important as standing your ground. Ultimately, prioritizing well-being and professional growth ensures that toxicity does not define one's career but instead serves as a catalyst for seeking healthier, more fulfilling opportunities.

> *Walk, fall down, get back up again, repeat. It's in the getting back up again that all the difference resides.* —Tamara Star, American author, life coach, and entrepreneur.

CHAPTER 8

Conflicts, Influence, and Negotiation

Character may almost be called the most effective means of persuasion. —Aristotle, Greek philosopher, and scientist.

Issues and disagreements exist at every company, and conflict resolution often requires patience and persistence. Committing to effective conflict resolution is extremely important, for without it, issues fester, and persistent conflict can poison working relationships and render the work environment toxic.

> *Conflict cannot survive without your participation.* — Wayne Dyer, American self-help author, and motivational speaker.

Ignoring or avoiding problems rarely leads to resolution and often exacerbates the situation. Whether a personal issue or a workplace challenge, addressing problems directly is essential for maintaining happiness and well-being. Even if a problem seems daunting or triggers strong emotions, running away from it isn't a winning solution. Instead, confront the issue head-on, seek input or support as needed, and work towards a successful outcome.

Remaining passive in the face of workplace issues is often the eas-iest path. Whether witnessing a colleague's mistreatment or encoun-tering poorly conceived leadership decisions, staying silent can be the safest option. Many opt for passivity to avoid drawing attention to themselves and the potential risks of speaking up, such as backlash or scrutiny. However, choosing silence as a means of self-protection per-petuates the problem and can lead to a toxic work environment.

When you see something that is not right, not fair, not just, you have to speak up. You have to say something; you have to do something. —John Lewis.

While addressing issues or conflicts head-on is usually desirable, it's possible to miss the mark by reacting too bluntly or without enough consideration for tact or empathy. This usually stems from prioritiz-ing expediency over human connection. Nevertheless, deliberate en-gagement usually earns appreciation from grateful colleagues, subordinates, and even superiors for being willing to speak up when others won't and advocating for those who face their challenges si-lently. Despite the occasional backlash from egotistical or autocratic leaders who prefer silence and compliance, most people value hon-esty, initiative, and courageous involvement over passivity.

I've learned that it is crucial to maintain a calm demeanor and show empathy when engaging others in challenging discussions. Sometimes, *how* you deliver your message matters more than the message itself. Unsurprisingly, being confrontational, especially with superiors, can have negative consequences, even when warranted.

Arguing with someone isn't necessarily bad or something to avoid. Arguments are more natural and commonplace than we realize or ad-mit. Plenty has been written about how we can better engage one an-other to drive more effective and less contentious arguments. Briefly, the following steps tend to work reasonably well in most instances:

- First, the notion of *winning* should be eliminated. This shifts the focus from competition to collaboration, enabling constructive arguments and reducing conflict. Removing the concept of winning encourages participants to prioritize shared goals, relationships, and collective problem-solving over short-term personal victories.

- Your relationship with the person you're arguing with should be prioritized over everything else. Rarely are issues or arguments worth destroying valuable working relationships or friendships.

- Compelling arguments and discussions require thoughtful consideration of the context and a willingness to appreciate varying perspectives. This creates an environment where diverse viewpoints can lead to more balanced and informed discussions and solutions.

- Embracing your vulnerability fosters trust and openness, allowing both parties to engage authentically and work toward a solution rooted in mutual understanding and respect.

- Allow yourself to evolve and transform your opinions as necessary and reasonable. Flexibility encourages openness to new ideas and perspectives. This adaptability strengthens relationships and enables people to address challenges collaboratively while embracing change for the greater good.

Following these steps enables people to engage with each other effectively, particularly on divisive issues.[171]

> *Before you argue with someone, ask yourself, is that person even mentally mature enough to grasp the concept of different perspectives? Because if not, there's absolutely no point.*
> —Unknown.

Persuasion and Influence

Have you ever noticed how easy, energizing, and exciting it is to follow inspirational leaders? They'll draw you in, and working for them feels like a kindred trek or an adventure you share. Influential leaders persuade by utilizing transparency, facts, logic, and emotion to present ideas and challenges and frame their arguments in ways that convince others. In my experience, teams are fully harnessed when they work for persuasive leaders. Those leaders unleash and enable the incredible power of their teams to accomplish seemingly impossible objectives.[172]

Communication, whether speech or writing, serves the dual purpose of informing and persuading others. Interestingly, the principle of persuasion can be traced back to Aristotle, who developed this skill over 2,000 years ago in *Rhetoric*, his treatise dedicated to persuading people. Aristotle's three devices for persuasion are logos (an appeal to reason), ethos (an appeal to credibility and character), and pathos (an appeal to emotion). These timeless principles continue to shape effective communication strategies today.

Compelling arguments are built on a foundation of factual evidence and data. When opinions or biases dominate an argument, dismissing or countering them becomes easier. However, when concrete facts and compelling data support arguments, they become more convincing and difficult to refute.

Additionally, personal credibility plays a crucial role in successful persuasion. Building trust, reliability, and consistency enhances your image among colleagues, making them more receptive to your ideas. Engaging actively with others, listening attentively, and leading with shared facts and assumptions can make your arguments more relatable and persuasive.[173]

To be persuasive we must be believable; to be believable we must be credible; to be credible we must be truthful. —Edward C. Morrow, American broadcast journalist, and war correspondent.

Persuading others can be challenging because many of us suffer from speech anxiety—we've never learned how to think about communication from a strategic standpoint. However, we can excel in this skill even if we can't overcome the anxiety element or our lack of self-confidence. The key is to learn how other people listen to us. The following steps can facilitate a persuasive argument:

- The most persuasive arguments begin by clearly understanding the audience, such as the number of participants, their race and gender, and their relevant subject knowledge.

- Clarify your objectives. Are you seeking to entertain, inform, or inspire, or do you seek approval or buy-in? Remember that *your* objectives may not align with your audience's. Speaking to others in terms of how *they'll* benefit demonstrates audience awareness.

- Speak in a common language that is relatable to the audience. For example, don't refer to feet and inches when presenting to people who use metric units.

- Refrain from presenting provocative information that will inflame your audience or bring specific attention to deficiencies or performance issues related to anyone listening.

- When you use humor, metaphors, and statistics, they should mean the same thing to your audience as they mean to you. As our workforce continues to expand in diversity, this can become challenging.[174]

- Offering a choice of ideas or solutions empowers others to contribute. Involving others in the planning phase by asking questions and seeking perspectives encourages personal investment in the plan. Action plans benefit from the insights of others, inspiring a sense of ownership in the execution process. Identifying gaps or weaknesses and inviting input to address them enhances alignment and increases buy-in from all involved parties.[175]

- Select your words carefully. Emphasize nouns rather than verbs. For example, consider using the statement "I am in favor of the cancellation of the program" rather than "I am in favor of canceling the program." The minor nuance of how we phrase statements can avoid emotions by stating a course of action rather than emphasizing the action itself.

- Describe how you're looking out for other people's best interests rather than telling them what to do. Start by understanding the other person's perspective and biases.

- Use "we" instead of "I" statements to build trust.

- Instead of trying to convince others, encourage them to persuade themselves.

- People are more easily persuaded by big ideas than small ones. Big ideas get people excited and energized.

- Workers are more persuadable when leaders offer positives and negatives, including risks. Avoid sugar-coating your idea—others will thank you.[176]

- If you seem doubtful or hesitant, or if you use words like "I think," "I hope," or "I feel," people will find it more difficult to commit fully. When attempting to persuade others to change their attitude, behavior, or approach, don't try to scare or guilt them into change. Instead, identify how a positive change will improve their situation. Focus on the positives.[177]

- If you have good and bad news to present, research shows that most people prefer to hear the bad news first.

- If you have an important request to discuss, present it after a break when your audience is relaxed and more likely to avoid a snap "no" decision. Studies show that people are more persuadable early in the day and immediately after breaks.[178]

Mastering the art of persuasion is invaluable for everyone, although it can be challenging and its effects temporary. Effective persuaders refrain from dictating to others and empower individuals to convince themselves. By guiding others to reach their own conclusions, persuaders cultivate stronger alignment and support for their positions. This approach cultivates deeper understanding and commitment, making persuasion more enduring and impactful.

> *The secret of all true persuasion is to induce the person to persuade himself.* —Harry Allen Overstreet, American writer, and lecturer.

Negotiation

Everyone negotiates, often without even knowing it. Seeking a "yes" from others, whether for a raise, a product purchase, or a deadline extension, constitutes negotiation. Negotiation is a form of collaboration, and collaboration requires trust between people.[179]

> *Let us never negotiate out of fear. But let us never fear to negotiate.* —John F. Kennedy, American politician, and 35th president of the United States.

When negotiating, arbitrators and opposing parties usually aim to compromise or meet halfway. However, achieving this middle ground can be challenging when stubborn principles or ideals obstruct progress. Some individuals, especially "driver" personalities, approach negotiations with a zero-sum mentality, viewing gains for one party as losses for the other. This mindset, known as the "100-0" mentality, involves keeping score of concessions made by each party, which can lead to exhaustion, disruption, and frustration.

Entrepreneurial coach Dan Sullivan suggests adopting an "abundance mindset" over a "scarcity mindset." This perspective encourages focusing on the bigger picture rather than fixating on deal *numbers*. Entering into engagements with partners, contractors, or customers in good faith with the shared goal of achieving something mutually beneficial creates opportunities for successful outcomes. It lays the foundation for productive, enduring, and fulfilling relationships.

> *Each party should gain from the negotiation.* —Dale Carnegie, American author, and lecturer.

If one party perceives a deal as unfair, it can erode trust and commitment, potentially damaging the relationship. Successful partners prioritize transparency and fairness, adjusting contract terms for mutual benefit. While reciprocity is ideal, prioritizing fairness ensures sustainable partnerships. Fair play and unconditional giving strengthen relationships in the long run.[180]

"Forced Empathy" is considered a powerful negotiating tactic. This technique focuses on encouraging the other person to empathize with you. By conveying your concerns, you aim for them to understand your perspective, challenges, and limitations. When the other party considers your viewpoint, they may be more inclined to propose a satisfactory offer or compromise. Utilizing phrases like "what" and "how" encourages them to view the issue from your standpoint. For instance, asking, "What am I supposed to do?" compels them to see things from your perspective.[181]

The following negotiating tactics combine practical wisdom and actionable tips to empower effective negotiation:

- Prepare thoroughly: Research the other party's interests, goals, and constraints to anticipate their position and develop a compelling strategy.

- Focus on interests, not demands: Seek solutions that address the core interests of both parties.

- Aim for win-win outcomes: Look for creative compromises and opportunities where both sides can gain value.

- Solicit expert advice when appropriate: Consult legal or industry experts to refine your strategy and avoid critical mistakes.[182]

- Lead with a compelling opening offer: Make the first move with an ambitious yet realistic proposal to influence the negotiation's trajectory.

- Use silence strategically: Pausing during discussions can prompt the other party to reveal more or reconsider their stance.

- Practice empathy and patience: Understand the other party's challenges and perspectives while allowing time for thoughtful decision-making.[183]

- Leverage data and facts: Present logical arguments supported by evidence to strengthen your position and counter objections.

- Remain flexible: Be open to adjusting your approach and exploring alternative solutions if circumstances change.

- Be willing to walk away: Recognize when a deal doesn't align with your goals and exit respectfully to preserve future opportunities.[184]

- Establish clear and unambiguous objectives: Identify your non-negotiables, desired outcomes, and acceptable trade-offs before entering negotiations.

- Build rapport: Establish trust and mutual respect through open communication and a collaborative tone.[185]

- Manage your emotions: Maintain composure and self-awareness, and don't let frustration or excitement lead to impulsive
  decisions.[186]

- Clarify and codify agreements and next steps: Summarize key
  points and confirm mutual understanding to ensure clarity and
  avoid misinterpretations. Establish the next steps when your negotiation requires follow-on effort.[187]

Mastering negotiation skills and tactics is crucial for specific roles. Being "likable" can be a positive factor when influencing and negoti-ating with those around you. Likable individuals often succeed in sales, attract support and assistance from others, and remain em-ployed even during challenging times. They are also more likely to be promoted or retained during layoffs, even over those with superior skills or experience who aren't particularly likable. Strike a balance by being confident, firm, and purposeful while offering fair and val-uable solutions in a friendly manner.[188]

Negotiation is a vital skill that extends beyond the boardroom, in-fluencing everyday interactions and critical business decisions alike. Professionals can create mutually beneficial agreements and nurture long-term relationships by mastering techniques such as thorough preparation, understanding interests over positions, building trust, and maintaining flexibility. Effective negotiation requires strategic think-ing, emotional intelligence, and adaptability. Whether seeking expert advice, leveraging facts, or practicing empathy, it's important to ap-proach each negotiation with clarity, respect, and an openness to col-laboration, ensuring sustainable success for all parties involved.

We've never succeeded in making a good deal with a bad person. —Warren Buffett.

Conflict Resolution

Arguments and conflict are genuine tests of leadership and emotional intelligence (EQ). While many individuals tend to avoid or shy away from arguments, some actively seek them out. They may view arguing as an opportunity to showcase their debating skills, assert intellectual superiority, or, unfortunately, belittle others. For these individuals, even minor disagreements can swiftly escalate.

Maintaining healthy interactions with coworkers is essential in business, as it preserves relationships that support teamwork and collaboration. Ideally, resolutions should benefit everyone involved, as nobody likes to lose, nor do they want to feel taken advantage of to get past an issue.

Negative emotions, such as anger and frustration, can dominate conversations and impair rational thinking. When tense or upset, the brain deviates from its rational state. Staying confident and calm is essential to retaining control. This enables active listening without judgment and prevents taking comments personally. Everyone has a right to their opinion and to be respected.

When a balanced, win-win solution becomes impossible or impractical, ensuring everyone's opinions are heard, acknowledged, and valued becomes particularly important. Respect and empathize with each person's needs or desires, and collaborate to find the best compromise or consensus.

Consensus is preferable to compromise, as it doesn't result in a winner and a loser. Identify a common goal in your debate, and acknowledge that both parties seek what's best, even with differing approaches. Create an environment of mutual trust where everyone feels confident expressing their opinions without fear of repercussion.

Avoid dismissing others' opinions, as it undermines trust and respect.[189]

If you're overseeing a negotiation, recognize that participants often seek an arbiter to make the final decision. Many resist allowing a peer to make the call, especially one who claims authority that hasn't been assigned. After listening to both sides and making a final decision, provide a rationale and justification so each party feels heard and understood—a decision without explanation lacks credibility. Once a resolution is presented, the team should support it and move forward unitedly. Passive-aggressive behavior, where the losing party undermines the decision over time, can harm team dynamics if left unchecked.

It's important to recognize and value the concept of diversity of thought. Different viewpoints enrich our understanding, and not every disagreement needs to escalate into an argument. Success thrives in environments where understanding, compassion, empathy, and positive intent prevail.

> *Conflict resolution starts by sharing your experience without blame or shame, and staying calm enough to listen to theirs.* —Unknown.

Disagreements and Misunderstandings

There is a substantial difference between a misunderstanding and a disagreement. Misunderstandings often stem from misinterpretations or errors in understanding or meaning and can typically be resolved through further discussion. In contrast, disagreements tend to involve arguments or debates where conflicting viewpoints may not find resolution through additional conversation, as the fundamental differences may be irreconcilable.

> *Honest disagreement is often a good sign of progress.* — Mahatma Gandhi, Indian lawyer, anti-colonial nationalist, and political ethicist.

Misunderstandings are usually worth resolving, as they can damage relationships if left unaddressed. Feeling misunderstood can be deeply unsettling for individuals. Often, misunderstandings arise due to insufficient communication. Therefore, the key to resolving them usually lies in enhancing communication and ensuring message clarity.

When faced with a disagreement, assessing whether it merits discussion or resolution is worthwhile. One option is to choose silence. By opting for this approach, the potential benefit is avoiding unnecessary conflict or tension. As I've grown older, I've become increasingly inclined to let minor disagreements slide. Often, ignoring and moving on results in minimal to no repercussions. Especially if the disagreement involves proving who is correct, avoiding escalation is usually advantageous—winning the argument yields little value. It can leave one or both parties feeling bad or angry, which is never the objective.

If you've determined that your disagreement warrants discussion, pay careful attention to your tone of voice. It's common for initial reactions to be influenced more by tone than content. Sometimes, you may perceive someone else's tone as anger directed towards you, but often, that isn't the case—they may simply be channeling a speech style they naturally adopt during disagreements. Not every disagreement evokes anger, despite the perceived tone.

Just because I disagree with you, does not mean that I hate you. We need to relearn that in our society. —Morgan Freeman, American actor, director, and narrator.

When dealing with a disagreement, it's important to eliminate sarcasm, anger, or frustration from your messaging. To control your voice, empathize with the other person's perspective. Nurture your positive thoughts and consider that they might be experiencing a difficult day or personal challenges. Approach the disagreement calmly and respectfully, selecting your words thoughtfully. Seeking more information can help refine your position, and phrases like "it seems to me" or "I'm not sure" can soften your stance. Avoid finger-pointing or adopting an aggressive posture that might put the other person on the defensive.

Remember, you don't need to apologize for your opinion or position; you have the same right to yours as they do to theirs. Diplomacy instills friendship and respect, making it the best approach to resolving disagreements.[190]

Most disagreements are caused by different perceptions that created different realities. —Unknown.

Facts and Opinions

What exactly is a "fact?" Within the scientific community, science is constantly changing and evolving. However, while much of science is still emerging, the amount of *settled science* increases almost daily. For reference, settled science represents knowledge that has undergone rigorous experimental validation and peer review by experts and has gained collective agreement within the scientific community. It provides a solid foundation for resolving conflicts, assuming the parties involved approach the discussion rationally and open-mindedly and are willing to set aside personal agendas or biases.

Arguments and debates can often be swiftly and effectively resolved when parties prioritize data and facts over opinions. Data provides invaluable guidance, perception, feedback, and insight on every subject and initiative. It informs good judgment and quality decisions. Data and facts are difficult to refute and can cut through arguments like a knife. Ideally, if you don't have the relevant data, you should secure it before presenting your case or attempting to resolve a conflict. You're unlikely to lose an argument when facts and data are on your side.

> *In God we trust. Everyone else: bring data.* —Michael Bloomberg, American businessman, politician, philanthropist, and author.

Despite the benefits of scientific reasoning and evidence-based discourse, many still rely on personal *intuition* and *feelings* to shape their beliefs and positions. Humans have evolved to rely on instinct and intuition for survival. Our natural instincts are deeply ingrained and powerful, often guiding our actions and decisions—our brains are not as adept at processing numbers and statistics as they are at processing emotions. The challenge lies in balancing our emotional responses and the rationality of facts and reason. While emotions are integral to human experience, we must temper their influence with logical analysis and evidence-based thinking to enhance our understanding and decision-making processes.

Consider the aftermath of the COVID-19 pandemic. Despite widespread efforts and clear guidelines from the CDC regarding vaccines, isolation, and hygiene, many needlessly lost their lives to various COVID variants. Tragically, some individuals ignored these guidelines, relying instead on personal intuition or succumbing to conspiracy theories. A significant portion of the American population remains hesitant to receive vaccinations, fearing the vaccines are part of a nefarious plot to control society or stubbornly doubting their efficacy without supporting data. Moreover, the persistent dissemination of fake news and conspiracy theories has led some to deny the existence of the COVID-19 virus altogether. This underscores the pervasive impact of misinformation in our society.[191]

In the workplace, it's essential to prioritize facts over opinions. This ensures that decisions are grounded in reality and evidence, leading to more effective and reliable outcomes. This practice creates a culture of accountability and transparency, driving success through informed action.

> *It is usually futile to try to talk facts and analysis to people who are enjoying a sense of moral superiority in their ignorance.* —Thomas Sowell, American author, economist, political commentator, social theorist, and educator.

CHAPTER 9

Supercharging Innovation

Innovation is where imagination meets ambition. —Unknown.

Innovation is rarely the product of a *lone genius*. Research shows that serendipitous encounters with others can often help trigger new ideas and inspiration.

What you *do* is based on what you *think*—innovation and creativity go hand in hand. Innovation is, at its best, an intensely collaborative activity that leverages a range of ideas and skills within a diverse team of people. It improves upon and validates an idea or invention, transforming it into something that people want and need, which can be manufactured with the attributes the market demands. Continuously and rapidly innovating through sustained creativity is necessary for companies to maintain relevance and avoid obsolescence, particularly in today's fast-paced global economy.

Innovation and invention are often used interchangeably, but there is a substantial difference between the two. I believe that the following quote may provide the best explanation:

> *Innovation connects the dots between inventions. Spotting potential for improvement, it cleverly fills a gap in the market and combines inventions into products that will attract customers and generate commercial success. Invention creates something new; innovation creates something that sells.*
> —Matthew Herbert, English marketing leader.

Inventors create new, novel, and original ideas, solutions, or processes for the first time. While inventions can create commercial value in and of themselves, we often need innovation that leverages and builds upon a novel and inventive idea to create a commercially successful product or process.

In the ideal sense, innovation differs from improvement or transformation—it involves doing something entirely *different* from current practices rather than just enhancing existing ones. Innovation encompasses the invention and its refinement, making it relevant, useful, marketable, and compelling.

Innovation and invention both fuel startups. While breakthrough inventions are sometimes essential, innovation provides the refinement necessary for market readiness. Through their creativity, innovators address and resolve errors, complexity, manufacturing challenges, and other deficiencies. Ultimately, innovation and invention are integral to creating value for a company.[192]

> *The heart and soul of the company is creativity and innovation.* —Bob Iger, American business executive.

The Dyson vacuum cleaner is an excellent example of how innovation applied to the industrial cyclone, which removes sawdust from the air in sawmills, created a bagless vacuum cleaner that reshaped the vacuum industry. While Dyson may have patented some aspects of its ingenious vacuum cleaner, it largely innovated a consumer product based upon an earlier invention or "prior art."

Apple likewise epitomizes innovation with its groundbreaking products. While the iPod wasn't the initial portable music device, and iTunes followed predecessors like Napster, Grokster, and Kazaa, Apple's innovation revolutionized the music industry. Apple created a compelling music ecosystem that changed how we consume and share music by integrating an MP3 player, a vast library of songs, and a music-sharing platform.

Successful companies embed innovation throughout the fabric of their entire organizations. They encourage every employee to think and behave like an innovator rather than treating innovation as a half-hearted priority for a handful of dabbling scientists. Their cultures encourage tangible action and substantial investment to ensure that great ideas are pursued and completed. Innovative companies are nimble and well-connected to the markets that they serve to ensure that their pursuits yield products and solutions that are timely, relevant, and valuable.

Facebook's popular hackathons and their intensely innovative teams exemplify how innovation is ingrained in everyone's daily responsibilities. It's a collective effort involving employees across all functions and disciplines. Regular company-wide gatherings ensure everyone stays informed about ongoing innovative pursuits, promoting a sense of unity around these efforts. This practice also allows support organizations, such as marketing, legal, and business development, to prepare for upcoming initiatives and contribute their expertise throughout the development lifecycle.[193]

Someone once said, "Ideas without action are regrets." Innovation demands that individuals overcome hesitation and uncertainty. It requires them to act on their ideas, setting aside fear of the unknown or failure. Innovators trust their intuition, analysis, judgment, and instincts. While they may not always succeed, taking action ensures progress, whereas inaction guarantees failure.[194]

> *You don't make progress by standing on the sidelines whimpering and complaining. You make progress by implementing ideas.* —Shirley Chisholm, American politician.

Innovation is rarely linear. "Aha!" moments often arrive seemingly out of the blue. I believe in tinkering—messing around in the lab and on the computer. If your company doesn't encourage people to spend at least some period each day exploring new ideas through creative noodling, mucking, and dabbling, then it's missing out on an essential innovative ingredient.

Most importantly, innovation encompasses more than just creativity, hackathons, and incubators. It's an end-to-end process, starting with identifying a problem or idea and culminating in successful deployment within the marketplace. Innovation and execution must occur concurrently, as they are interdependent and inherently linked. Without execution, innovation remains a mere idea without the potential to generate income, otherwise known as *research*.[195]

> *Do the impossible, because almost everyone has told me my ideas are merely fantasies.* —Howard Hughes, American business magnate, aviator, engineer, film producer, and philanthropist.

Acquisitions and Innovation

How often have you witnessed an innovative company being acquired only to succumb to the pressures of assimilation? Why do acquired companies struggle to maintain their creative edge and success post-acquisition?

Selling one's startup is a difficult decision for any founder. The most important considerations include future prospects, competitive landscape, acquisition price and terms, investor outcomes, and employee impact. While optimistic leaders may believe they can maintain the status quo post-acquisition, this is often unrealistic in the long term.

Priorities in large companies differ significantly from those in small firms, often resulting in a slower pace of execution. While small companies may fail more frequently than large companies, *products* are more prone to failure in large organizations. New products in large companies receive less individual attention, face internal obstacles, compete for resources, and may not be assigned to top talent.

Startups are agile and willing to take substantial risks, while large companies tend to be more conservative. For small companies, the success of a new product is vital for survival, unlike in large firms where products can be overlooked or neglected.

Some founders mistakenly believe they can enact change within the acquiring company. However, this is seldom the case. While there may be promises of autonomy and freedom, the startup's dynamics inevitably shift after the acquisition, only partially returning to their original state.

This doesn't imply that an acquired company can't still innovate and contribute value to the acquirer. However, setting realistic expectations and proactively addressing the potential downsides typically associated with acquisitions is essential.

Consider the following steps to enhance the long-term prospects of an acquisition:

- Cohesion: The startup team should remain intact post-acquisition to sustain the same level of innovation. Acquiring leaders have a keen eye for exceptional talent, and siphoning those exceptional talents away from the acquired startup can doom the acquired company's prospects.

- Separation: Maintaining the innovative culture of the acquired startup usually requires a physical separation between the startup and the acquirer. This keeps the team together and minimizes distraction and cultural bleed-through.

- Autonomy: The acquired startup should be granted near-complete autonomy, maintaining separate administration, processes, and IT systems. While this approach may be challenging, less efficient, and more costly, it can yield significant benefits in the long run.[196]

- Resources: Allocate sufficient resources and support to the acquired startup to sustain continued innovation. This includes financial investment, access to necessary tools and technologies, and professional development and collaboration opportunities.

- Focus: To avoid diluting the acquired startup's innovative focus, avoid imposing excessive bureaucracy or diverting resources to non-essential activities. Instead, prioritize initiatives that align with the startup's core strengths and strategic objectives.

- Collaboration: Facilitate collaboration and knowledge sharing between the acquired startup and other teams within the larger organization. Cross-functional collaboration can stimulate creativity and expose employees to new perspectives and ideas. Accordingly, HR must expertly manage personnel transfers to ensure that the critical skills necessary to innovate are maintained within the acquired startup.

- Incentives: Financial incentives should be established for the acquired team. When a startup is acquired, its stock options and vested ownership shares usually convert to cash or options in the acquiring company. However, the replacement compensation package can be less appealing to the startup employees. Ensuring they're adequately incentivized is critical for retaining their skills, experience, and knowledge.

- Evaluation: Regularly assess the acquired startup's innovation performance and progress. Solicit employee feedback, track critical metrics, and adjust strategies to address challenges or barriers.

Innovation will inevitably suffer if the acquiring company's processes and systems are allowed to infiltrate the acquired startup. Maintaining the startup's independence, culture, and *magic* for as long as possible increases the likelihood of retaining its creative employees.

> *Large corporations welcome innovation and individualism in the same way the dinosaurs welcomed large meteors.* — Scott Adams, American author, and cartoonist.

Creativity

Creativity and innovation go hand in hand. But what exactly is creativity? Creativity is often perceived as an innate trait—either you have it or you don't. We may envision creative innovation as a spark of inspiration reserved for the fortunate few—artists, geniuses, or inventors. However, the reality is quite different.

Creativity is a cognitive ability that manifests through a combination of skills, behaviors, and mindset:

- As a skill, creativity can be developed through practice, such as problem-solving, brainstorming, or artistic expression.

- As a behavior, it's reflected in how people approach challenges, take risks, and think outside the box.

-   As a mindset, it thrives on curiosity, openness to new experiences, and a willingness to challenge norms.

Creativity can be cultivated and developed by anyone. Insights from psychology, neuroscience, and business validate this notion. Creativity doesn't happen instantly; it results from dedication, expended energy, and the continuous accumulation of knowledge. It thrives through collaboration and effective leadership that prioritizes it within the workplace. Behind every significant innovation lies effort, persistence, iteration, and refinement. While we often hear about moments of sudden, unexpected insight, they typically emerge from a foundation of hard work. Like most endeavors, success in creativity seldom comes from shortcuts, but rather from consistent effort and perseverance.[197]

To promote creativity, one must fully engage with the subject matter, absorbing its nuances and complexities to fuel new ideas and discoveries. The most transformative innovations often emerge from patient collaboration and inspiration driven by diverse teams of contributors. Leadership plays a crucial role in facilitating this level of innovation by promoting creative risk-taking, patience, and mentoring others to embrace processes that nurture ongoing creativity. Innovators should be trained to embrace the frustrations inherent in the creative process and persist until they reach the optimal outcome, even in the face of diminishing returns.

While solitude can facilitate deep thinking, boredom can stifle creativity. Innovation thrives on a balance of introspection and external stimuli. Surprisingly, even procrastination can allow creative insights to emerge during ideation. The key is recognizing that innovation takes time, and rushing the process is counterproductive. Innovative breakthroughs often occur organically and cannot be forced. They require patience and the right conditions to manifest.[198]

In today's fast-paced work environment, workers often struggle to find dedicated time for creativity, given their busy schedules filled with meetings and emails. To encourage innovation, companies must cultivate a work culture that allows innovators reasonable chunks of uninterrupted time to contemplate problems deeply and draw upon their memories and experiences for solutions.

If you want to be more creative, become less productive. — Unknown.

Some psychologists argue that openness to new experiences is the most influential personality trait for predicting creative success. Rather than "thinking outside the box," true creativity often involves drawing from various sources of knowledge and experience. Creative individuals are frequently described as "jacks of all trades," possessing diverse skills and interests. For example, Steve Jobs' creativity stemmed from his fusion of technology with knowledge of liberal arts and humanities. While entrepreneurs typically look within their industry for product ideas, exceptional innovation often arises from exploring diverse fields and perspectives.

Consider the many groundbreaking healthcare innovations that benefit humanity, like the hospital X-ray system, MRI, and ultrasound. These innovations were conceived by physicists with no prior interest in healthcare, which underscores how new ideas often emerge from tangential fields and unexpected connections. Creativity thrives when inventors engage in spontaneous conversations across disciplines fueled by mutual curiosity. Rather than fixating on practicality, exploring diverse interests can spark innovation. Sometimes, focusing too narrowly can impede creativity.

Creative ideation often starts with individuals independently generating ideas, drawing from their deep expertise, unique perspectives, and knowledge. Following this initial phase, group brainstorming sessions encourage sharing, discussing, and refinement. Alternatively, when group brainstorming *initiates* the creative process, there's a risk of groupthink stifling innovation. The influence of the first or strongest voice can dominate, hindering diverse perspectives and creative exploration.[199]

Creativity and innovation demand persistence, while superficial thinking leads to ordinary solutions. To uncover groundbreaking ideas, you must push beyond initial possibilities. For instance, aiming for three strong ideas might require generating twenty to unearth the best options. This process is arduous and often frustrating, leading many to abandon their pursuit of genuine innovation. However, those who commit to extensive contemplation are rewarded with original insights.

Achieving breakthrough ideas typically requires more iterations and resources than anticipated. Additionally, I've observed that tackling the biggest and most challenging problem first works best; easier tasks can be done later. Generally, if you can't conquer the most difficult problems, the easier ones won't matter anyway.[200]

> *The first thing you consider is probably what everyone else is considering, which means that they're not novel. So, you have to push past those to get to the things that are a little more unique.* —Brian Lucas, professor of organizational behavior.

The most impactful innovations frequently result from incremental, data-driven improvements that are continuously optimized over time. This iterative approach relies on trial and error, close collaboration with customers, and feedback from testing and actual use to refine and enhance the product or service.

Encouraging creativity and innovation is essential, but these traits must be directed toward solving real-world problems to achieve meaningful business success. This involves expanding the focus beyond internal concerns to include external factors such as the customer's challenges, needs, and overall human experience with the product or service. This customer-centric approach often leads to enhanced solutions, a critical product development objective.

Innovative organizations establish a feedback loop between development teams and operations to capitalize on lessons learned. Insights gained during design and development inform future investments in IT, capital equipment, and talent. Deficiencies in equipment, tools, and processes are often identified throughout the innovation process, prompting the need for upgrades. Access to cutting-edge tools is essential for effectively addressing complex problems, ensuring innovators can unleash their full potential.[201]

Research indicates that individuals often underestimate the value of their own ideas, leading them to discard them prematurely and waste time on less promising ventures. On average, a person's first choice is often not the best. We tend to rank our choices in favor of being concrete and easy to apply. The value of this first-choice idea is already relatively apparent, leading us to overlook slightly more abstract concepts that are perceived as not immediately practical. However, with further refinement of subsequent abstract options, their potential uses and utility soon become apparent, making them more attractive.

When evaluating ideas, it is worthwhile to focus on both their positive attributes and potential drawbacks. Listing the pros and cons of each idea allows for a more comprehensive assessment of their feasibility and possible challenges. Soliciting feedback from others, especially those who may be interested in the product or service, can provide valuable insights and help counteract personal biases. This collaborative approach to ranking ideas ensures a more thorough and balanced evaluation process, increasing the likelihood of selecting the most promising and achievable concepts.[202]

Innovation is a state of mind, not a *one-and-done* pursuit. Whether you're at a startup or a large company, great innovators are constantly looking for ways of doing things better. They're continually questioning the status quo, asking questions like "Why are we doing it this way?" They get excited by change, not annoyed or afraid. Given that most great innovations require the contribution of others, innovators don't usually go it alone—they inspire others to join them in their pursuits. Innovation never ends at the most successful companies; even when something new has been developed, further iteration and optimization are pursued relentlessly.[203]

Invention and Patents

"Necessity is the mother of invention," goes the saying. Correspondingly, invention is the engine that propels economies forward. Most innovations trace their roots back to invention. A unique concept or product must be imagined, envisioned, conceptualized, and put into practice before being sold for profit. Invention typically emerges from experimentation, often accompanied by numerous failures.

> *Failure and invention are inseparable twins. To invent you have to experiment, and if you know in advance that it's going to work, it's not an experiment.* —Scott Galloway, marketing professor, speaker, author, podcast host, and entrepreneur.

Inventions solve problems, and the best inventions can even change the world. Inventions have enabled humans to evolve and modernize, permeating every aspect of contemporary life. Our daily routines are filled with invented items and devices, and their significance is often overlooked or taken for granted. When we contemplate the living standards and life expectancies within impoverished nations, we begin to appreciate the profound impact inventions have had on those fortunate enough to enjoy their benefits.

Some inventions are famous, while others are obscure or forgotten. Behind every invention is someone who identifies a problem or opportunity and crafts a solution. While some inventions may seem like strokes of luck or chance discoveries, the majority result from keen observation, creativity, and hard work. Many are impactful and even life-saving, while others are silly or rather useless. They can be the brainchild of a lone inventor or, more commonly, the result of a deeply collaborative team effort.

> *If I have seen further, it is by standing on the shoulders of giants.* —Isaac Newton, English mathematician, physicist, astronomer, alchemist, theologian, and author.

The cost of pursuing patents can be significant, encompassing labor, capital investment, and attorney fees. Therefore, each invention must offer substantial value to the business. Patents should protect your core technology and your overall business interests. To safeguard your competitive advantage, it's advisable to patent not only the specific solutions intended for the market but also similar or tangential embodiments that competitors might develop. This proactive approach helps fortify your intellectual property portfolio and defend against potential challenges to your patents, ensuring the sustainability of your advantage in the market.

Be sure to include all contributors as co-inventors when drafting patent disclosures to ensure fair recognition of their contributions. While your patent attorney can help determine which contributors qualify as inventors, fundamentally, an inventor has participated in the *conception* of the invention—this can be anyone who suggested or conceived of any of the steps or features listed in a patent application *claim*. Other people who contributed to authoring the patent application, identifying the original problem, or reducing the invention to practice are *not* considered *inventors* from the application standpoint.[204]

Failure to correctly identify *all* inventors within a patent application can result in severe consequences—it may even invalidate the patent. Unfortunately, some inventors may resist acknowledging others' involvement, driven by ego or a desire to maintain sole credit. This attitude undermines the collaborative spirit essential for innovation and goes against patent laws governing inventorship. Encouraging a culture of inclusivity and fairness leads to the proper recognition of contributors and ensures that the company upholds legal standards related to patenting.

It's also important to avoid inventing when perfectly acceptable solutions already exist. Don't waste resources on unnecessary inventions driven by curiosity or ego. Instead, prioritize high-value, high-impact work and remain open to leveraging existing solutions when appropriate.

> *You can learn from experience, but smarter people learn from the experience of others.* —Unknown.

Innovation Timing

Timing plays a critical role in innovation. Being late to an opportunity allows entrenched competition to dominate, while being too early risks a lack of customer interest. I've experienced the frustration of introducing a great innovation ahead of its time only to find the market unready for it. To ensure successful adoption, it's important to gauge customer demand and readiness before introducing new products or services.

Effectively timing new projects can be a strategic advantage. Steve Jobs exemplified this skill with the iPhone project. Despite a compelling proposal, he delayed its launch for three years to focus on Apple's strategic priorities: growing iTunes and completing the development and rollout of the iPod. Jobs' deliberate postponement ensured that the iPhone had the best chance of success in the market when it was introduced.[205]

E. M. Rogers' "S-Curve Model of Diffusion" is a valuable technique for determining the optimal time to launch new projects. This model explains how innovation is accepted and spreads within society, and offers insights into adoption trends and economic patterns across various disciplines. By modeling the adoption life cycle, one can project backward to identify the most advantageous time to initiate a project. This approach helps ensure that the project aligns with market readiness and maximizes its chances of success.[206]

In addition to employing the S-Curve Model of Diffusion, traditional assessments and project definition activities are helpful. These include ideation sessions to generate innovative ideas, thorough market and competitive analyses, evaluation of corporate fit, definition of project scope and requirements, financial and investment cost assessments, staffing and skill evaluations, and development of detailed timelines and schedules. By conducting these comprehensive assessments, organizations can ensure their projects are well-defined, strategically aligned, and positioned for success from the outset.

Innovation is everything. When you're on the forefront, you can see what the next innovation needs to be. When you're behind, you have to spend your energy catching up. —Robert Noyce, American physicist, and entrepreneur.

Rapid Ideation

In today's rapidly evolving global market, a team's ability to rapidly innovate is critical for success, profitability, and even corporate survival. Consequently, tools facilitating rapid iteration toward a final design have become a priority in corporate investment strategies.

What good is an idea if it remains an idea? Experiment. Iterate. Fail. Try again. Change the world. —Simon Sinek.

Rapid prototyping is one of the most effective and impactful techniques for facilitating real-time modifications and enhancements to product design. Often dubbed "making to think," it is a powerful technique for uncovering flaws and continuously validating performance. This iterative process provides designers with crucial data and insights, informing further optimization in a rapid, almost immediate fashion.

Beginning with a hypothesis on how a product should be envisioned, rapid prototyping involves multiple quick cycles of iteration, testing, and refinement. Throughout this process, valuable information and feedback are collected, guiding the evolution of the product. While experiments are decentralized, the learning is centralized, contributing to organizational scale, efficiency, and resilience.

In recent years, 3D printers have taken center stage, revolutionizing the prototyping process by swiftly producing physical objects through layered printing techniques guided by digital input files and robotic applicators. These devices have transformed how prototypes are developed, offering rapid and cost-effective solutions.

Another notable tool in product development is the Raspberry Pi. This small and affordable single-board computer enables developers to create a wide range of applications and devices with remarkable speed.

Advanced electromagnetic simulation tools, such as HFSS, harness sophisticated mathematical algorithms for high-frequency design to accurately model antenna performance. These tools enable engineers to tackle complex radio frequency and microwave design challenges.

For example, during my time at Endgate, we harnessed an advanced antenna modeling program, coupled with a genetic algorithm optimizer, running on our internally constructed Beowulf cluster 'supercomputer.' Operating together, they drastically reduced our iteration cycles from weeks to hours. This accelerated pace enabled us to introduce market-leading designs in a fraction of the time it would have otherwise taken.[207]

While many consider these rapid tools and computer models in the context of faster prototyping, they're even more impactful as ideation tools. They enhance traditional ideation activities like brainstorming and whiteboard concept sketching by facilitating rapid iteration and prototyping. For instance, instead of merely analyzing the performance of a new widget under specific conditions, prototypes can be quickly built and tested under real-world conditions, enabling immediate design adjustments based on actual test results. This iterative process can be conducted faster and more confidently than relying solely on analysis.

Additionally, rather than presenting concept sketches to customers for feedback, physical prototypes can now be provided within the same timeframe. This allows customers to interact with and manipulate potential designs, facilitating optimization.

Another significant advantage relates to expanding the solution space during the ideation phase. By leveraging these advanced ideation tools, designers can sample and evaluate a much more extensive range of potential designs within a larger realm of possibilities. This broader exploration often exposes surprising, non-obvious options and solutions that may not have been considered within traditional development time constraints. Faster iteration enables designers to delve more deeply into the search for extraordinary solutions, ultimately enhancing the creative process and increasing the likelihood of groundbreaking innovations.[208]

It's important to *iterate* persistently before launching into *optimization*—achieving success often involves multiple iterations before finding the optimal solution. Rather than striving for perfection from the outset, embracing the inherent chaos and discovering the creative process is essential. Google, for instance, emphasizes the importance of appreciating the early, scrappy iterations, often referred to as "Version 0.crap." Managers who attempt to circumvent or truncate the natural progression of iterating to save time or money do so at the expense of deep innovation.

The speed at which innovation occurs can significantly impact a company's corporate strategy and competitive advantage. Rapid prototyping tools have revolutionized the ideation process, empowering teams to generate ideas quickly and efficiently. In organizations with time constraints, leveraging these rapid ideation tools becomes essential for meeting aggressive deadlines and staying ahead of the competition.

Great design will not sell an inferior product, but it will enable a great product to achieve its maximum potential. — Thomas Watson, American industrialist, and business executive.

Sprints and Hacks

Innovation *sprints* offer a method for rapidly injecting new ideas into the product development pipeline. Hackathons, also known as Hacks, have proven highly effective in the tech industry for innovating, refining products and services, and enhancing processes. A key ingredient in these sprints and hacks is a culture that routinely encourages spontaneous collaboration and innovation, as well as leaders who embody that culture.

As a quick route to innovation, hackathons are intensely focused, creative, and collaborative. —Unknown.

In business, the journey often feels like a marathon, but there are moments when a sprint is necessary to tackle unforeseen challenges or inspire fresh ideas. Sprints and hacks typically involve short-term initiatives where employees with diverse skills unite as a "Tiger Team" to confront a new problem or opportunity. While some companies integrate quarterly sprints into their routines, others promote ongoing hackathons. The approach to these endeavors varies, with some emphasizing structure and rigor and others prioritizing autonomy and flexibility. However, they all share excitement, energy, and sometimes healthy competition. These initiatives generate innovative ideas that are created, shared, discussed, evaluated, and refined within a framework of urgency, ensuring that sprint activities do not become prolonged drains on resources.

Hackathons are common at companies like Facebook, offering significant benefits for innovation and team morale. They drive business outcomes and fuel creativity and camaraderie among employees. By empowering staff to ideate and pursue projects they are passionate about, hackathons invigorate teams and strengthen the bonds between workers and leadership.

The key to innovation is to create a culture in which ideation is fluid and encouraged. When a manager hesitates to allow a key team member to divert even temporarily from their primary responsibilities for a hack or sprint, it undermines the viability of these initiatives. Everyone must be fully committed, and managers must lead by example. Further, once approved, hacks and sprints should be allocated the resources necessary for success, including personnel time and financial investment. Any hesitation or withholding of resources can quickly derail these efforts, potentially harm employee morale, and jeopardize the hacker-fueled culture.[209]

> *The hacker way is an approach to building that involves continuous improvement and iteration. Hackers believe that something can always be better and that nothing is ever complete.* —Mark Zuckerberg, American business magnate, internet entrepreneur, and philanthropist.

Constructive Deviants and Neurodiversity

A company's culture typically revolves around rules and policies that promote stability, productivity, and efficiency. In large corporations, policies often accumulate over time, leading to maximum rigidity.

However, regardless of size, every company can nurture ground-breaking innovation that profoundly boosts the entire enterprise's success, potentially disrupting or creating entirely new markets. More often than not, this newfound success can be attributed to the efforts of a select few individuals known as "rare breeds," "pirates," "rebels with a cause," or "constructive deviants."

Psychologists have found compelling evidence that rebelliousness plays a vital role in enhancing creativity. In a study examining the creative tendencies of 22 Nobel Laureates, researchers found that they were all emotionally motivated by a strong desire to innovate rather than maintain the status quo. They envisioned opportunity through fresh mindsets rather than following established wisdom. They tended to think and act in ways that were in direct opposition to what is commonly observed in conformist personalities.

Unfortunately, leaders frequently view creative renegades as troublemakers who resist established norms. These mavericks propose entirely new and sometimes seemingly absurd ideas, which are often received with indifference or dismissal. They are inclined to challenge rules, manipulate the system, and defy authority, the status quo, and dogma. Additionally, they may exhibit audacity, obsession, eccentricity, or intellectual intensity.

Researchers also found that rebels are typically promotion-focused, goal-oriented, and motivated by personal growth. They are deeply and even overtly focused on the positives that might be achieved, while remaining reasonably comfortable with the possibility of failure. This can create conflict in organizations that refuse to tolerate or encourage risk-taking.

Rebels often care deeply about the organization, feeling discomfort when they observe opportunities for improvement that fail to secure the necessary interest, attention, leadership approvals, or funding to pursue. These individuals represent a minority in the workforce, possessing unique perspectives and valuable strategic insights that can catalyze remarkable innovations when given the opportunity. They care less about fitting in or avoiding criticism than being true to themselves.

Challenging paradigms and thinking differently demand courage and persistence. Regrettably, many companies fail to create environments where these rebels can thrive. Rules and processes inherently breed inertia that impedes innovation. Further, historical precedents and entrenched culture often perpetuate the status quo. When employees align with and endorse the established paradigm, accepting and evaluating new and seemingly crazy ideas and proposals with an open and unbiased mindset becomes challenging.

Instead, leaders striving for innovation should cultivate a culture that values challenging the status quo and pushing boundaries as legitimate behaviors rather than relying solely on a few renegades to champion unconventional ideas. When leaders prioritize creativity, they take tangible steps to facilitate progress and provide workers with the necessary resources, funding, and time to pursue innovative concepts. Individual differences that contribute to positive outcomes should be acknowledged and celebrated within the organization.

Steve Jobs delivered a memorable commencement speech to the graduating class of Stanford University in 2005. In his address, he imparted the wisdom that pursuing something we love leads to a deep emotional commitment, compelling us to do what is *right* even when faced with opposition or differing perspectives. Jobs unequivocally advocated for thinking *differently*, a sentiment that coincidentally became synonymous with Apple's brand as it ascended to become the world's most valuable company. While rebels may sometimes be perceived negatively, they can accomplish extraordinary feats in the appropriate environment with the right motivation and incentives.[210]

Rebels are relatively rare and often create complexities and challenges. While their ideas and determination can galvanize a team, they also have the potential to incite chaos or discord. Sometimes, they may disrupt meetings by expressing oppositional behavior, challenging ideas, or posing questions that unsettle others. If they exhibit antisocial behavior, they may cause significant turmoil within the organization. Despite their disruptive tendencies, their contributions provide substantial value, but shielding the rest of the organization from their disruptive or antisocial tendencies is often necessary.

For example, in certain tech companies, entire departments are composed of high-functioning individuals with neurodiverse conditions like Asperger's. Managers are assigned to guide their efforts and represent their work to the broader organization. The key is channeling, directing, and mediating their efforts. Ultimately, the goal isn't conformity; it's innovation.[211]

Many companies continue to experience the value and impact of neurodivergent employees. The following abbreviated list summarizes some of their unique strengths and attributes:

- Dyspraxia: Strong verbal skills and empathy, creative thinking and problem-solving, ability to connect with others, exceptional verbal communication skills, and determination and resilience in overcoming challenges.

- Dyscalculia: Innovative problem-solving, creativity in visual and artistic tasks, strong verbal reasoning and critical thinking skills, and attention to abstract concepts.

- Dyslexia: Strong creative and visual thinking, holistic problem-solving, exceptional verbal communication, and storytelling skills.

- ADHD: Energetic and hyper-focused contributions, creativity and out-of-the-box thinking, resilience and adaptability in dynamic environments, and quick decision-making in fast-paced situations.

- Autism: Attention to detail, memorizing and learning information quickly, visual thinking and logical thinking ability, exceptional honesty and integrity, dependability, and reliability.[212]

Ultimately, constructive deviants and neurodiverse individuals bring invaluable perspectives, creativity, and problem-solving abilities to businesses. They challenge conventional norms and drive innovation, inclusivity, and organizational success.

> *Somewhere in your organization, groups of people are already doing things differently and better. To create lasting change, find areas of positive deviance and fan the flames.*
> —Richard Pascale, American Management educator, theorist, author, and business advisor. —Jerry Sternin, author, and social change expert.

CHAPTER 10

Teamwork Unleashed

Teamwork makes the dream work, but a vision becomes a nightmare when the leader has a big dream and a bad team. —John C. Maxwell, American author, speaker, and pastor.

When you realize you're not the brightest person in the room, consider yourself fortunate, as it means you can learn from the many remarkable and brilliant colleagues surrounding you. As a young manager, I discovered that hiring the best and most capable individuals empowers the entire team to thrive. I've also observed that exceptional subordinates and coworkers can propel you to success under the right circumstances, even if you're not a great manager. The most significant achievements often arise when collaborative teams driven to excel are led by managers who provide gentle guidance to ensure direction and focus, then step back to allow progress to unfold organically.

Teamwork is really a form of trust. It's what happens when you surrender the mistaken idea that you can go it alone and realize that you won't achieve your individual goals without the support of your colleagues. —Pat Summitt, American women's college basketball coach, author, and philanthropist.

Every individual within an organization plays an important role and contributes to its success. This becomes evident when considering something as essential as securing a customer order. A company's future is fundamentally tied to orders placed, services rendered, or products shipped. Consequently, every member of an organization supports the sales process in one way or another.

In business, purchase orders aren't simply handed to us; they must be earned. When orders are shipped, the revenue generated supports critical aspects of our operations, such as procuring parts, paying employee wages, maintaining infrastructure, and investing in research and development to enable future growth. When every aspect of the business operation aligns successfully, customer revenue translates into sustainable profitability, fulfilling a primary corporate objective.

While salespeople bear primary responsibility for securing orders, it's important to recognize the collateral contributions of the broader workforce. Engineers innovate products and provide customer support through training and documentation. Lawyers ensure compliance with laws and regulations, safeguarding the interests of the company, its employees, suppliers, and partners. Quality assurance teams ensure product reliability while driving for zero defects, so product failures don't impact future orders. HR oversees personnel hiring and training and resolves personnel issues to maintain an effective workforce. Leadership drives overarching strategy and execution, guiding the company toward success. Assemblers and technicians are instrumental in building and testing products, while procurement secures a continuous supply of parts and subcontractor support. Each function is integral, and any failure or setback in one area jeopardizes the future and success of the entire company.

The razor blade is sharp, but it can't cut a tree. The axe is strong but it can't cut the hair. Everyone is important according to their own unique purpose. Never look down on anyone, unless you're admiring their shoes. —Bishop Mutendi, Zimbabwean religious figure.

Brainstorming

Great ideas rarely appear out of thin air—they're sparked through curiosity, collaboration, and structured creativity. That's where brainstorming comes in, transforming scattered thoughts into breakthrough solutions.

The following list details the many benefits of brainstorming:

- Brainstorming encourages diverse perspectives by bringing together unique viewpoints from individuals with different backgrounds and experiences, which promotes superior innovation.

- It cultivates creativity by helping participants think beyond conventional solutions, collaboratively building on others' ideas.

- It builds team cohesion and enhances employee engagement by promoting a sense of inclusion and shared purpose.[213]

- It breaks mental blocks and encourages risk-taking by creating a safe environment for sharing unconventional or risky ideas.

- It accelerates problem-solving by generating a wide array of potential solutions quickly.

- It stimulates mental flexibility by challenging participants to approach problems from different angles, improving adaptability and cognitive agility.[214]

- It reveals hidden talents by uncovering previously unseen skills, creativity, or expertise.

- It improves communication skills by encouraging active listening, respectful debate, and the articulation of ideas.

- It promotes cross-functional understanding by encouraging departments or disciplines to discuss one another's challenges and perspectives.[215]

- It generates unexpected connections by facilitating the combination of unrelated ideas into novel solutions, which can lead to breakthrough innovations.

- It reduces hierarchical barriers by creating an egalitarian environment where all voices are heard and considered.

- It leverages collective intelligence by tapping into the group's shared knowledge and experiences, often producing better solutions than individual efforts.[216]

- It encourages ownership and accountability. When participants contribute to solutions, they are more likely to take responsibility for implementing them effectively.[217]

While extensive literature exists on brainstorming methods, here's a concise overview of the key ingredients based on my experience:

- Diversity: A diverse group of participants generates a broader set of ideas. If the only people you invite share a common background and are like-minded, you can confidently predict a mediocre brainstorming outcome.

- Preparation: Avoid attending a brainstorming session unprepared. Provide essential context, objectives, and ground rules beforehand. Assign a pre-meeting homework task to encourage team members to contemplate the objective, ensuring that the discussion doesn't start from scratch. This approach helps kickstart the brainstorming session with momentum and purpose.

- Time constraints: To maintain focus and momentum, set a specific time limit for brainstorming sessions. This will encourage rapid idea generation without overthinking.

- Quantity: During the initial brainstorming phase, prioritize quantity over quality. Encourage participants to generate as many ideas as possible, regardless of feasibility or practicality.

- Compounding: Create a collaborative atmosphere where team members can build upon and expand each other's ideas. Encourage piggybacking and combining ideas to create new possibilities.

- Creativity: The main objective of brainstorming is to generate numerous ideas, which can only occur in an unrushed, interruption-free setting. Taking your brainstorming session offsite and turning off all cell phones can encourage fresh perspectives and open-mindedness. Prompting participants to leave biases behind and embrace creative, unconventional thinking is essential. Explore wild and out-of-the-box ideas.

- Safety and trust: Team members actively participate in discussions only when they feel assured that their contributions will be respected and valued, free from ridicule or rejection. Everyone should be encouraged to contribute without fear or judgment.

- Judgment and filtering: Effective brainstorming prioritizes ideation above all else. Judgment, filtering, and down-selecting should only occur after the initial ideas have been presented and discussed. Some ideas initially perceived as suboptimal may eventually be the best upon further examination—avoid hastily judging or dismissing ideas that appear less promising at first glance.

- Cooperative criticism: Recent studies have revealed that *cooperative* criticism can enhance ideation and creativity. It thrives in environments where participants share aligned, non-competing goals. However, in competitive settings, criticism may have adverse effects, as it can be perceived as destructive and lead to intra-group conflict. Criticism from peers may be constructive, whereas criticism from managers may be perceived as stifling and inhibiting.[218]

- Leadership: An experienced facilitator is essential for effective brainstorming. Without oversight or structure, brainstorming sessions can quickly devolve into chaos. The leader must establish the tone, communicate the rules of engagement, and clarify that destructive criticism or real-time critiquing will not be accepted. The facilitator is vital in moderating participation, ensuring that quieter voices are heard and dominant voices do not overshadow others.

- Documentation: Document all ideas generated during the brainstorming session for future reference and further discussion. Use visual aids like whiteboards or sticky notes to capture and organize ideas.

- Have fun: The more involved, invested, and engaged your participants are, the more they will interact, create, and ideate. Lower the temperature, lighten the mood, and encourage unencumbered conversation. Inspire participants to speak their minds without pre-filtering or self-editing.

- Next steps: After the brainstorming session, the evaluation, filtering, selection, and elimination of ideas should follow. However, take your time with this process. End the first brainstorming session on a positive note and transition to the next phase later, allowing time for the ideas to marinate. Even after the session concludes, additional thoughts, suggestions, or refinements may emerge.

Effective brainstorming enriches creativity and innovation, allowing teams to generate diverse ideas and solutions. By encouraging open dialogue and creating an inclusive environment, organizations can harness the collective potential of their workforce and drive successful outcomes.

I sometimes compare brainstorming to the drilling of oil wells. The only way to strike oil is to drill a lot of wells. — Tom Monaghan, American entrepreneur.

Cohesion

Cohesion is the invisible thread that binds teams together, transforming a group of individuals into a unified force capable of extraordinary achievements. In business, cohesive teams are the bedrock of success—they inspire deep collaboration, trust, and a shared sense of purpose. When cohesion thrives, it amplifies collective problem-solving, encourages innovative thinking, and ensures resilience when facing challenges. But cohesion doesn't happen by chance—it results from intentional leadership, mutual respect, and a culture that values diversity and inclusivity.

> *We are not a team because we work together. We are a team because we respect, trust, and care for each other.* —Unknown.

Cohesive team members engage in ongoing discussions about their teammates' needs and challenges to identify ways they can contribute to the team's success. They understand that their individual contributions are part of a larger collective effort. By actively supporting each other, team members increase the likelihood of achieving a positive overall outcome.

Cohesive teams also prioritize mutual recognition when presenting their work to others. During meetings, they avoid drawing attention to themselves and their own achievements, instead acknowledging and commending their teammates. Whenever an individual seeks to stand out by appearing superior or more important than their team members, exaggerating their progress, or criticizing their colleagues' efforts, their behavior reflects poorly on the team and its leader.

Team and corporate success require personnel alignment and commitment. While not everyone on the team may ultimately agree on a decision or chosen path, every member must commit to supporting them uniformly. There should be no room for holdouts or individuals undermining progress, overtly or covertly. Those who adopt passive-aggressive behaviors when faced with decisions they disagree with are particularly disruptive.

Cohesive team members understand how their contributions intertwine with the rest of the team's efforts and influence their colleagues. When a team member acts as a detractor or, worse yet, a saboteur instead of supporting and integrating, it poses significant risks to the project. Further, most complex endeavors entail dependencies, where team members rely on one another's work to fulfill their own obligations. A failure to deliver on commitments or adhere to schedules by one team member can trigger a cascading effect on others, making recovery challenging.

I agree with Jeff Bezos' approach to securing buy-in. When faced with conflicting opinions or a lack of consensus, Bezos advocates for the concept of "disagreeing and committing." This approach involves acknowledging disagreements but committing to supporting the decision despite them. Allowing individuals to express their opposition and then move forward with the decision creates an opportunity for everyone to voice their concerns while ensuring unified action. Commitment from team members signifies their willingness to support the team's objectives, even if they harbor reservations or doubts. In this context, commitment holds greater significance than achieving uniform consensus.[219]

Team members facilitate each other's success by recognizing how their tasks interact with and affect others. Upholding commitments and diligently executing tasks are critical to achieving overall team success. Strong team cohesion isn't just about getting along—it constitutes a foundation of trust, collaboration, and peak performance. When teams unite around shared goals and mutual respect, they become more resilient, innovative, and ultimately unstoppable.

> *You've got to be all in. There's no way to have one foot in the canoe.* —Dave Kaval, American entrepreneur, professional baseball executive, board member, and lecturer.

Nothing is Somebody Else's Problem

The best employees refuse to hide behind job titles or rigid roles—everyone takes ownership. The mindset of "that's not my job" creates bottlenecks, stifles innovation, and breeds resentment. Success arrives when individuals step up, collaborate, and take responsibility, knowing that shared goals require shared effort.

I first encountered the phrase "Nothing is somebody else's problem" at Facebook. Sherly Sandberg, our COO, discussed it thoroughly at one of our all-hands meetings, and posters reiterating the theme were easily found randomly throughout the campus.

When you notice an issue, take charge of the situation—it's everyone's responsibility to ensure success. Companies that promote this proactive approach cultivate a culture where individuals willingly go above and beyond because they understand it's their responsibility to do so. They routinely demonstrate initiative by taking charge of solving problems without waiting for someone else to assign them.[220]

Here are some key benefits of embracing a "nothing is somebody else's problem" mindset:

- Increased team cohesion: Encourages a culture of support, accountability, and shared success.

- Greater innovation: Team members think beyond their roles, leading to creative problem-solving.

- Increased productivity: Eliminates bottlenecks and ensures tasks don't stall due to rigid role definitions.

- Improved morale: Employees feel valued and empowered when their contributions go beyond job descriptions.

- Stronger adaptability: Teams pivot quickly in response to challenges and unexpected needs.

- Enhanced leadership development: Encourages initiative and helps cultivate future leaders.

- Improved customer and stakeholder outcomes: A proactive approach leads to faster issue resolution and improved service.

- Reduced workplace tension: Prevents resentment that arises when people refuse to step up.

- Higher retention and engagement: Employees in dynamic, collaborative environments tend to stay longer and perform better.

- A culture of excellence: Reinforces high standards where success is a shared responsibility, not an individual burden.

Embracing a "Nothing is Somebody Else's Job" mindset transforms workplaces into collaborative, resilient, and high-performing environments where everyone takes ownership, innovation thrives, and success is shared.

Teamwork appears most effective if each individual helps others to succeed, increasing the synergy of that team; ideally, every person will contribute different skills to increase the efficiency of the team and develop its unity. —Andrew Carnegie, Scottish-American industrialist, and philanthropist.

Lazy Teammates

In business, everyone must contribute cooperatively. A team member who is a "slacker" can create bottlenecks, hinder productivity, erode morale, and jeopardize overall success. Most employees dislike relying on or collaborating with a lazy colleague.

> *Hard work spotlights the character of people: some turn up their sleeves, some turn up their noses, some don't turn up at all.* —Sam Ewing, American athlete.

Below are some behavioral indicators that signal that an employee is being lazy:

- Absenteeism and tardiness.

- Lack of productivity, initiative, or impact.

- Frequent blame-shifting or excuses for personal underperformance.

- Minimal output and effort.

- Outward signs of disengagement.

- Lack of ownership, responsibility, or accountability.

- Chronically missed deadlines.

- Wasting time and taking excessive breaks.

Addressing performance issues *before* they escalate is critical when dealing with lazy employees. It's best to avoid assigning someone to a team who is likely to underperform or disrupt team dynamics. Resist the urge to transfer a problematic individual to another team—take a proactive approach to finding an effective resolution rather than sluffing them off on others or waiting for the situation to resolve itself.

Below is a list of strategies to effectively address and manage lazy employees while maintaining a productive and positive work environment:

- Root cause: Determine whether laziness stems from a lack of motivation, burnout, unclear expectations, or personal issues. The person might not be lazy; other factors, such as feeling overwhelmed or dealing with external problems, could be at play.

- Set clear expectations: Clearly define job roles, responsibilities, and performance standards to ensure employees know what is expected of them.

- Provide constructive feedback: Offer specific examples of underperformance and discuss the impact on the team while focusing on solutions.

- Motivate through incentives: Use positive reinforcement such as rewards, recognition, or opportunities for advancement to encourage improved effort.

- Encourage open communication: Have a one-on-one conversation to understand the employee's perspective and address any barriers to productivity.

- Offer support or training: Provide resources, coaching, or mentoring to help employees improve their skills and confidence.

- Monitor progress closely: Set measurable goals with timelines and follow up regularly to track performance improvements.

- Redistribute tasks: Assign work that is better aligned with the team member's strengths and interests or reassign critical tasks to more motivated team members.

- Address team dynamics: If an employee's behavior affects team morale, address the issue promptly to prevent resentment or a culture of complacency.

- Institute accountability measures: Implement performance reviews and check-ins to ensure accountability.

- Lead by example: Demonstrate strong work ethics and commitment, to inspire the same behavior in employees.

- Provide consequences for underperformance: If the employee fails to improve despite intervention and coaching, implement disciplinary actions, such as written warnings or probation periods.

- Evaluate fit for the role: If the employee fails to meet expectations despite support, training, and other interventions, consider whether they are a good fit for the role or organization.[221]

Make sure that a problematic employee doesn't monopolize your time. Stay focused on your primary responsibilities to prevent underperformance in your own role. As a mentor, explore techniques or strategies to help the worker improve without doing their work for them. Simply acting as a sounding board can sometimes resolve a performance issue. Additionally, offering temporary assistance may help a struggling employee overcome obstacles and get back on track.

Brook's Law states, "When a person is added to a project team, and the project is already late, the project time becomes longer rather than shorter." Experienced program managers understand this truism, which is why it's so important to be proactive and stay ahead of the curve.

Fortunately, teams consist of multiple experts, each possessing various skills. Sometimes, it makes sense to rotate responsibilities among team members to play to their strengths and minimize weaknesses. This practice facilitates cross-training and better aligns each task with individuals' interests.[222]

Bill Gates once stated: "I will always choose a lazy person to do a difficult job—because he will find an easy way to do it." While this approach may apply in certain unique instances, I haven't found it to be a winning strategy in general. When faced with a difficult task requiring swift resolution, success is more likely to come from someone who energetically and aggressively dives in, performing the heavy lifting expertly and expediently. While a lazy worker might excel in finding a simple, non-optimal solution, in my observation, most challenging and complex problems aren't amenable to shortcuts. Tasks are usually completed most efficiently by those uniquely qualified to perform them and willing to commit the energy and persistence to succeed.

A team is only as strong as its weakest link. A productive team thrives on shared effort and accountability. Addressing laziness requires setting clear expectations, holding individuals responsible for their contributions, and providing the necessary support to help them succeed. By encouraging open communication and reinforcing a culture of fairness and collaboration, teams can ensure that every member pulls their weight. When everyone is committed to the collective goal, productivity increases, morale improves, and the team's overall success is strengthened.

Collaboration

In recent years, there has been a significant surge in the development of collaboration tools. Two decades ago, communication primarily relied on phone calls, emails, and face-to-face meetings. Today, we benefit from team and group chats, virtual meetings, instant messaging, social networks, and many other powerful tools—all easily accessible at our fingertips, facilitating around-the-clock communication and collaboration.

The proliferation of collaboration tools has made people more accessible and interactive. However, unintended consequences, such as increased stress, burnout, and a decline in meaningful face-to-face interactions, are emerging. We're observing a shift towards indirect messaging, with fewer direct conversations, even among physically co-located individuals. Many opt for electronic communication methods, sometimes appearing selectively deaf to their immediate surroundings. While headphones are valuable for uninterrupted concentration, they can also create a sense of isolation throughout the day.

Employers increasingly use advanced sensors and analytical tools to collect interaction data, understand their workforce's collaboration styles and behaviors, and drive more optimal behavior. A recent study involving two Fortune 500 firms found that transitioning to an open-office layout *reduced* face-to-face interactions by 70% while electronic interactions increased accordingly.

One explanation for this finding is that individuals establish virtual or physical barriers in open offices to define their personal space, and colleagues respect these boundaries. Interruptions are less frequent, especially when someone appears intensely focused. Additionally, the proximity between desks directly impacts physical and digital interactions.

Research has found that people on the same team were six times as likely to interact on the same floor, and people from different teams were nine times as likely to interact if they were on the same floor. In another study, 10% of all communications were found to occur between employees whose desks were less than 500 meters apart. Collaboration is maximized when workers are within the same building and, ideally, on the same floor.

As remote work becomes increasingly prevalent worldwide, leaders should assess the *types* of interactions they desire and develop effective strategies to maximize those while decreasing ineffective ones. This may require running experiments to generate valuable data, which can be analyzed for cause and effect.

Interactions in the workplace encompass various dimensions, including communication, efficiency, collaboration, productivity, and overall impact. However, changes to the work environment can also influence factors such as worker concentration, health, psychological well-being, stress levels, and other intangible yet significant aspects. Considering the complexity of human interaction, it's important to thoroughly assess the potential downsides of any proposed changes to avoid unintended consequences and costly mistakes.

Conducting experiments and studies on human behavior that involve behavioral data collection may raise concerns about worker privacy. Adhering to local laws and regulations and prioritizing ethical practices, transparency, and sensitivity to employees' feelings and concerns is essential.

Collaboration is often a journey of gradual improvement. Significant progress doesn't always necessitate sweeping, large-scale infrastructural changes. Sometimes, even minor adjustments can yield substantial returns on investment. Once a change is implemented, it is worthwhile to encourage further refinement and customization on an ongoing basis. For example, employees should have the flexibility to tailor their workspaces and interaction methods within reasonable bounds. By observing these tweaks, organizations may uncover additional opportunities for improvement that can be scaled or applied elsewhere.

The physical layout of office items like coffee makers or snack bins can enhance collaboration by creating natural gathering spots. Additionally, positioning support or stakeholder groups adjacent to core teams can facilitate cross-functional collaboration. However, there's no one-size-fits-all solution—each company is unique and thus requires a tailored approach to meet its specific needs.[223]

Understanding human behavior and its implications for workplace dynamics is necessary when considering how to encourage increased collaboration beyond physical workspaces and tools. Traditionally, scientists proposed that humans are inherently self-centered, a perspective that informed approaches to promoting collaboration in the workplace. Strategies centered on rewards, monitoring, and punishments were often employed to encourage cooperative behavior among employees. However, research has shown mixed results, casting doubt on the effectiveness of such methods.

Contemporary experts suggest that creating an environment where collaboration flourishes may yield better outcomes. This shift toward organic collaboration underscores the importance of workplace cultures that encourage mutual respect, open communication, and intrinsic motivation among team members.

Learning cultures thrive on collaboration, which is enabled when individuals are encouraged to take risks and view mistakes as valuable learning opportunities. Collaborative work cultures celebrate diversity and uniqueness, recognizing the strengths and skills that each individual brings to a team's pursuit. As a result, collaboration flourishes, contributing to happier and more engaged workforces. In contrast, *performance-driven* cultures often discourage mistakes and prioritize avoiding blame. This can lead to a culture of CYA (cover your ass), where errors are buried rather than addressed, ultimately stifling innovation and collaboration.[224]

Collaboration within large teams and organizations demands ongoing attention from managers and leaders. While collaboration may begin with enthusiasm, it can gradually diminish as silos develop and employees become more isolated in their work. Sustained collaboration necessitates consistent cross-functional communication and engagement across the organization.

Workers tend to participate at the level that they feel is desired or required and no further. If they're under pressure to meet a deadline, they should be empowered to opt out of meetings that impede their productivity at crucial times. Effective leaders provide their workers with flexibility in managing their participation and attendance.[225]

Collaborative failures can occur for various reasons. Common culprits are siloed groups, divergent incentives among team members or multiple teams, and unclear decision-making processes or authorities. Sometimes, conflicting priorities overwhelm teams. Strategic planning, clear structuring, and thoughtful organization can lay the groundwork for successful collaboration, while ad hoc team formation may lead to eventual failure.

When I worked at Facebook, I was impressed by their deeply collaborative work environment and culture. Project teams regularly embedded cross-functional expertise within their pursuits, hacks, and workshops, spanning legal, finance, facilities, sourcing, policy, and product and program management. Collaboration was ingrained in their culture, with everyone working together to achieve success. Managers were encouraged to adopt a growth mindset, coaching others to excel while scaling back their own involvement as positive performance and self-reliance became evident. This approach prevented managers from becoming bottlenecks or micromanagers.

In summary, collaboration is the backbone of a successful workplace. When teams work together effectively, they leverage diverse skills and perspectives to solve problems, drive creativity, and achieve common goals. Open communication, mutual respect, and a willingness to support one another create an environment where individuals can thrive, morale stays high, and productivity soars. In today's fast-paced and interconnected world, success isn't about working in isolation—it's about building strong relationships, breaking down silos, and recognizing that the best results come from collective effort.

Collaboration divides the task and multiplies the success. — Unknown.

Team Leadership

Team leadership involves coaching, guiding, and empowering others to do their best work. Great leaders inspire trust, set clear expectations, and create environments where collaboration and innovation thrive. They lead by example, balancing authority with approachability while ensuring every team member feels valued and motivated. In an ever-evolving workplace, effective leaders transcend achieving results; they create resilient, engaged teams that can adapt, grow, and succeed together.

When you are thrust into leading a team composed of unfamiliar individuals, it's only natural that earning respect and inspiring confidence in your leadership and judgment will take time. I've encountered this situation multiple times—the journey to success can be challenging and time-consuming.

Take, for instance, team members who initially adopt a "wait and see" approach, withholding their trust until you've proven yourself. It often feels like everyone is eager to point out even the slightest misstep. However, you'll gradually win over the most skeptical members through consistent, mindful, respectful leadership and steadfast advocacy for the team and its goals. Over time, they'll warm to your coaching style and leadership approach, especially as they witness positive progress and shared team success.

Leaders play an essential role in setting the tone for both individuals and the organization as a whole. When we adopt a clear communication style and model the highest standards of integrity, we establish expectations for others to follow suit. Further, when we demonstrate tolerance for risk-taking and view failures as opportunities for learning, we create environments that are conducive to growth and innovation. These behaviors lay a solid foundation for team success.

As a team leader, you embody your team's spirit, representation, and voice. Avoid singling out and blaming underperforming individuals, especially if they are well-liked by other team members, as this can quickly erode respect. Instead, when leaders take responsibility for failures and attribute successes to the team while rewarding and recognizing individual contributions, they earn admiration, appreciation, and respect over time.

Ultimately, the leader bears the responsibility for the team's success. Any failure—whether due to inadequate planning, communication, goal-setting, accountability, resource allocation, executive support, funding, staffing, or addressing toxic behavior—falls squarely on the shoulders of the team leader.

Whether a team operates together in the office or remotely, team leadership involves a variety of techniques to ensure overall success:

-   Conductor: The conductor ensures that plans, decisions, information, and accomplishments are shared to coordinate and motivate team members.

- Catalyst: The catalyst encourages collaboration, ignites creativity and innovation, cultivates a shared culture, and nurtures dedication within the team.

- Coach: The coach works with team members individually to guide them toward peak performance. This involves building trust and prioritizing their well-being and professional growth. It necessitates strong emotional intelligence (EQ), empathy, and the ability to effectively navigate and overcome personal performance obstacles.

- Champion: The champion advocates for the team, secures team resources, taps essential information sources, communicates accomplishments, and builds trust with peers and key stakeholders, both in-person and virtually. This requires skills in negotiating, influencing without authority, and building alliances.

Ultimately, team leaders must prioritize building and maintaining connections and trust beyond task execution. As remote work becomes increasingly prevalent, the challenges for team leaders in fulfilling their roles and responsibilities intensify. Particularly as leaders ascend higher within the organization, the role of champion becomes even more crucial.

While proficiency in the conductor role is expected among successful team leaders, mastering the catalyst and coach roles demands specific skills and attitudes. To thrive in today's dynamic and hybrid work environment, effective leaders must focus on skill development to enhance their competency across the range of roles they're expected to fulfill.[226]

There are many important considerations regarding the tactical aspects of leading a team. Here's an abbreviated list that describes the roles and actions of a successful team leader:

- Vision: The team leader sets a clear vision for the team's goals and coordinates the development of the necessary plans to achieve them. They align the team's objectives with the company's mission, engage stakeholders, and establish metrics to measure success.

- Resources: Team leaders recruit and assemble the resources needed to accomplish the team's goals.

- Objectives: The team leader establishes clear, measurable, and achievable objectives for everyone on the team. Some will lead efforts, while others will contribute. The effort can begin once the plans and work responsibilities are established and approved.

- Guidance: The team leader proactively motivates and guides the team, monitors progress, inspires achievement, and maintains a global perspective. Their team relies on the leader to resolve issues, make tough decisions, and overcome obstacles. Constructive criticism is offered sparingly.

- Communication: The team leader ensures that everyone, including stakeholders and leadership, is involved and informed throughout the process. Concealing issues or working in isolation can lead to personal and team failure.

- Accountability: The team leader holds their team members accountable. Though they may object initially, this accountability is crucial for achieving team success.

- Empowerment: The team leader empowers team members to determine how best to accomplish their tasks and objectives while providing adequate maneuvering room and autonomy.

- Recognition: The team leader celebrates successes and provides recognition routinely.

- Calm: The team leader exudes a steady calm, which is the default tone for collaboration, especially during stressful and challenging periods.

- Responsibility: The team leader accepts personal responsibility for team failures but generously distributes credit and praise to others.[227]

If you're new to team leadership, seeking guidance from more experienced individuals is often helpful when faced with challenges. Find a coach or mentor who can offer valuable advice and support. Avoid isolation; while the team leader's role is pivotal, success, especially in large and complex programs, relies on the support and expertise of numerous contributors.

Effective team leaders guide teams toward their goals, inspire confidence, and create a supportive environment. By demonstrating strong communication, empathy, and strategic vision, leaders can empower their teams to perform at their best and achieve collective success.

Leaders relentlessly upgrade their team, using every encounter as an opportunity to evaluate, coach, and build self-confidence. —Jack Welch.

Team Building

Building a team can be straightforward, but sustaining collaboration and high performance can be challenging and frustrating. Effective teamwork demands unity among individuals, pooling their strengths to achieve what each cannot do alone. It doesn't emerge spontaneously; it requires a cohesive leadership team to motivate and uplift workers and guide them to innovate collectively toward shared goals. Teamwork, after all, empowers ordinary individuals to achieve extraordinary outcomes.

*When building a team, I always search first for people who
love to win. If I can't find any of those, I look for people who
hate to lose.* —H. Ross Perot, American business magnate,
politician, and philanthropist.

Team building requires active leadership and a commitment to build
on what works while removing elements of dysfunction. Dysfunctional teams can transition to high performance when they focus on
the following priorities:

- Trust and safety: High-performing teams leverage the strengths
  and passions of contributors to help the team. Encouraging open
  communication and a culture of safety encourages risk-taking
  and builds confidence and trust.

- Conflict: Great teams are exceptional at solving problems. They
  focus on issues, support one another, encourage energetic participation, and avoid toxic blame-shifting and scapegoating.

- Commitment: Teams excel when roles and responsibilities are
  clearly defined, goals are achievable, and they align with the
  corporate vision and mission.

- Accountability: When team members take ownership of their responsibilities and hold themselves and each other accountable
  for the plans, obligations, and tasks that they've been assigned
  and committed to, they inspire trust, reliability, and collective
  success.

- Results: High-performing teams are results-driven. They work
  well together, supporting and collaborating to maximize output
  and innovation.[228]

Leaders nurture genuine relationships among team members to create
an environment where teams function and thrive at their highest potential. While team-building activities can promote positive transformation, they can also go awry. When executed effectively, they can
significantly enhance team performance, creating trust and respect
among members. When mishandled, they can embarrass or shame

team members, weaken bonds, and harm existing interpersonal relationships.

> *Successful people build each other up. They motivate, inspire, and push each other. Unsuccessful people just hate, blame, and complain.* —Unknown.

In my experience, effective team-building involves engaging coworkers in enjoyable activities that are neither frightening nor threatening. Changing the scenery for a few hours and spending time together in a relaxed setting creates stronger and deeper working relationships.

At ARGOSystems, our company hosted regular beer bashes in the cafeteria, which created a strong camaraderie across the organization. Within my group, we often gathered spontaneously at a local outdoor Biergarten, where we mingled with colleagues from different departments. These impromptu gatherings, especially when we met up before quitting time, added an element of fun and mischief to our interactions.

At Endwave, we organized regular offsites, typically at a local brewpub, which allowed everyone to come together, share laughter, and relax. Additionally, we held off-site Christmas parties, and summer picnics with food and games at a local park. Our CEO arranged leadership offsites that reinvigorated our relationships while collaborating on long-term planning. My wife Elaine and I hosted my team for water ski trips to the local Delta every summer, followed by dinner and poolside relaxation at our house.

At Facebook, we enjoyed various off-site activities, including visiting a local Escape Room, experiencing a local Ropes Course in the Santa Cruz mountains, trips to the Santa Cruz Boardwalk, local scavenger hunts, wine tastings, and more.

These activities all had one thing in common—moving to an off-site locale. This allowed us to relax and enjoy non-work-related activities in comfortable and safe environments. It also provided opportunities to bond and connect on a personal level away from the confines of the office.

When we're together in a non-work setting, silly things happen, strengthening our bonds. Creating a shared sense of experience, a memory of being there and doing (that) together, becomes vital to our sense of team and belonging.[229]

Team-building activities facilitate collaboration, build trust, and enhance employee morale, directly contributing to a more cohesive and productive workplace. While it may be tempting for leaders to minimize team-building expenses, being penny-wise and pound-foolish can undermine long-term gains. A well-planned team-building initiative can pay dividends through improved communication, higher employee engagement, and reduced turnover—benefits that far outweigh the initial expense. However, leaders should strike a balance, ensuring that activities are impactful and aligned with organizational goals without unnecessary extravagance. Judicious funding within practical limits, focused on outcomes rather than frills, ensures that team-building efforts remain effective and affordable.

> *Without trust we don't truly collaborate; we merely coordinate or, at best, cooperate. It is trust that transforms a group of people into a team.* —Stephen Covey.

CHAPTER 11

Project Mastery

By failing to prepare, you are preparing to fail. —Benjamin Franklin, American writer, scientist, inventor, statesman, diplomat, printer, publisher, and political philosopher.

Project management is the backbone of turning ideas into tangible results, bridging vision and execution. It requires a strategic blend of planning, leadership, communication, and adaptability to guide teams through complex challenges and deliver outcomes that align with goals. Whether managing a minor initiative or a large-scale endeavor, mastering project management principles is essential for ensuring success in today's fast-paced and competitive workplace.

According to a "Pulse of the Profession" survey from the Project Management Institute, there has been a notable increase in global attention toward project management. However, only 56% of corporate strategic initiatives typically achieve their goals and business intent. While high-performing organizations successfully complete 89% of their projects, low-performing ones only reach 36%, resulting in a staggering collective loss of $109 million for every $1 billion invested in projects.

Low-performing organizations waste nearly 12 times more money on project pursuits than high-performing ones. Furthermore, projects aligned with an organization's strategy boast a 71% success rate, while misaligned projects have a success rate of only 48%. Additionally, agile and nimble organizations achieve a success rate of 69%, compared to 45% for those less agile.[230]

Investing in project management can significantly impact a company's success and bottom line. However, many companies fail to prioritize this crucial function. Contrary to common belief, programs *do not* run themselves, nor are they consistently well-run by novices. This is particularly true for complex pursuits and teams with high-maintenance or uncooperative personnel. There are many ways in which projects can derail, resulting in wasted capital and failure to meet objectives.

While some companies have been slow to recognize the importance of effective program management, there has been a recent uptick in the role's identity, maturity, and reputation, mainly due to the efforts of various project management associations worldwide. Today, there is a growing demand for seasoned program managers with extensive experience in their field who have been formally trained and certified by recognized institutes.

Effective program management delivers corporate advantages and offers fulfilling, meaningful, and rewarding career opportunities to those prepared to take on the challenge.

> *Operations keeps the lights on, strategy provides a light at the end of the tunnel, but project management is the train engine that moves the organization forward.* —Joy Gumz, project management and audit expert.

Projects, Programs, and Products

While "project management" and "program management" are often used interchangeably, they represent distinct concepts. Projects are typically short-term, finite endeavors with a tactical focus, usually consisting of a single cycle or phase. Alternatively, programs commonly involve multiple projects aligned and coordinated to achieve a more significant organizational impact. Programs are complex, multidisciplinary initiatives that span numerous phases or cycles and are typically more strategic. While project managers oversee outputs (results and deliverables), program managers focus on outcomes—the collective result of combined project outputs.

Successful project managers must demonstrate effective leadership skills when overseeing all aspects of their projects and the personnel involved. They are responsible for coordinating the efforts of vendors, consultants, and contractors, ensuring that all tasks are planned, executed, and completed on time, within budget, and according to specifications. Additionally, project managers are expected to deliver high-quality work products or services to their clients or customers.

Program managers often oversee and coordinate multiple projects and teams to achieve overarching strategic program goals. Collaborating with executives, sponsors, customers, and stakeholders, they conceptualize and plan the overall program. They negotiate personnel assignments with team leaders and secure phased investments from executives. Additionally, they demonstrate their business analysis skills by creating business requirements documents and process maps and conducting data-gathering sessions with stakeholders.

The scope and complexity of a program dictate the scale and intricacy of its schedules, often necessitating various monitoring and control tools. Professional schedulers and planners are enlisted for large and complex programs to manage daily details and coordinate with the many project pursuits feeding into a program. Program managers closely coordinate with all project or subsystem managers who oversee cross-functional developments to ensure alignment with schedules, interfaces, interdependencies, and functionality.

Successful program managers combine strategic, interpersonal, and operational skills to achieve success. They are also highly effective communicators, exceptional problem solvers, and demonstrate strong emotional intelligence. These qualities are essential for effectively navigating the complexities and challenges inherent in program management.[231]

Recognize that project and program manager role definitions can vary between companies and industries. These definitions may overlap, and they can evolve and adapt based on organizational needs and the skill levels of program personnel.

Product managers often hold a more strategic position than program managers. They typically oversee entire product lines, where products are developed under the leadership of project or program managers and then handed over to the product manager for new product introduction, marketing, and sales. Product managers typically own the product roadmap and spend significant time collaborating with customers, marketers, designers, and corporate executives to formulate plans for addressing customer or market needs. Critical metrics for product managers include conversion rates, revenue, profit margins, and churn, in contrast to program management metrics focused on meeting schedule, cost, and performance objectives.

The following list further delineates the responsibilities of each role while showcasing how they contribute to organizational success:

Project Manager:

- Defines project scope, objectives, and deliverables.

- Creates detailed project plans, timelines, and budgets.

- Oversees resource allocation and task prioritization.

- Coordinates and manages cross-functional teams to ensure successful project completion.

- Monitors project progress and status and addresses risks or delays.

- Communicates project updates to stakeholders.

- Ensures that projects are completed on time, within budget, and to quality standards.

Program Manager:

- Oversees multiple related projects within a program to achieve broader organizational goals.

- Aligns program objectives with business strategies and priorities.

- Manages interdependencies, risks, and resource allocation across projects.

- Develops and maintains program budgets and schedules.

- Ensures consistency and alignment across projects to maximize outcomes.

- Serves as the primary point of communication between project managers and senior leadership.

-   Monitors overall program performance and outcomes, adjusting strategies as needed.

Product Manager:

-   Defines and articulates the product vision and strategy.

-   Conducts market research and gathers customer feedback to identify opportunities.

-   Develops and maintains the product roadmap.

-   Collaborates with engineering, design, marketing, and sales teams to bring products to market.

-   Prioritizes features and improvements based on business value and user needs.

-   Manages the product lifecycle, from concept to launch and beyond.

-   Tracks product performance and implements updates to optimize user experience and profitability.

-   Serves as the primary point of communication between project managers and senior leadership.[232]

-   Engages with early customers, demonstrates compelling product value, secures early orders, and refines messaging before transitioning to the sales team.

Project, program, and product managers each play a distinct yet interconnected role in driving organizational success. Together, they form a cohesive framework, each contributing uniquely to operational excellence and innovation. Their collective impact enables organizations to meet immediate objectives, achieve sustainable growth, and attain long-term success.

For simplicity, I'll use the abbreviation "PM" throughout the following sections to refer to project, program, and product management.

PMs are the most creative pros in the world; we have to figure out everything that could go wrong, before it does. — Fredrik Haren, Swedish author, and speaker on Business Creativity.

Technical Program Management

The Technical Program Manager (TPM) role has emerged as a significant addition to the broader category of program managers, particularly within the tech industry. Many tech companies have recognized the importance of experienced program managers with technical expertise. TPMs have become integral to shaping the technical strategies at major companies such as Facebook, Google, Amazon, Apple, Robinhood, and others.

These highly skilled leaders take ownership of leading, defining, and building end-to-end solutions and solving complex, cross-functional, and high-impact technical challenges. TPMs possess a deep understanding of the technical systems they work on and demonstrate exceptional cross-functional leadership and strategic execution skills necessary to drive success in the most challenging corporate pursuits.

Product TPMs drive organizational scale and efficiency and engage deeply with product teams. They are responsible for driving strategy and execution for product platforms and cross-team initiatives, with a specific emphasis on scaling products. These experts demonstrate a deep understanding of the technology stack and possess comprehensive industry and partner knowledge.[233]

If you're considering a TPM role, your résumé and qualifications must stand out. While leading companies are highly selective when hiring for TPM positions, don't let that discourage you from applying.

Here are some typical skill requirements for TPM roles to guide you:

- Program Management: TPMs are expected to execute complex, multi-disciplinary programs. During the interview, you'll need to demonstrate evidence of this ability, spanning the traditional aspects of program management.

- Facilitation: TPMs solve complex problems, overcome obstacles, and advocate for resources and strategies. They represent their programs and teams when advocating for and coordinating support and collaboration from support personnel, customers, stakeholders, executives, and sponsors.

- Technical: TPMs lead or contribute to the technical activities within their programs. While they don't need to be experts in every technical detail, they must demonstrate technical excellence and have a broad understanding of interconnected systems. Successful TPMs are adept at navigating technical discussions and setting strategic directions for engineering activities. They are also keen to discern valid engineering discussions from distractions, ensuring effective decision-making for program success.

- Problem-solving: TPMs demonstrate a strong aptitude for analyzing complex problems, identifying solutions, and making data-driven decisions.

- Strategic thinking: TPMs align program objectives with overall business strategy and drive innovation.

- Leadership and Communications: TPMs lead their teams, develop plans and strategies, and coordinate end-to-end efforts. They navigate a diverse array of personnel, skills, and roles, excelling in inspiring, persuading, facilitating, and, above all, communicating effectively. Strong written and verbal communication skills are critical in this role.[234]

Fortunately, TPM roles exist at multiple levels, from entry to senior positions. Those with a technical background can prepare for TPM roles by gaining experience in management, leadership, and program management over time. Entry-level TPM positions provide opportunities to develop expertise that can lead to upward advancement. Additionally, obtaining business and program management certifications can further substantiate qualifications for TPM roles.

When I joined Facebook as a TPM within their renowned "Connectivity Lab," I embarked on one of my career's most stimulating and fulfilling roles. My responsibilities centered around innovating revolutionary communication systems to provide affordable internet access to developing countries. One of my more interesting assignments was to lead Facebook's efforts to innovate optical and millimeter-wave communication systems for use on high-altitude platforms (HAPS), which are solar-powered, unmanned drones that will orbit for months at 60-80,000 feet. Constellations of these drones are intended to operate as pseudo-satellites, beaming low-cost internet to countries that lack deep telecom infrastructure or can't afford traditional internet access.

My efforts as TPM involved technical and program leadership and coordination of cross-functional experts to create an entirely new industry and ecosystem. This involved substantial collaboration with legal, policy, regulatory, various product teams, and external partners to drive a holistic approach to innovation.

TPMs at Facebook and elsewhere enjoy their reputation as leaders who work horizontally, vertically, and diagonally, accomplishing the nearly impossible while continuously 'getting the tough shit done.'

Portfolio Management

A program portfolio comprises projects and programs managed collectively to achieve strategic goals. Portfolio managers work closely with individual PMs to maintain alignment and provide oversight. They oversee multiple programs to promote consistency and uniformly apply best practices. Additionally, portfolio managers allocate shared resources strategically to optimize organizational objectives. They resolve conflicts and guide PMs, driving performance improvement across the portfolio. In large companies, portfolio managers represent their organizations and collaborate with peers in other organizations to address high-level, cross-functional program challenges and enhance overall corporate success.

The portfolio manager sets the standard for oversight and governance across the organization, ensuring that all projects and programs align with the overall strategy. The portfolio manager provides guidance, coaching, and mentoring to other PMs and team members, leading to improved program outcomes.

> *Portfolio managers bridge the gap between strategy and execution.* —Unknown.

A portfolio manager often involves resolving conflicts between and within programs, prioritizing tasks across programs to address constraints or bottlenecks in facilities, personnel, or equipment, and ensuring consistent application of best practices in project management.

As a portfolio manager at Space Systems Loral, I also dedicated significant effort to advocating for finance and sourcing priorities and support, developing and refining reporting tools and dashboards at the portfolio and program levels, and collaborating with counterparts in other organizations to streamline and enhance cross-organizational processes. Furthermore, I invested a fair amount of time addressing delays from key subcontractors that impacted multiple programs.

Admittedly, my least favorite responsibility as a portfolio manager was reporting to and liaising with executive leadership. As the accountable owner of our portfolio of programs, I absorbed the heat when things occasionally went sideways while shielding my PMs from the direct line of fire. This buffering role was crucial as it ensured that program teams could focus on solving problems and driving progress without being distracted by executive-level concerns. By acting as a bridge between the executives and my teams, I could distill leadership discussions into actionable insights, nurture trust on both sides, and focus on driving uninterrupted progress. While this role often felt thankless, ensuring the organization's projects and programs continued to excel under pressure was essential.

Portfolio management is instrumental for aligning projects and programs with an organization's strategic objectives, ensuring optimal resource utilization, and managing risk. By effectively overseeing projects and programs at the portfolio level, organizations can achieve greater transparency, prioritize initiatives, and maximize overall value and impact.

Portfolio Management is an ongoing process that includes decision-making, prioritization, review, realignment, and reprioritization. —Unknown.

The Triple Constraint

Every successful PM learns how to expertly manage the "triple constraint," also known as the "iron triangle" or "project management triangle."

The Triple Constraint framework consists of three key elements:

- Scope (performance): Defines the work required to complete a project, including deliverables, features, and objectives.

- Time (schedule): Represents the schedule and deadlines for completing the project, ensuring tasks are finished on time.

- Cost (budget): Encompasses the funding and resources allocated to the project, including labor, materials, and other expenses.

These three constraints are interdependent—changing one affects the others. Expanding the scope often requires more time and cost. Reducing time may increase costs due to the need for additional resources. Cutting costs can limit the scope or extend timelines. A project's quality is constrained by its budget, schedule, and scope. It's the program manager's responsibility to judiciously trade between these constraints to deliver the best overall solution for the company.

Good, fast, cheap. Choose any two. —Unknown.

Within this truism lies an Euler diagram that illustrates a few of the several possible permutations, a concept often covered in entry-level PM training courses:

- Higher Cost and Less Time => Faster

- Lower Cost and Less Quality => Cheaper

-    Higher Cost and Higher Quality => Better

While the project management triangle offers insight into the inherent complexity of any project, it's an oversimplified model that often falls short when applied to complex programs. Manipulating these priorities and constraints can be complicated and typically involves assessing various risks, tradeoffs, and consequences.[235]

For instance, increasing staff to expedite progress on a program may escalate costs unless compensatory savings are realized elsewhere. However, if not managed effectively, expanding staffing can introduce coordination challenges and hinder collaboration, potentially compromising program performance, product quality, or team efficiency. Scope, representing performance, is susceptible to "scope creep," which means that the project can unintentionally increase in extent or complexity. This can occur when designers expand a product's features or functions, which drives longer schedules and higher project expenditure. If not carefully controlled, scope creep can undermine performance, particularly if corners are cut to maintain the budget or schedule. Such compromises may ultimately result in program failure or diminished reliability and quality.

The successful PM is adept at juggling and managing the many program constraints while coordinating the inputs of leadership, stakeholders, customers, and other influencers and benefactors. Successfully managing the Triple Constraint—scope, time, and budget—requires careful balancing, as changes to one element inevitably impact the others. Effective PMs continuously assess these trade-offs, leveraging clear communication, risk management, and stakeholder alignment to maintain equilibrium. By proactively navigating these constraints, teams can optimize resources, minimize disruptions, and successfully complete projects while meeting business objectives.

First have a definite, clear practical ideal; a goal, an objective. Second, have the necessary means to achieve your ends; wisdom, money, materials, and methods. Third, adjust all your means to that end. —Aristotle.

Project Success

Statistically, most projects are *not* completed successfully (on time, on budget, and with all objectives met). A 2015 survey found that 71% of the 50,000 projects reviewed failed to meet their goals. What's concerning is that these figures aren't substantially improving despite the abundance of powerful project-management tools available today. While companies often excel at driving strategies, aligning teams, and boosting productivity, those efforts alone are insufficient to ensure project success.

Prior preparation and planning prevent piss poor performance. —Military adage.

I've found that projects usually fail due to any of the following:

- Lack of accountability from the project lead or the project team.

- Poor planning or execution.

- Frequent scope changes, which create confusion and rework.

- Lack of clear direction, which stalls decision-making and progress.

- Shifting priorities, which disrupt focus and resource allocation.

- Executive interference, which manifests as bullying or micromanagement, undermines team autonomy and efficiency.

- Poor cross-functional communications lead to siloed efforts.

- Misalignment of project goals or strategy.

- Lack of adequate resources.

- Lack of executive (or sponsor) buy-in and support.

- Overly optimistic or aggressive budget, schedule, or requirements (unrealistic demands).

- Overly constrained project parameters.

- Failure to mitigate risks.

Teams often fixate on just one or two program constraints, neglecting the others, which can jeopardize overall success. Achieving a balanced approach is crucial, but external factors sometimes disrupt this equilibrium, leading to unproductive outcomes.

Consider an example where an overly influential quality manager prioritizes quality above all else, imposing expensive design enhancements or exhaustive testing procedures that strain the program's budget. Similarly, a determined CTO may insist on surpassing performance specifications, leading to over-engineering the product while eroding the schedule and budget. Furthermore, leaders often underestimate the importance of competent program management, training, or tools, erroneously believing that projects can run themselves.

Projects and programs often falter because their plans are unreasonably optimistic. When confronted with cost overruns, schedule delays, or the inability to achieve all performance requirements, compromises are inevitable, which can undermine the program's success. The leadership team often demands optimistic plans in their drive for accelerated completion or cost savings. Leaders struggle to avoid placing their thumbs on the scale when the PMs are developing their program plans (especially when establishing schedules).

Project success is enabled when the following steps are taken:

-   Collaborate: Effective collaboration across the entire project team, including executives, support organizations, external stakeholders, and customers, is critical for success. Cross-functional teams should be viewed as a source of diverse knowledge, enhancing the overall team's capabilities.

-   Communicate: Effective communication is necessary to drive alignment and prevent confusion. Regular communication helps prevent surprises and ensures everyone stays informed about plans, issues, status, risks, and other important updates. Selecting the appropriate communication tools is essential.

-   Plan: Planning is essential for project success. Achieving desired objectives becomes challenging without a comprehensive effort to specify and plan a project.

-   Schedule: Scheduling is crucial for project success. It is an essential management tool that substantially improves outcomes. Timely task completion ensures that dependent and follow-on efforts align with the plan, avoiding unplanned resource consumption for mitigation pursuits. Projects lacking achievable, detailed schedules face a high risk of not meeting objectives.

-   Stretch goals: Assigning "stretch" goals leads to better program outcomes. However, the PM must maintain sufficient management reserve when schedules or budgets are skewed toward ambitious targets. Falling short of a stretch goal should not result in penalties or negative consequences for team members. Stretch goals are inherently challenging and may even be impossible to achieve. Still, they are worth pursuing because aiming for something difficult often yields higher performance than targeting easier objectives.

-   Critical path: Modern scheduling tools enable schedulers to identify the critical path, which consists of task sequences that determine the overall project duration. Any delay in a critical path task jeopardizes the project timeline, prompting immediate attention and corrective action.

- Control: Project management and oversight are not passive or shared activities. Task ownership and responsibility must be clearly established for all essential efforts. While the PM is assigned overall responsibility, they should receive adequate support from the team, partners, and stakeholders to ensure success.[236]

Achieving project success requires meticulous planning, clear communication, and continuous monitoring to ensure goal alignment and timely delivery. PMs can effectively navigate challenges and achieve outstanding results by championing collaboration and adaptability. Additionally, prioritizing stakeholder engagement and maintaining flexibility to adjust strategies as necessary ensures that projects remain on track and deliver maximum value.

Success is a project that's always under construction. —Pat Summitt.

Scheduling and Planning

"Nothing ever goes according to plan." This truism resonates deeply, particularly in the corporate world, where deadlines are frequently missed. Effective scheduling and planning are the backbone of successful project execution. Without a clear roadmap, teams risk missing deadlines, resource shortages, and inefficiencies that can derail progress. A well-structured plan aligns tasks with objectives and provides flexibility to adapt to unforeseen challenges. Organizations can enhance productivity and ensure smoother project delivery by priori-tizing realistic timelines, resource allocation, and risk management.

To ensure success, managers, especially PMs, must invest time in establishing specific instructions, goals, and guidelines for projects in advance. They must actively lead their programs, harnessing their teams' skills, abilities, and tendencies while providing effective over-sight and orchestration to sustain productivity throughout the project lifecycle. Leading programs demands active engagement, courage, and perseverance, traits unsuited for the passive, timid, or lazy.

If you talk about it, it's a dream. If you envision it, it's pos-sible. If you schedule it, it's real. —Tony Robbins, American author, coach, speaker, and philanthropist.

Long-term planning is necessary but time-consuming. Unexpected events or deliberate detours often necessitate revisions to plans and schedules, adding further complexity. Sometimes, the unexpected be-comes the norm, making long-term planning all the more challenging. Recognizing this, many successful corporations adopt a more com-pressed time frame for their planning activities, understanding that "long-term planning" can be a contradiction in terms. Plans should be guided by a clear vision and a deep understanding of strategic direc-tion.

Humans have evolved to respond to deadlines, as time constraints create urgency, focus, and a call to action. This also applies to com-panies and projects. However, I've found scheduling and deadlines to be a double-edged sword. When individuals are provided a specific task timeframe, they often adjust their efforts to fill that span. Con-versely, if workers are asked to set their own deadlines, they pad their estimates to ensure ample time. Ideally, tasks should take only as long as necessary to complete and no longer. If everyone works diligently without compromising quality, tasks can often be completed sooner than *planned*, allowing for more time to tackle other priorities or engage in creative endeavors.

Planning also encompasses budgeting. Each team member should estimate the expenses related to their assigned tasks. They should collaborate with vendors and subcontractors, coordinating with the company's procurement and sourcing teams to gather detailed quotes and delivery estimates. The PM consolidates these inputs to formulate the top-level budget requirements, which include a detailed spreadsheet of planned expenses and their approximate timing. After reviewing the budget assessment for omissions or duplications, including clearly defined contingency reserves to account for risk, estimate errors, and surprises, the budget request is presented to management for approval.

It's important to review your plans with sourcing, procurement, and other support functions before project launch to secure the required level and timing of support. Schedules should reflect realistic procurement durations and part deliveries, including uncertainties.

While leaders responsible for providing project approvals should carefully scrutinize the details and underpinnings of the PM's budget request, schedules, and other critical project plans, they should not dictate changes without a clear explanation and rationale. If they challenge the PM and the project team to stretch goals, such as an accelerated schedule or reduced budget, the risk management plan and contingencies should be adjusted accordingly, delineating the increased risk imposed on the project.

When procuring products or services to support product development, the team members utilizing, consuming, or integrating supplier products or designs are best positioned to evaluate their capability, technical approach, strategy, and associated risks. They lead or oversee vendor engagements, assess and negotiate specifications, and determine the frequency and timing of oversight and review activities. They specify or approve vendor test plans and strategies, ensure compliance with specifications or performance requirements, and authorize shipment and invoicing approvals. Close coordination between the project team, sourcing, and procurement personnel is required to ensure optimal vendor performance and successful contract execution.

Typically, in project execution, tension exists between engineering teams and procurement or sourcing functions—a dynamic rooted in differing priorities and responsibilities. Engineers, focused on innovation and technical progress, often seek open, direct communication with vendors and contractors to troubleshoot, iterate, and accelerate development. However, procurement and sourcing teams are rightly concerned that, without proper oversight, engineers may inadvertently commit the company to additional scope or cost by offering guidance that vendors interpret as contractual direction. This can lead to uncontrolled scope creep, budget overruns, or misalignment with contract terms. Organizations should establish clear communication protocols to manage this dynamic effectively, ensuring all vendor interactions are documented and routed through designated channels when discussions could influence scope or cost. Joint training sessions on contract awareness for engineers and regular alignment meetings between engineering and procurement can facilitate mutual understanding. Empowering technical staff while maintaining contractual discipline is critical to innovation and control.

Responsible team members embrace planning and scheduling tools as essential components of their responsibilities. Everyone must understand that planning and scheduling contribute significantly to project success rather than viewing them as unnecessary, burdensome activities.

Consider the following guidelines when preparing your plans and schedules to maximize the probability of success:

- Clearly understand Parkinson's Law and its implications: "Work expands to fill the time allotted for its completion." Loose deadlines can encourage procrastination, while a fast-approaching end date provides a much-needed incentive to buckle down, focus, and accelerate efforts.

- Clearly outline your vision statement and drivers: By clearly laying out the project impact and how it relates to and creates value for the team and organization, you can ignite the team's motivation and sense of ownership over their assigned tasks and milestones.

- Clarify roles and responsibilities: Establish clear roles and responsibilities for each team member and ensure they take full ownership of their tasks. Address any obstacles that could hinder the team's availability or ability to achieve its goals, which may involve rescheduling conflicting tasks or removing barriers.

- Clarify scope: Describe what is and is *not* included in the project scope. Define the parameters and control the limits so extraneous scope creep doesn't sabotage your plan or timeline.

- Work Breakdown Structure: Any comprehensive project plan begins with a Work Breakdown Structure (WBS). The WBS lists the tasks and resources required to achieve all program objectives. For large or complex projects, the detailed WBS evolves through iterations as the project progresses.

- Detail your schedule: To improve fidelity, create a sense of urgency, and resist procrastination, set your task durations in days rather than weeks or months.[237]

- Work calendar: Project schedules should be predicated on standard working hour assumptions and account for planned holidays and vacations. Overtime should never be baselined in the schedule—it should only be employed to overcome slips, delays, and surprises, and utilized occasionally and sparingly.

- Milestones: Milestones are critical tasks or sub-project end dates that define significant achievements or the completion of dependent tasks. They often trigger subsequent activities by other team members or organizations. Milestones are crucial for large or complex programs as they enable the monitoring and communication of project handoffs spanning multiple teams.

- Schedule baseline: After finalizing and approving your schedule, "baseline" it by exercising the baseline function within your scheduling software. This establishes a *reference* schedule that remains unchanged, allowing you to monitor and evaluate schedule changes over time as the project progresses.

- Risks and opportunities: Risks are events that, if left unaddressed, can negatively impact the project, while opportunities present unexpected benefits. Identifying risks allows for proactive measures to avoid, mitigate, or eliminate them. When opportunities are realized, the team capitalizes on favorable outcomes.

- Deal with the unexpected: Surprises are inevitable, so be prepared to make on-the-fly trade-offs to resolve issues swiftly. In overly constrained projects, something may have to give—avoid clinging to a baseline plan when it becomes unfeasible. Instead, be ready to modify, adapt, re-plan, and execute without delay. This skill becomes a PM's superpower.

- New hires: When scheduling, remember to include reasonable schedule spans for personnel recruitment, onboarding, and training for the tasks that new hires will perform.

- Procurements: Always include realistic procurement spans in your schedule. Schedule time for contractor surveys, down selections, and contract negotiations (including NDAs, T&Cs, and legal reviews). Incorporate vendor schedules into your project schedule and require your vendors to update their schedules regularly.

- Avoid omissions: Ancillary activities can consume valuable schedule time. For example, if your project involves a testing phase, allocate sufficient time to develop test plans and procedures and secure access to bottlenecked test facilities.

- Scheduling tools: Computer-based tools are more effective for project planning than manual methods or simple spreadsheets. Investing in the best PM tools can improve overall success. While maintaining tool consistency can moderately benefit the organization, scheduling tools are not one-size-fits-all.

Effective project planning and scheduling are fundamental to project success. They provide a structured approach to organizing tasks and resources. A well-planned schedule ensures that teams stay aligned, meet deadlines, and adapt to changes smoothly, ultimately leading to the successful completion of projects. By establishing clarity, accountability, and coordination, robust planning and scheduling frameworks empower teams to manage complexities and consistently deliver high-quality results.

Plans are worthless. Planning is essential. —Dwight D. Eisenhower, American statesman, military officer, and 34th president of the United States.

Budgeting and Cost Control

Budgeting, like scheduling, underpins any successful project endeavor. The project budget accounts for all the costs and expenditures associated with completing a project. These costs can be internal (personnel headcount, general and administrative, travel, supplies, capital expenses, etc.) or external (subcontracted efforts, purchased items, services, consultants, etc.).

Budgets play a critical role in project management for two main reasons. First, the approved budget dictates the project's funding.

Inadequate funding can make successful execution difficult or even impossible. Second, the approved budget is a baseline for cost tracking and control. When certain expenditures exceed their budgeted allocation, adjustments must be made elsewhere to maintain the overall spending plan. Budgeting is not an afterthought or busywork; like any other type of plan, you need a budget to know if you're spending too much or too little, too fast or too slow... until you run out.

> *A budget isn't about restricting what you can spend. It gives you permission to spend without guilt or regret.* —Dave Ramsey, American personal finance personality, radio show host, author, and businessman.

While the overall project budget may be approved before the project launch, funding can occur in stages, often triggered by specific milestone completions. For large programs, approval might be granted sequentially. For instance, the initial exploratory or proof-of-concept phase might need to be completed, evaluated, and accepted before follow-on or full program approval is granted.

Maintaining a graph that compares the approved budget with actual spending over time can be particularly helpful. This enables the PM to track how expenditures align with the planned budget. Any deviations from the plan can inform corrective actions.

Budget contingency (or "reserve") should be allocated as a separate line item to account for any risks that materialize during the program. Conversely, "opportunities" are favorable events or outcomes that provide program savings or other benefits as they occur. It's important to actively pursue and capitalize on these advantages, even if it requires investment, as the overall benefit to the program often justifies the expenditure.

PMs are often challenged to remain on budget, particularly when their plans and forecasts are overly optimistic. Experienced PMs recognize that unexpected events occur, tasks frequently take longer than anticipated, and actual costs exceed initial estimates. Therefore, they rely on their intuition and experience to identify when estimates are overly optimistic and strategically incorporate management reserves into their plans. These reserves help mitigate the impact of surprises and underestimated costs, allowing for more realistic budget management.

Controlling costs is a critical skill for PMs. Although denying team members' spending requests can be challenging, maintaining strict control over resources is essential for a project to stay within budget.

When plans go awry, it's common for individuals to resort to blame-shifting rather than addressing the root causes. Successful PMs navigate projects' natural fluctuations while proactively monitoring and controlling costs.

A budget tells you where your money should go, and when, instead of wondering where it went. —Unknown.

Sponsorship and Advocacy

Successful projects don't thrive in isolation—they require robust sponsorship and active advocacy from leadership. Project sponsors provide the vision, resources, and strategic alignment needed to drive initiatives forward, while advocates help secure buy-in, remove roadblocks, and maintain momentum. Without engaged sponsorship, projects risk stagnation, misalignment with business goals, or failure due to a lack of support. By championing initiatives and ensuring they receive the necessary attention and resources, sponsors and advocates play a critical role in turning plans into impactful results.

Leaders, sponsors, and advocates support project success through the following actions and behaviors:

- They prioritize recruitment activities to accelerate the hiring of key project personnel.

- They prioritize procurements to ensure on-time deliveries of critical purchased or subcontracted items.

- They allocate the use of constrained facility assets in support of the project's schedule requirements.

- They approve and assign legal, procurement, and other essential support functions in a timely fashion.

- They prioritize and facilitate approvals for spending and travel requests, avoiding unreasonable signature hurdles.

- They provide introductions to mentors and industry experts who act as project advisors.

- They critically review and approve project plans, schedules, and budgets without imposing unreasonable influence.

- They participate in project reviews, including peer reviews, design reviews, etc. They recognize that their involvement stimulates team engagement and reinforces the importance of the project pursuit.

- They offer constructive coaching, mentoring, strategic guidance, and problem-solving insights, empowering the team rather than undermining them with unreasonable challenges, intimidation, or excessive second-guessing.

Management and executives play a crucial role in program oversight. They routinely check in with PMs to ensure that team efforts are progressing as planned. When they personally engage, they reinforce executive support for the project, provide guidance to resolve obstacles, and allocate additional resources when necessary to accelerate progress or recover from setbacks. These periodic check-ins demonstrate the organization's commitment to the project's success and facilitate effective communication between leadership and project teams.

When leaders meet with PMs, the focus should be on constructively and collaboratively addressing issues, conflicts, delays, risks, and opportunities. Before each meeting, leaders should familiarize themselves with the program status, team accomplishments, and future projections to facilitate meaningful discussions. Expending valuable meeting time to discuss or review status can be an expensive waste of time. All attendees should arrive at each meeting pre-informed of the status, ready to dive into resolving critical issues.

Occasionally, I've observed senior-level program reviews that descend into hostile interrogations, scapegoating, and toxic fear-mongering when leaders bully PMs and their teams into working harder, especially when attempting to recover lost time. Demands for excessive overtime, canceled vacations, daily tiger-team meetings, and additional executive oversight are typical go-to methods leaders choose when programs struggle or slip. These behaviors create a culture of self-preservation, where fear-driven "cover-your-ass" (CYA) tactics replace accountability and innovation, ultimately draining morale and undermining the teams the organization relies on for success.

Instead, high-performing teams thrive under leadership that exhibits empathy, respect, and a collaborative spirit. Rather than resorting to fear-based tactics, effective leaders engage with team members to address conflicts and issues as they arise and before they become significant problems. When leaders actively support and *inspire* their teams, the atmosphere becomes one of shared determination and commitment to success. Positive and supportive leadership behaviors are critical for promoting a culture of excellence and achievement.

Dashboards and Reporting

Transparency and efficiency in delivering regular project updates are a cornerstone of effective project management. Achieving success hinges on continuous learning, adaptation, and optimizing reporting methods, tools, and strategies to ensure efficiency and efficacy. Status updates must be brief, clear, and concise. I've always adhered to the principle that leaders and customers should receive the information they *need to hear* rather than what I might *want to convey*, acknowledging the significance of this differentiation.

When reporting to higher-ups, take the necessary time to consider your objectives and then focus on achieving them. If your focus is to inform, then concentrate on prioritizing critical, timely, and relevant information—avoid burdening leaders with unimportant details. Alternatively, if your goal is to solicit a decision, then focus on presenting unbiased facts and data, clearly outlining the decision you're seeking, and providing reasons to support it. Ensure you leave each meeting having accomplished your objectives, and take proactive steps to follow up if further action or information is required.

Large and complex programs require comprehensive reporting schemes to communicate effectively. Project dashboards are invaluable for this purpose, allowing for the graphical display and tabulation of critical metrics and trends. With just a few slides or pages, dashboards can convey essential information regarding status, issues, risks, progress, and plan variances. This concise and visual representation enables efficient communication and explanation of key program concerns to leaders.

Portfolio managers find dashboards particularly useful for reporting the status of multiple programs. In addition to critical metrics, dashboards can also indicate cumulative risk and opportunity, personnel satisfaction, stress levels, engagement, cross-program trends or inefficiencies, and other collateral yet essential factors that affect the success of multiple projects.

The standardized or unified usage of dashboards across multiple programs offers several advantages. By comparing common metrics from multiple programs, portfolio managers can quickly rank performance and identify areas of strength or weakness. They can audit the best-performing projects to understand the factors contributing to their success, such as superior practices, processes, or techniques. These insights can be communicated and applied to other programs, allowing teams to learn from each other and improve overall performance. This sharing of best practices helps create a culture of collaboration and continuous improvement within the organization.

It's worthwhile to develop dashboards that auto-populate data whenever possible. Linking to other spreadsheets or data sources that are routinely generated significantly reduces the workload for maintaining the dashboard. This ensures the dashboard remains current and relevant without becoming burdensome and time-consuming.

Out-briefs and dashboards consolidate and communicate important information efficiently. They also serve as tools to highlight critical issues that require team discussion, resolution, or leadership intervention. Focusing on current and future challenges is far more impactful when presenting to leadership than dwelling on prior issues or performance deficiencies.

Be proactive in addressing both near-term critical items and long-term strategic concerns. This demonstrates forward-thinking and shows you are focused on driving success. Avoid the temptation to impress others or draw attention to yourself. Recognition comes from tangible success and effective leadership, not from flashy presentations. Stay humble and focus on delivering value to the organization through informed and actionable reporting.

Dashboards are more than just communication tools; they are essential management tools. When done right, they focus management and team members' attention on important information, facilitating informed decision-making and impactful action. They also provide a snapshot of critical metrics and trends, enabling leaders to assess a project's health quickly and take appropriate action.

> *The key metric of whether you've succeeded is what fraction of your employees use that dashboard every day.* —Keith Rabois, American technology executive, and investor.

Project Reviews

Project reviews are essential for ensuring alignment, accountability, and continuous improvement throughout a project's lifecycle. They provide a structured opportunity to assess progress, identify risks, and make necessary course corrections before minor issues become major setbacks. Effective reviews promote transparency, facilitate stakeholder collaboration, and reinforce best practices, ultimately driving better outcomes. Whether conducted at key milestones or upon project completion, these evaluations help organizations refine processes, enhance decision-making, and optimize future initiatives.

Project reviews are structured checkpoints, each serving a specific purpose. Reviews should be constrained to what is critical and necessary based on the project's size and complexity, given the associated expense and time invested to prepare and present. The following list describes several reviews typically encountered in projects and programs:

Project Initiation and Planning:

-   Kickoff Review: Aligns stakeholders on project launch objectives, scope, and responsibilities.

-   Project Charter Review: Ensures that the project's purpose, objectives, and resources are communicated, understood, and formally approved.

Design and Development:

-   Concept/Feasibility Review: Evaluates the viability and risks of proposed concepts or solutions.

-   Requirements Review: Verifies that all stakeholders agree on the documented requirements.

-   System/Preliminary Design Review (PDR): Assesses the preliminary design to ensure it meets requirements and is ready for detailed design.

-   Peer Reviews: Deep dives, customized to address specific concerns, often held multiple times as necessary.

-   Critical Design Review (CDR): Confirms that the detailed design is complete and satisfies all technical and programmatic requirements.

Implementation and Execution:

-   Test Plan Review: Ensures testing methodology and criteria align with project goals.

-   Manufacturing Readiness Review (MRR): Confirms that production processes are in place and ready for execution.

- Build Readiness Review (BRR): Verifies the readiness to proceed with system assembly or production.

Monitoring and Control:

- Phase Gate Reviews: Conducted at the end of each phase to confirm that the project is ready to proceed to the next phase.

- Status/Progress Reviews: Regular check-ins to monitor performance, timelines, and budgets. Leadership attendance enhances problem-solving and expedites issue resolution while modeling supportive collaboration.

- Risks and Opportunities Review: Focuses on identifying, analyzing, and mitigating project risks, and formulating strategies to realize opportunities that could benefit the project.

- Configuration Review: Ensures project scope or deliverable changes are controlled and documented.

Testing and Verification:

- Test Readiness Review (TRR): Confirms that all systems, resources, and conditions are prepared for testing.

- Integration Readiness Review (IRR): Ensures that individual components are ready to be combined and tested as an integrated system.

- Validation/Verification Review: Confirms that the system meets design specifications and fulfills the intended purpose.

Delivery and Closure:

- Operational Readiness Review (ORR): Verifies that the system or product is ready for operational use.

- Final Acceptance Review (FAR): Confirms that the client or customer has accepted the deliverable and that it meets contractual obligations.

- Lessons Learned Review (or Final Closeout Review): Identifies successes and areas for improvement regarding future projects and evaluates the project's outcomes against its objectives after completion.

The project Kick-Off Review is often the most crucial. It aligns everyone involved and ensures they understand the bigger picture and potential pitfalls before the project begins. An effective kick-off involves team members, stakeholders, support personnel, managers, and executive leadership. The project leader and the executive sponsor set the preliminary vision and mission for the project, explaining why valuable resources are being invested. The kick-off review links team efforts to larger corporate objectives, showing how they advance the company's goals. It aligns objectives, workflows, and priorities, creating a cohesive direction.[238]

Team members often resist project reviews, considering the preparation involved. However, I can't recall a well-transacted review that did not substantially benefit the project, offsetting the investment of time and effort. Each review is a valuable opportunity to identify and address issues early on, ensuring that the project stays on track and efficiently meets its objectives.

We improve our work when multiple expert, diverse, and experienced perspectives are applied to program pursuits during critical stages. Collaboration is a force multiplier, allowing us to enhance our work through collective effort. Reviews must be structured and expertly led to maintain a tone of support, kindness, and respect.

Reviews represent critical milestones that signify interim progress and task completion. They can also facilitate public recognition for programs and their team members. They put a *bow* on completing a particular effort phase once the review action items have been closed. They mitigate project risk and ensure the entire team is aligned.

Reviews also serve as prerequisites for approvals to proceed. They can signal accomplishments worthy of celebration for team-building, stress release, recognition, and rewards. Further, formal reviews constitute critical deadlines, inspiring a team's sprint to the finish line.

The ultimate inspiration is the deadline. —Nolan Bushnell.

Reviews offer additional benefits through their associated documentation. Review preparation compels the team to document their strategies, designs, analyses, justifications, specifications, data, and plans. This focused scrutiny ensures that each phase meets the necessary standards before advancement. Additionally, documentation packages provide a historical accounting and foundation upon which future pursuits depend.

When scheduling project reviews, it is recommended that review packages be provided to participants at least one week before the meetings. Encourage participants to thoroughly review the material beforehand and come prepared with questions and feedback. During the meeting, focus the discussion on areas of particular interest or concern. Much of the detailed information in the review package is for reference only, so discussing the entire content is unnecessary as long as everyone has adequately prepared.

Conducting a Final Close-Out Review is a vital retrospective exercise. It encourages teammates to reflect on *what* they've done and *how* they've done it. This review encourages communication and builds trust and honesty within the team. It also enables the team to evaluate the project's successes and shortcomings and understand their causes. It's a platform to celebrate achievements and learn from mistakes, which can be applied to future programs. Additionally, it serves as a forum to explore potential follow-on pursuits extending beyond the current project's scope.

Successful final reviews depend on a culture that prioritizes transparency and encourages honest, constructive criticism. Without a safe environment where teams feel free to provide respectful and empathetic feedback, the value of final reviews diminishes rapidly. Similarly, if executives view the final review as an opportunity to criticize or punish individuals or teams for project issues or deficiencies, participation in future reviews will suffer accordingly.

A retrospective has huge potential for learning. It should not be off limits for any team member. —Luis Goncalves, entrepreneur, author, agile coach, and speaker.

In summary, project reviews are instrumental in assessing progress, identifying areas for improvement, and ensuring alignment with objectives. They contribute to project success by reinforcing accountability, facilitating timely course corrections, and enhancing learning. Thus, they drive better project outcomes and continuous improvement.

Leading by Example

In my experience, many workers, particularly engineers, procrastinate on tasks like developing schedules, writing status reports, and preparing for reviews and test plans. This isn't surprising, as people often prefer the creative aspects of their work over everything else. However, these oversight activities are crucial for program success. As a PM, it's essential to use persuasion tactics like reminders, encouragement, cajoling, nudging, and sometimes more assertive measures to ensure that deadlines are met, especially for tasks that team members may resist prioritizing.

When confronted with a hesitant team, I often take the initiative and lead by example. I'll prepare initial drafts of technical project review outlines, presentations, reports, or schedules well ahead of deadlines. Then, I share those drafts with the team, emphasizing the importance of timely completion. I set clear expectations for review and final draft deadlines and monitor progress continuously. This proactive approach sets a precedent for accountability and encourages the team to follow suit.

People, by nature, have difficulty starting things. Launching efforts yourself can help others build upon your work on their path to completion. Further, by establishing the preliminary structure or outline, you're nearly assured that the final product will meet your minimum expectations. This approach accelerates progress and enables greater influence over the content and structure of the final work product.

Remember that a PM's primary objective is to ensure the project's overall success. Sometimes, this involves stepping in to facilitate progress, even temporarily assuming tasks outside your domain. By doing so, you can influence team performance and impactfully contribute to the project's success.

Leading by example often creates a sense of camaraderie and reciprocity within the team. When team members see the PM actively contributing and taking initiative, they are more inclined to reciprocate with their own efforts. Demonstrating a willingness to roll up your sleeves and tackle tasks firsthand sets a precedent for teamwork and collaboration. Ultimately, it reinforces the notion that everyone is working together towards a common goal, with each member doing their part to contribute to the project's success.[239]

Great leaders don't just tell you what to do. They show you how it's done. —Unknown.

CHAPTER 12

Philanthropy and Citizenship

We rise by lifting others. —Robert Ingersoll, American lawyer, writer, and orator.

Engaging in philanthropy and embracing citizenship allow individuals and organizations to create lasting positive impacts on their communities and the world. By contributing time, resources, and expertise, we can address pressing societal challenges and help build a more equitable and thriving future.

The personal rewards of giving back to society are well-studied and documented. Offering our time or resources to those in need can reduce stress while elevating our well-being, morale, and happiness. Compassion and generosity create a sense of fulfillment that can surpass other pursuits.

Many of us aspire to contribute to a cause greater than ourselves. We seek to make a positive difference in our local communities, our nation, and globally. Nearly a third of American adults volunteer, and charities receive billions of dollars in donations each year. 84% of those with significant wealth consider *giving back* a vital goal. Regardless of circumstances, we can all donate our time, ideas, creativity, resources, or influence to create meaningful change. Engaging in impactful endeavors benefits others and gives us a profound sense of purpose and fulfillment.[240]

> *What we have done for ourselves alone dies with us. What we have done for others and the world remains and is immortal.* —Albert Pine, English author.

The concept of *giving* is deeply rooted in the cultural context in which we are raised. Individualistic cultures emphasize personal success and achievement, often prioritizing self-interest and maximizing personal gain. In contrast, collectivistic cultures place greater emphasis on communal well-being and addressing the needs of others. Humanistic psychologists like Maslow, Seligman, and Kaufman have shed light on these cultural tendencies and their impact on human development. They advocate for a shift towards a focus on enriching the lives of others as the ultimate goal, promoting a sense of interconnectedness and social responsibility.[241]

At their core, giving and serving extend beyond mere acts of generosity or contribution. They also involve intentional actions to combat injustice and advance shared objectives. When individuals are harmed, society becomes responsible for offering support, empathy, and defense.

For example, despite decades of efforts to combat discrimination, it persists in various forms in the United States and elsewhere. Many individuals choose to look the other way or actively contribute to the continuance of prejudice and hatred. This is evident in the divisive rhetoric and fearmongering perpetuated by many politicians and media figures, which polarize society further and marginalize certain groups in pursuit of power, influence, and political gain, creating tangible harm to many.

Citizenship involves actively opposing leaders' divisive and harmful agendas to counter and suppress this dangerous trend. Truth is the antidote to falsehoods and misinformation, so promoting accurate information and holding those spreading lies accountable is essential. Peaceful protests are fundamental to our democracy, providing a platform for advocating for change and challenging unjust systems.

Despite extremist threats of violence, individuals committed to society's well-being often consider public service as a means of counteracting harmful influences and safeguarding democratic values. While this endeavor demands courage and patriotism, it is essential for preserving the nation's health, integrity, and future.

A quote from William Bloomberg, father of magnate and philanthropist Michael Bloomberg, encapsulates a powerful sentiment: "We're in this together, and if you have an opportunity to help, you have an obligation to act—to fight to help wrongs wherever they might exist."

Regardless of our circumstances or resources, we can all make a positive impact through our actions, voices, and participation. Contributing to meaningful and positive change can be a gratifying achievement.[242]

Anyone can be great, because anyone can serve. —Martin Luther King Jr., American minister, and social activist.

Pay it Forward

Embracing the spirit of giving and philanthropy doesn't require grand gestures or substantial resources. Even small acts of kindness and generosity can have a meaningful impact on others, especially considering the compounding effects of many small contributions. Getting started can be as simple as identifying causes or organizations that resonate with you and finding ways to support them through donations, volunteering, or spreading awareness. By taking small steps and persistently seeking opportunities to make a positive difference, you can cultivate a compassionate mindset and create a better world for everyone.

> *The road to success is dotted with many tempting parking spots. If you've put it in park, thrust it into drive to get unstuck.* —Jeff Bezos.

It's heartening to see how families can come together to positively impact their communities by giving back. By involving children in philanthropic activities from a young age, parents instill values of compassion and empathy and provide them with opportunities to actively participate in making a difference.

For example, my wife Elaine and I are proud to have donated to many great causes through various school drives, sporting events, and scouting activities, to name a few. We encouraged our children to join local organizations that sponsor community volunteering, and we set an example by donating to worthy causes that each of us is passionate about. We've spent time at soup kitchens, retirement homes, and fundraisers. Our children have donated their time towards maintaining and renovating local parks and open spaces, as well as cleaning up trash on beaches and parks. When our children were very young, we encouraged them to regularly set aside a portion of their allowance to be donated to their favorite charities. We helped them list the local causes that carried meaning for them and watched them proudly donate their savings, ensuring that they understood the value and impact of their benevolence. Through these types of activities and experiences, families can bond over shared values and create lasting memories while making a meaningful difference in the lives of others.

Embracing the concept of Karma and practicing random acts of kindness are powerful ways to spread positivity and make a difference in the lives of others. Demonstrating kindness and generosity brightens someone else's day and inspires those around us to do the same. As we sow seeds of kindness, we can trust that they will eventually come back to us in ways we may not expect, reinforcing the belief that small gestures of kindness can have a ripple effect of positivity far beyond the moment.

> *You will never understand the damage you did to someone until the same thing is done to you... That's why I'm here.* — Karma, spiritual concept.

The *butterfly effect* poignantly reminds us of the profound impact our actions can have on the world around us. Just as the flutter of a butterfly's wings can set off a chain reaction leading to significant changes in weather patterns, our minor acts of kindness and compassion can spark transformative shifts in the lives of others.

When we embrace the interconnectedness of our actions and recognize the power of collective goodwill, we are inspired to cultivate positivity and generosity in our interactions with others. When applied to our daily deeds, we contribute to a more compassionate and harmonious world where even the simplest acts of kindness can create meaningful and lasting change.

> *Every pebble of thought—no matter how inconsequential— creates endless ripples of consequence.* —Edward Lorenz, American mathematician, meteorologist, and chaos theory pioneer.

The tradition of "Caffè Sospeso," or *suspended coffee*, exemplifies the power of collective generosity and compassion to uplift those in need within a community. Originating in Europe, this practice allows individuals to purchase a coffee for someone less fortunate, creating a chain of positive pay-it-forward actions. Those facing hardship are offered a warm beverage, instilling a sense of solidarity and support.

By participating in such acts of kindness, communities address immediate needs and cultivate a culture of empathy and mutual aid, contributing to the advancement of society as a whole.[243]

> *My wish for you is that you continue to astonish a mean world with your acts of kindness.* —Maya Angelou, American memoirist, poet, and civil rights activist.

My wife and I occasionally pay road tolls for random cars behind us. We hope our gesture brings happiness to unsuspecting drivers and inspires similar acts of kindness in others. On occasion, we've also covered the drink tab for people we've met in bars or restaurants, especially those who are young or facing financial challenges. It's gratifying to secretly pay their bill, knowing they'll be pleasantly surprised later.

Most recently, we joined our friends on a trip to West Maui following the devastating Lahaina fire. We spent a few days volunteering at the local food pantry and then purchased and delivered a van full of food and supplies to their smiling volunteers. We can all find creative ways to bring unexpected aid and joy to others when we commit to doing so.

> *Your beliefs become your thoughts, Your thoughts become your words, Your words become your actions, Your actions become your habits, Your habits become your values, Your values become your destiny.* —Mahatma Gandhi.

We often admire remarkable individuals like Bill Gates, Michael Bloomberg, Marc Benioff, Warren Buffett, and Richard Branson, who have significantly changed the world. However, the cumulative impact of small, individual contributions can be even more profound over time. Everyone possesses ability, knowledge, and skills. Making a real difference often only requires the motivation to identify problems that need attention and a commitment to contribute. The world benefits immensely when each person gives a little to worthy causes.

Bill Gates dedicates considerable effort to exploring how technology can uplift the lives of the world's poorest individuals. Today, it's increasingly straightforward for people from diverse backgrounds to volunteer their free time to support initiatives that advance global health and development. Engaging in such endeavors can be profoundly fulfilling, offering the chance to collaborate with capable individuals from various backgrounds on meaningful causes. For example, the Bill and Melinda Gates Foundation curates a list of volunteering opportunities. Likewise, the internet is an excellent source of information that we can tap to find opportunities aligned with our passions.

Another impactful way to give back to society is to innovatively utilize our professional expertise, especially as we approach or enter retirement. My Uncle, Don Roberts, is a personal inspiration in this regard. Trained as a geologist and civil engineer, he blazed a trail in multidisciplinary environmental planning. His career transitioned from specialized geotechnical engineering to tackling various ecological challenges, including natural hazards and human-induced pollution.

In the late 1980s, instead of retiring, he embarked on a new chapter by joining a different company for the first time in his 36-year career. His new role empowered him to pursue his passion for environmental causes. His groundbreaking work significantly influenced the discourse on sustainability in engineering and spurred changes in engineering education across America. Ultimately, his efforts contributed to creating the World Engineering Partnership for Sustainable Development, and Engineers Without Borders.[244]

We can all contribute to society in countless ways, from small gestures to monumental initiatives. Each contribution, regardless of its scale, holds significance. Like the ripples in a pond, every individual effort merges with others, gradually altering the landscape. The cumulative effect of these small and incremental influences, when combined with those of others, ultimately drives global change.

The smallest act of kindness is worth more than the grandest intention. —Oscar Wilde.

Corporate Citizenship

Throughout history, businesses have often operated with selfish motives. For example, John D. Rockefeller (founder of Standard Oil) said of his company's monopoly: "The growth of a large business is merely a survival of the fittest. The American Beauty Rose can be produced in the splendor and fragrance, which brings cheer to its beholder, only by sacrificing the early buds, which grow up around it. This is not an evil tendency in business, it is merely the working out of the law of nature and of God."

By the middle of the 20th century, the prevailing profit-centric leadership philosophy regarding business practices and corporate morality was challenged and re-evaluated. Under the visionary leadership of its founders, Hewlett-Packard recognized that employees do a better job when they're treated respectfully as human beings. In 1966, Dave Packard proposed that profit should be seen as a return on investment and the best measure of a business's contribution to society. He advocated for corporate leaders to begin focusing on creating jobs and improving the lives of employees, customers, the public, and those who invest in the business.

> *...today's business manager must add to this heritage, not merely use it. He can best do this by first realizing that profit is not the proper end and aim of management, but only that which makes all of the proper ends and aims possible.* — David Packard, American entrepreneur, co-founder of Hewlett-Packard, and philanthropist.

Many benevolent companies and their workforces have significantly evolved in recent years. Their overarching strategy now extends beyond mere profit-making and wealth accumulation for shareholders. Today, employees are increasingly drawn to companies that actively contribute to society, share their social values, and uphold truth, transparency, and ethical principles. Forward-thinking companies recognize that attracting the next generation of workers hinges on aligning their mission and philosophy with potential recruits, who increasingly prioritize social responsibility and the pursuit of a better world.

Companies should be responsible corporate citizens, considering their impact on the communities where they operate. From affecting traffic flow to influencing neighboring businesses, large companies should recognize their role in the local ecosystem and give back accordingly. This involves showing appreciation for the benefits they receive by investing in initiatives that support the community. Ethical and empathetic corporate leaders actively seek opportunities to contribute to the well-being of their local surroundings.

> *We can have a world that is livable for humans or we can have great wealth concentrated in the hands of the few; but we can't have both.* —Louis Brandeis, American lawyer, and associate Supreme Court justice.

Corporate citizenship creates fringe benefits, including increased support and loyalty from those who recognize or benefit from philanthropic initiatives. Additionally, local politicians may be more inclined to advocate for companies that contribute significantly to their communities. Moreover, corporate giving enhances a company's reputation, respect, and brand perception. Examples abound of large companies donating to schools and parks, with lasting positive effects on children's educational and extracurricular experiences.

The high-tech industry, in particular, has undergone a notable shift in corporate stewardship, departing from solely profit-driven objectives. Numerous studies indicate that companies prioritizing corporate social responsibility, sustainability, and societal enhancement alongside profit-making have experienced positive impacts on their bottom lines.

Microsoft's Brad Smith, for example, is working to restore public faith in Big Tech. He suggests, "If you don't figure out how to make things work from a broad societal perspective, you will pay a steep price for many years."

Smith's concern about how the high-tech industry handles its latest innovations, including AI, social media disinformation, electronic hacking, and cyberattacks, is well-founded. The rapid evolution of technology has outpaced our ability to establish robust processes for protecting, managing, and regulating it.[245]

Some leaders have started to redefine their companies' missions by integrating an element of *soul* into their strategies. Tadashi Yanai, CEO of Fast Retailing, is guided by 23 management principles that he calls the *soul* of his company. He believes that the soul is the most crucial thing in life.

The soul of an organization has also influenced the visions of other U.S. business leaders, such as Microsoft CEO Satya Nadella and Salesforce co-founder Marc Benioff. Nadella views his company's higher purpose as assisting every person and organization in achieving more. He links soul and strategy, asserting that reconnecting with the company's soul will lead to crafting the right approach, ultimately enhancing the lives of its customers, employees, partners, and members of society.

Benioff ties purpose even more explicitly to the organization's role in society, claiming that it's no longer feasible for a company to conduct business as usual. Over time, your employees and customers, as well as your investors, partners, host communities, and other stakeholders, will want to clearly understand your philosophy for doing business. They want to know if you have a *soul*.[246]

Facebook has maintained its mission to "make the world more open and connected" by dedicating significant effort and resources to connecting the unconnected and underconnected to the internet. They believe that providing access to the wealth of online knowledge will help alleviate poverty globally, a notion supported by historical data. Microsoft is also committed to expanding broadband coverage to 3 million rural Americans and investing $500 million in creating more affordable housing, a goal shared by other tech giants like Apple and Google. Google is set to become the Bay Area's most prominent land developer, with plans to invest $1 billion in building 20,000 new homes to address the region's chronic housing shortage.[247]

Of particular significance, in 2019, a business roundtable convened with over 180 CEOs of prominent U.S. companies. They collectively endorsed the *Business Roundtable's New Statement of Corporate Purpose*, pledging to focus their attention beyond shareholder profits by expanding their attention to consumers, customers, communities, workers, and the environment. However, at the 5-year mark, the practical impact of this commitment presents a mixed picture. Despite their pledge, many companies continue to prioritize shareholder returns exclusively, with boards not formally approving their stakeholder commitment, and their CEO compensation remains primarily tied to shareholder value.[248]

While the benefits of corporate benevolence are diverse and numerous, there are powerful voices among the contrarians who argue against companies focusing on anything beyond maximizing shareholder value or profit. They contend that prioritizing profit enables companies to reinvest in improving goods and services, leading to more employment opportunities with better jobs and benefits, thus indirectly providing social benefits. Some argue that increased corporate profitability can result in improved wages, motivating *workers* to engage in individualized charity, which they see as an advantage over corporate giving. Additionally, they assert that philanthropy is not a core competency of companies, suggesting that charitable efforts are best left to individual citizens.

We also witness a troubling trend in American politics that threatens corporate advocacy and philanthropy. There's now a notable backlash against companies that engage in cultural and policy issues, particularly when their actions clash with certain political ideologies. When this occurs, it's necessary to acknowledge that businesses and individuals are responsible for solving social and cultural issues and supporting their communities. Each company must find the right balance among its various stakeholders: customers, employees, investors, suppliers, and communities. Plans for philanthropic actions and how profits will be used must be transparently communicated upfront. Investors who disagree with those plans have the option to invest elsewhere.[249]

Upholding moral principles and doing the *right* thing should be core principles of American leadership. Corporate citizenship underscores the interdependence of business and society, demonstrating that thriving communities and a healthy planet are essential for sustainable economic growth. By prioritizing transparency, inclusivity, and social equity, corporate citizenship reinforces a company's role as a steward of shared resources and a catalyst for positive change.

> *The purpose of life is not to be happy. It is to be useful, to be honorable, to be compassionate, to have it make some difference that you have lived and lived well.* —Ralph Waldo Emerson, American essayist, lecturer, philosopher, abolitionist, and poet.

DEI and ESG

In today's interconnected and socially conscious world, corporate citizenship extends beyond financial performance and charitable giving. Corporate responsibility includes cultivating a workplace culture that reflects the diverse society in which businesses operate. Diversity, equity, and inclusion (DEI) are not just ethical imperatives but strategic necessities that drive innovation, employee engagement, and long-term business success. Companies prioritizing DEI don't just improve internal morale; they contribute to a more just and equitable society, reinforcing their role as responsible corporate citizens. By embedding DEI into their core values and operations, businesses can enhance their reputation, attract top talent, and cultivate a better-equipped workforce to serve an increasingly diverse customer base.

Diversity, Equity, and Inclusion (DEI) and Environmental, Social, and Governance (ESG) initiatives have emerged as essential frameworks for businesses striving to build a more sustainable, ethical, and high-performing future. DEI promotes workplace environments where diverse perspectives are valued, equitable opportunities are ensured, and inclusive cultures drive innovation and engagement. By integrating DEI principles, companies enhance employee morale and retention and improve decision-making and market competitiveness.

Meanwhile, ESG principles guide businesses toward responsible corporate citizenship, emphasizing environmental sustainability, social responsibility, and ethical governance. ESG initiatives encourage companies to reduce their carbon footprint, uphold human rights, and maintain transparency in leadership, ultimately mitigating risks and ensuring long-term profitability.

DEI and ESG reflect a modern corporate imperative—aligning business success with societal and environmental well-being to create lasting value for stakeholders and the planet.

Diversity, equity, and inclusion (DEI) are critical drivers of business and educational success. Research consistently shows that diverse teams outperform homogeneous ones in creativity and decision-making, leading to better financial performance. DEI encourages inclusive learning environments in education, where diverse perspectives enhance critical thinking, broaden understanding, and improve student outcomes.

> *Don't tolerate me as different. Accept me as part of the spectrum of normalcy.* —Ann Northrop, American journalist, and activist.

Despite the long-standing benefits of DEI and ESG, both frameworks have been aggressively weaponized and mischaracterized by political and religious extremists seeking to undermine their progress. For decades, businesses have leveraged DEI to cultivate diverse talent pipelines and ESG to drive sustainability and ethical governance, contributing to economic growth, corporate resilience, and societal well-being. However, in recent years, opposition forces—driven by ideological agendas rather than business realities—have reframed these initiatives as threats rather than assets. Through misinformation and fearmongering, they have portrayed DEI as racism in disguise and ESG as radical environmental overreach, distorting their true purpose. Some experts suggest that attacks on DEI are simply a sanitized substitute for the racist comments that can no longer be spoken openly. Others claim that eliminating DEI is akin to affirmative action for straight, white, Christian males.

These oppositional efforts have escalated rapidly, persuading corporate leaders and shareholders to abandon or dilute their initiatives to avoid backlash. The speed of this shift reveals how fragile corporate commitments can be when faced with coordinated ideological attacks, making it necessary to reframe and reinforce the value of DEI and ESG in a way that withstands manipulation.

Influencers, politicians, and extremists have leveraged their platforms and budgetary powers to pressure organizations and schools into defunding or eliminating DEI, equal opportunity, and other anti-discrimination efforts. They argue for a so-called "color-blind" approach, asserting that systemic racism is no longer an issue, despite significant evidence to the contrary. Their narrative misrepresents DEI's purpose as a rhetorical tool to undermine progress toward equitable workplaces and educational environments while perpetuating the very inequities these initiatives seek to address.

Those who weaponize DEI often distort its intentions, portraying it as divisive or discriminatory. By framing DEI as a threat, these individuals obscure its underlying value, promoting fairness, tapping into a workforce's full potential, and preparing businesses for a globalized world. Their agenda undermines progress, stifles innovation, and risks alienating talent and customers who value inclusive practices.

Some individuals and groups resist DEI, often operating under a veneer of other concerns, such as fears of losing meritocracy, fairness, or personal freedoms. These arguments serve as a smokescreen for a deeper, often unspoken motive: preserving systemic privilege. By couching their opposition in more socially acceptable terms, they avoid being labeled as advocates for white male supremacy while effectively working to sustain the power structures that benefit them.

People who characterize DEI as political indoctrination misrepresent DEI initiatives as partisan tools rather than practical strategies for enhancing innovation, fairness, and inclusion. Eliminating DEI initiatives does not prevent indoctrination—it *enables* it. Without DEI, educational and workplace environments default to existing power structures, effectively granting affirmative action to those who enjoy persistent advantage and reinforcing systemic biases. This absence creates a vacuum where bad actors can shape narratives unchecked, promoting exclusionary ideologies while silencing diverse perspectives that fuel critical thinking and social progress.

DEI opponents may also falsely claim that DEI initiatives lower the caliber of personnel by prioritizing diversity over merit. This deception ignores key evidence and misrepresents the goals of DEI. The idea that DEI compromises merit is based on the flawed assumption that merit is evaluated without bias and that all candidates have equal opportunities to demonstrate their talent. In reality, DEI initiatives strengthen organizations by reducing bias, expanding access to top talent, and promoting environments where diverse perspectives drive innovation and success. Hiring purely on "merit" in a biased system perpetuates inequities; hiring with a DEI focus ensures that merit is identified, recognized, and rewarded.[250]

Recently, corporations and colleges, under political pressure, have reversed DEI policies at an alarming rate. Yet many of these same institutions still rely on legacy admissions, cronyism, and nepotism—fundamentally anti-meritocratic practices. If truly committed to a merit-based system, they would eliminate preferential hiring for executives' children, alumni networks, faculty preferential admissions, legacy admissions, and old boys' clubs. The hypocrisy is defending these unearned advantages while simultaneously dismantling the DEI efforts that actually level the playing field.

Business mogul Kevin O'Leary's recent claim that merit-based hiring naturally leads to diversity absent DEI initiatives is a convenient but flawed oversimplification. The assumption is that diversity will automatically follow if companies hire purely on qualifications and ability. However, research consistently shows that systemic biases—both implicit and explicit—continue to shape hiring and promotion decisions, even in supposedly meritocratic environments.[251]

The meritocracy myth has been further debunked by studies that confirm the following:

- Bias in hiring and promotion: Studies have shown that identical resumes with minority-sounding names receive fewer callbacks than those with white-sounding names. Meritocracy assumes a level playing field, but that's not the reality.

- Network disparities: Many jobs are filled through referrals, and because professional networks are often homogenous, diverse candidates may have fewer opportunities to enter the pipeline.

- Historical exclusion: Certain demographics have been systematically excluded from industries for decades. Without active measures, those historical imbalances don't correct themselves.

- The fallacy of 'best fit': Many hiring managers unconsciously favor candidates who "feel" like they belong, which often means selecting those with similar backgrounds and experiences. This reinforces the status quo rather than enhancing diversity.[252]

These behaviors reflect a broader societal reluctance to confront privilege and inequity, which makes addressing these issues even more challenging. Therefore, it is essential to recognize the subtle and covert ways this resistance manifests when advocating for DEI.

The following list describes various other ways in which DEI is being weaponized or misrepresented:

- Denying systemic inequities: Some dismiss the need for DEI by falsely claiming that society is already fair and equitable, ignoring clear evidence of racial, gender, and economic disparities.

- Promoting a false narrative of "reverse discrimination": Opponents falsely claim that DEI initiatives unfairly disadvantage majority groups, ignoring systemic barriers that have historically excluded marginalized communities.

- Deflecting accountability with "equality" arguments: Opponents insist on treating everyone equally, even in the presence of deeply rooted inequities, perpetuating privilege for already-advantaged groups.

- Weaponizing fear of change: Resistance to DEI often exploits fears of shifting cultural norms, portraying progress toward inclusion as a threat to tradition or personal freedoms.

- Contradicting conservative values of hard work: By resisting DEI, some seek to preserve default advantages that shield them from the need to compete or excel on an even playing field. This contradicts the conservative ideal of rewarding success through effort and commitment.[253]

While DEI has largely been mischaracterized by those who claim it is a form of racism, certain aspects of DEI are legitimately flawed, or at least non-optimal. Here are a few examples of legitimate criticisms:

- Quotas over qualifications: Some DEI efforts rely on rigid diversity quotas rather than facilitating inclusion, leading to concerns that hiring decisions prioritize demographics over merit.

- Superficial compliance ("Checkbox DEI"): Many companies treat DEI as a PR exercise, implementing surface-level initiatives without real structural change, accountability, or measurable outcomes.

- Unintended resentment and backlash: Poorly implemented DEI programs can create workplace tension, reinforcing divisions rather than enhancing collaboration and shared success.

- Bias training limitations: While implicit bias training is common, research suggests its long-term effectiveness is questionable, and it can sometimes reinforce stereotypes rather than mitigate them.

- Failure to address economic inequality: Some DEI initiatives focus narrowly on race, gender, or identity while overlooking broader socio-economic disparities impacting opportunity.[254]

The effectiveness of DEI initiatives depends on thoughtful implementation. When reduced to quotas, superficial compliance, or ineffective bias training, they can generate backlash, reinforce divisions, or fail to drive meaningful change. To succeed, DEI efforts must go beyond performative gestures, addressing deeper systemic inequities with accountability and measurable impact.

While little evidence exists that validates claims that white men are being discriminated against in the workplace or at school, many men legitimately feel disadvantaged today due to significant economic, cultural, and societal shifts that have upended traditional norms and expectations. The erosion of industries that once provided stable, well-paying jobs for men, combined with changing gender dynamics and the growing emphasis on equity, has left some men feeling uncertain about their place in the modern workforce. Additionally, the recent decline in male college attendance and graduation rates has compounded the problem, limiting opportunities for advancement in an increasingly knowledge-driven economy. These challenges, coupled with rising mental health struggles, have led some men to experience depression and a loss of direction and motivation to excel.

Unfortunately, instead of addressing the root causes of these issues, some men have channeled their frustration into blaming women and minorities, fueled by false narratives that suggest DEI initiatives or equity efforts unfairly disadvantage them. This scapegoating is often perpetuated by influential figures manipulating these grievances for personal or political gain, fueling division and resentment. This tactic detracts from the real issues—systemic changes in the economy, education, and culture—and obstructs progress toward collective success.

> *It's always easy to blame others. You can spend your entire life blaming the world, but your successes or failures are entirely your own.* —Paulo Coelho, Brazilian lyricist, and novelist.

To move forward, we must address men's legitimate concerns while rejecting narratives that pit groups against each other. This means investing in education, workforce training, and mental health support to empower men to adapt to modern challenges. It also requires dismantling harmful ideologies that seek to subordinate women and minorities for male advantage.

Corporate leaders, educators, and policymakers must champion collaboration and mutual respect, emphasizing that equity is not a zero-sum game. When everyone has the tools and opportunities to thrive, society benefits. We must also encourage men to embrace the hard work and resilience necessary to build a foundation for long-term success. This includes promoting educational advancement, skills development, mentoring young men to help them navigate modern challenges, and encouraging open discussions about mental health to break down stigmas.

Schools, employers, and communities should work together to provide targeted support, ensuring men feel empowered to adapt, grow, and thrive in today's evolving world. By addressing the deeper structural issues while promoting unity and shared purpose, we can create a future where men, women, and minorities all succeed together.

Unfortunately, these steps are insufficient to overcome the hardened opposition seeking to sustain a durable advantage for white males. DEI must be retooled for broad acceptance. Instead of the divisive branding of "DEI," we need a rebranding rooted in universal principles of fairness, opportunity, and economic pragmatism.[255]

Perhaps we might consider replacing DEI with a framework that emphasizes the following:

- Fair access and equal opportunity: Ensuring all candidates, regardless of background, have equal opportunities (this appeals to conservative values of fairness and individual responsibility).

- Talent optimization: Focusing on expanding talent pipelines to include the most skilled individuals naturally leads to a broader, more diverse workforce (a strong business argument). This only occurs when companies proactively expand access to high-quality candidates from underrepresented groups by recruiting beyond their usual networks, refining evaluation criteria, and removing systemic barriers.

- Workforce readiness and mobility: Investing in skills development and mentorship programs so underrepresented groups can compete on a truly level playing field.

This new framework could be called *Workforce Excellence & Opportunity (WEO)* or *Inclusive Talent Strategy (ITS), which is* focused on strengthening businesses and increasing innovation rather than a politically loaded acronym like DEI. By framing the issue to ensure access, optimize talent, and boost economic growth, we can make it politically and socially indefensible to oppose, except by those who explicitly wish to preserve exclusion and inequality.

This type of framework neutralizes the most common criticisms of traditional DEI efforts while maintaining their core objectives. Instead of focusing on identity-based hiring, it prioritizes ensuring all individuals have a fair shot at success, a principle that is nearly impossible to argue against without exposing bias.

This modified approach doesn't mandate diversity quotas or promote exclusionary identity-based policies. It simply ensures equal access to compete, which is the very definition of meritocracy. It also doesn't assume bias—it merely acknowledges that barriers to opportunity exist and seeks to optimize the workforce by ensuring everyone can contribute at their highest potential. Even those skeptical of bias can't argue against expanding access to qualified talent.

This proposed framework is based on a strategy that directly improves business outcomes rather than just ticking diversity boxes. It's also not about social justice—it focuses on economic pragmatism, national competitiveness, and the pursuit of the best-equipped and most skilled talent. Opponents who try to fight this approach will argue against fair competition, business efficiency, and national economic strength, which is a losing battle.

Ultimately, DEI and ESG were designed to strengthen businesses and society, yet relentless attacks have distorted their intent, forcing many companies into retreat. The path forward requires reframing these initiatives with clear, common-sense principles that emphasize fairness, innovation, and long-term value. This will make them impervious to bad-faith arguments and ensure their lasting impact.

The beauty of the world lies in the diversity of its people. — Unknown.

CHAPTER 13

Joyful Living

The two most important days in your life are the day you are born and the day you find out why. —Mark Twain.

It's easy to lose sight of what's truly important in life amidst the daily grind of work, commuting, mindless gaming, and mundane chores. Days blur together as we go through the motions, caught in a cycle of routine and repetition. We wake up, go to work, and come home; another week has flown by before we know it. We get so caught up in the hustle and bustle of everyday life that we forget to pause and reflect on what truly matters.

Time, however, is invaluable and irreplaceable. We often fail to appreciate its worth until we face a moment of reckoning, wishing we could reclaim the time we squandered. We cannot buy more time or rewind the clock. It slips away silently, leaving us longing for a second chance at life.

Make the most of this precious resource—to excel in our endeavors, cherish our loved ones deeply, and diligently prepare for each stage of life. This will ensure that we're poised to achieve our most significant goals.

Joyful living means embracing each day with intention, curiosity, and gratitude. It's about finding meaning in small moments, aligning your actions with your values, and cultivating a rich life, not just in accomplishments but also in fulfillment and connection.

Joyful living offers many benefits, including improved mental and physical health, stronger relationships, increased productivity, and a greater sense of purpose and fulfillment. By embracing a lifestyle that prioritizes happiness and well-being, we can better navigate challenges and cultivate resilience. Joyful living also promotes a positive outlook, inspiring those around us and contributing to a more harmonious environment in both personal and professional settings.

To achieve joyful living, consider the following suggestions:

- Practice gratitude: Focus on the positive aspects of life and express appreciation for them.

- Nurture meaningful relationships: Spend quality time with loved ones and build supportive connections.

- Engage in activities you love: Dedicate time to hobbies and interests that bring you joy and fulfillment.

- Adopt a growth mindset: Embrace challenges and view failures as opportunities to learn and grow.

- Prioritize self-care: Ensure adequate rest, nutrition, and physical activity to maintain overall well-being.

- Live in the moment: Practice mindfulness to fully experience and appreciate the present.

- Give back: Volunteer or engage in acts of kindness to positively impact others' lives.

Assess your accomplishments, consider your most important objectives, and spend your time wisely. Find your purpose and leave your unique imprint on the world.

> *Ubuntu tells us that we can create a more peaceful world by striving for goodness in each moment, wherever we are.* — Desmond Tutu, South African Anglican theologian, and human rights activist.

Quality of Life

How often do we pause to assess our quality of life, to ponder what truly holds significance, and to evaluate our progress toward our most vital life goals? Some may focus solely on work output, income, or business success, inadvertently neglecting crucial metrics like enriching others' lives or nurturing meaningful relationships with loved ones.[256]

Interestingly, artificial intelligence (AI) has recently been applied to some of humanity's most profound, spiritual, and awe-inspiring texts in search of life's meaning. Throughout this exploration, AI consistently returned to three fundamental principles:

- Love is the meaning of everything. It provides purpose in our lives and is the reason we're here.

- Heaven and paradise are found within the present moment. As we leave the present, we dwell on the past or become anxious about the future, which leads to suffering.

- We are all fundamentally connected to one another and the universe around us. These connections represent our humanity.[257]

As an adolescent and even a young engineer, I equated success with climbing the corporate ladder as high and fast as possible. Initially, that was my focus. Within a decade, I went from a junior engineer to a corporate co-founder, and 10 years later, I became an engineering VP. However, upon reflection, I realized that while my career was reasonably satisfying, my overall quality of life was lacking. Surprisingly, the higher I ascended within each organization, the less content I felt.

Thankfully, marrying and having children provided the fulfillment I was missing. They brought a new depth of meaning and purpose to my life. The joy and deep connection I discovered in building a family added a richness to my life that no professional success could match.

> *Your true inner happiness does not come from the material things of this world. Whether you're flying first class, or economy class—if the plane crashes, you crash with it. —* Unknown.

As I spent more time on family pursuits, I often grappled with guilt— I began to worry that my career would suffer. Perhaps my boss and co-workers would see me as less than dedicated or committed, which might jeopardize my employment or even my professional reputation.

When confronted with this dilemma, I've found that setting boundaries around family priorities first and then boundaries at work can eliminate the ambiguity between competing priorities. Establishing a predictable and dependable foundation for your personal life is essential, which, in turn, facilitates a more focused, efficient, and ultimately satisfying lifestyle in which both work and family receive the attention they deserve.[258]

For those striving for balance in life, the challenge is finding employers and managers who share your values and actively promote outside interests and pursuits. You may choose to seek out companies and leaders committed to creating work cultures that support personal success, whatever form that may take for each individual. This entails tolerance and genuine encouragement of employees' diverse passions and endeavors beyond the workplace.

Improving your quality of life requires intentionality and balance, ensuring that your time and energy are aligned with your values and priorities. You can create a rich and rewarding life by nurturing meaningful relationships, focusing on personal well-being, and pursuing activities that bring joy and fulfillment. Remember, success isn't just about achievements—it's about the quality of your experiences and the legacy you leave behind.

> *A good family life, is the building block of society.* —George P. Shultz, American economist, businessman, diplomat, and statesman.

Reimagining Success

Success can be defined as "the accomplishment of an aim or purpose" or "the good or bad outcome of an undertaking." To measure success, an objective must first be established against which progress or attainment can be measured. While it's tempting to live an open-loop life, setting visions and goals and regularly assessing progress can help transform aspirations into reality.

We all follow our unique paths in life, so pursuing success is a deeply personal undertaking. It's worthwhile to periodically assess whether our decisions and actions align with our understanding of success and whether fear or practicality, rather than courage and optimism, guides our choices. Our willingness to take reasonable risks can fuel personal growth and unlock our full potential. Succumbing to excuses, worries, and self-doubt can be limiting; instead, embracing opportunities with boldness and conviction enables us to explore new possibilities and experiences, contributing to personal and professional fulfillment.

While it's easy to set objectives around money, wealth, advancement, and other tangibles, I've learned that career success is rather hollow without a happy life rich in love and affection. Contributing to others and positively impacting the world can produce profound satisfaction, underscoring the importance of a holistic approach to success.

> *Let us reflect on what is truly of value in life, what gives meaning to our lives, and set our priorities on the basis of that.* — The Dalai Lama, Tibetan spiritual and temporal ruler, former head of state, speaker, and author.

Even wealthy or otherwise successful individuals can fail in life. We see this repeatedly in the news and tabloids. We should adopt the word *accomplishment* to describe the attainment of specific goals, while *success* is the consequence or outcome of an accomplishment. By embracing this nuanced perspective, we recognize that genuine success encompasses achieving objectives and the impact and fulfillment derived from our endeavors.

Committing to doing our best results in prideful accomplishments and protects against regret during periods of self-doubt. Central to success is a steadfast belief in oneself. This trait may not come naturally or easily, but it is a critical characteristic of highly successful individuals. Embracing this mindset empowers us to navigate challenges with resilience and determination, ultimately propelling us toward our goals with confidence and purpose.

Enriching your life with abundance, including love, family, friends, and purpose, cultivates a deep appreciation for your blessings. Engaging in acts of kindness and altruism contributes to a better world and creates a reciprocal cycle of support, where others are inspired to extend assistance in return. When we contribute to a collective environment of compassion and mutual aid, we enhance the well-being of ourselves and those around us.

Living a life of integrity, which involves knowing the difference between right and wrong and consistently acting in alignment with those principles, promotes confidence and pride. When integrity is coupled with persistence, passion, and grit, it forms a powerful combination that propels individuals toward accomplishment. By consistently adhering to ethical standards and embracing determination in the face of challenges, individuals achieve their goals and uphold their self-worth and integrity.

When we acknowledge that our destiny is controlled by us and not by others, we become empowered to take responsibility for our actions and their consequences, enabling increased success. Loving and being loved open our hearts and empower a fulfilling life. However, it's essential to recognize that we must be lovable to be loved. [259]

Success isn't a mere coincidence. No one else dictates your path or the pace at which you pursue it. Your life is yours to shape according to your unique desires. What you *do* reflects who you *are*, underscoring the importance of purposeful action in achieving your aspirations.

Nobody cares more about your success than you do. Success is based on choice, motivation, action, persistence, and hard work. There are no shortcuts. There is no right or wrong way—only *your* way.[260]

If asked to define my life's most profound source of joy and fulfillment, I wouldn't hesitate: it's my family. Not a success in the traditional sense, but a shared journey filled with love, growth, and enduring connection—something we've all built together. Whether we choose parenthood or it finds us unexpectedly, navigating the parental journey involves learning as we go. Parenthood often brings moments of uncertainty and worry as we ponder the unknowns. Yet, the memories we create as a family are priceless. Nothing brings me greater joy or pride than the bonds we share and the experiences we cherish.

> *Your greatest contribution to the universe may not be something you do, but someone you raise.* —Unknown.

Whether your family consists of children, a spouse or partner, extended family, or close friends, they provide a foundation of support, love, and motivation that fuels personal success. Their presence in our lives offers encouragement during challenges and celebrates our achievements, reminding us that true success is often shared with those who matter most.

Extreme Success

Work success, whether in terms of money, fame, reputation, or career accomplishment, is substantially dependent on hard work and persistence. But circumstances, timing, and serendipity also play a role.

Achieving extraordinary success often requires exceptional skill and a stroke of good fortune, yet even this may not suffice. Many immensely talented individuals fall short of reaching the pinnacle of success. However, one aspect within our control is defining what success means to us personally. By shaping our definition of success, we can tailor our lives to align with our aspirations, significantly increasing the likelihood of achieving fulfillment.[261]

Success can be challenging to quantify, describe, or define. It carries a unique meaning within each of us. Some prioritize their private or family lives over professional pursuits, while others strike a balance or prioritize work above all else. Those who relentlessly dedicate themselves to advancing their careers to the utmost epitomize the highest levels of ambition and aspiration. Like Elon Musk, these individuals are willing to go to extraordinary lengths, often working grueling hours and sacrificing sleep to pursue their goals.

> *Extreme success requires extreme sacrifice.* —Joe De Sena, American entrepreneur, and author.

While working hard is necessary for success, focusing on the right tasks in the proper sequence is equally important for making meaningful progress. Much of our work success hinges on sweat equity, unwavering dedication, persistence, and time invested—to attain exceptional success, one must be prepared to work tirelessly.

In the end, it boils down to your priorities. If you aim to disrupt an industry or amass significant wealth, you'll likely need to devote extensive time and effort, often working longer and harder than individuals prioritizing family over career ambitions.[262]

> *I've learned that success comes in a very prickly package.* — Sandra Bullock, American actor, and producer.

Happiness

Finding true happiness seems more elusive these days. We work longer and harder, yet productivity, growth, and job satisfaction remain stagnant. Even with the shift to remote work spurred by the pandemic, which affords more flexibility and freedom, many find themselves working longer hours and experiencing heightened levels of stress and burnout. Despite the benefits of reduced commuting time, the line between remote work and personal life has blurred, leaving less time for life outside of work.

When we explore the relationship between money and happiness, we find that well-being rises with income at low socioeconomic levels because it eliminates poverty. Money enables access to better nutrition, education, and healthcare, which reduces unhappiness. However, once basic material needs are met, the correlation between money and happiness diminishes.

While achieving success through work can create happiness across all income levels, the ceaseless quest for more material possessions can detract from time spent on meaningful pursuits such as building memories, nurturing relationships, supporting others, and seeking genuine fulfillment.[263]

Beyond a certain point, money fails to enhance our capacity to prioritize what truly matters for emotional well-being. While material possessions acquired through money can offer *temporary* joy, they often provide only fleeting moments of happiness. True fulfillment and lasting contentment stem from experiences and connections beyond the material realm.

Studies indicate that individuals with little free time experience greater stress, are less active, and are less likely to help others. This suggests that spending a little money to buy some additional *time*, which can be spent on more satisfying pursuits, is worth the investment. Buying time might include hiring a gardener, a house cleaner, or ordering delivered food as an occasional luxury.

How we spend our time is also critical. One study found that spending free time on socializing or active forms of leisure substantially outperforms passive activities like napping, staring at a phone or computer, or watching TV. So, when you have more time on your hands, using it effectively can increase your happiness.

In another study, researchers found that people who spent money on vacations created happiness before (anticipation), during (the experience), and after the vacation (remembering the experiences they had).

Yet another study found that friendships significantly influence health and happiness, even more so than relationships with family members. However, nurturing these friendships demands ongoing effort and shared experiences, which require planning and execution. Recognize that some friends are poor initiators, meaning you might need to take charge. Resist the urge to take it personally or overanalyze why the organizing always falls to you. Instead, celebrate that you have good friends and make the best of it.[264]

Nobody can go back and start a new beginning, but anyone can start today and make a new ending. —Unknown.

Some people assume that success will naturally lead to happiness. However, chasing success carries certain *costs*, which can eventually reduce our happiness. This suggests that instead of focusing on success, we should work on our happiness, which can ultimately lead to success.

Happiness can lead to success in marriage, friendship, health, income, and work performance. It can also make us more productive, which further inspires success. When we display positive emotions, we get rewarded.[265]

Research has determined that our early life choices significantly shape how happy we are later in life. Findings suggest that when we're young, we essentially invest in a "Happiness 401(k)" based on our choices, health, and lifestyle, which we enjoy when we are older. Within one such study, the happiest respondents didn't smoke, watched their drinking, maintained a healthy body weight, prioritized physical activities like walking, developed effective coping mechanisms that helped them deal with life's curveballs and distresses, and embraced continuous learning, which encourages active minds in old age. The most influential investment in this *happiness fund* lies in cultivating healthy relationships with spouses, family, friends, and partners, underscoring the profound impact of social connections on overall well-being.[266]

> *Blessed is he who expects nothing, for he shall never be disappointed.* —Alexander Pope, English poet, translator, and satirist.

Many people believe they must first *have* something before they can *do* something that will enable them to be happy or successful. For instance, they may think, "If only I had the time or money, then I could travel, start a business, or establish a relationship, which could bring me happiness or success." Instead, this paradigm should be reversed. First, be whatever you want to be (i.e., happy, loving, etc.). With a successful mindset, you can begin pursuing other endeavors. This will lead to doing, accomplishing, and possessing what you truly desire. Results translate from attitudes and behaviors, not the other way around.

Psychologists have found that showing gratitude for what we have is another way to improve well-being. Grateful people tend to be happier and show lower levels of stress hormones like cortisol. Gratitude also reduces stress and depression and improves sleep quality and overall mood. Sharing gratitude with others can strengthen the bond with those who matter most in your life. Consider how much happier we could all be if we focused on accepting what we already have as being *enough*.[267]

Experts have explored how people describe and achieve happiness. For example, Finland is consistently rated among the happiest countries. They channel their inner grit, or *sisu*, by embracing the extreme weather to find an inner glow. The Dutch embrace the concept of *niksen* (the art of doing nothing) to reduce anxiety and boost creativity and productivity, which leads to contentment. The Greeks embrace their food as *meraki* (labor of love) to bring each other happiness. In South Africa, the Bantu people embrace *ubuntu* as the greatest gift—they care for others to achieve happiness and fulfillment. The Japanese embrace imperfection, impermanence, and incompleteness through *wabi-sabi*. Their joy is found through appreciating the beauty in their most natural and imperfect state. In Turkey, happiness is found through *keyif*—the pursuit of a moment of idle pleasure. The Aloha Spirit, deeply rooted in Hawaiian culture, creates happiness by encouraging a mindset of kindness, compassion, humility, and respect for others and oneself. It's more than a greeting—it's a way of life that values empathy over ego, community over individualism, and connection over competition. There are various ways in which peace and happiness can be found when we look for them.[268]

Happiness can also be affected by the body's chemicals, which are naturally generated through certain activities:

- Dopamine (reward) is produced when we eat food, celebrate a small win, perform a self-care activity, or complete a task.

- Serotonin (mood) is produced when swimming, walking in nature, cycling, running, meditating, or soaking in some sunshine.

- Oxytocin (love) is produced when hugging, holding hands, complimenting someone, interacting with a baby, or playing with a dog or other animal.

- Endorphins (painkillers) are produced when laughing, exercising, eating dark chocolate, or watching a comedy.

Avoid comparing yourself to others, find contentment in your accomplishments and possessions, and embrace the journey rather than fixate on reaching a destination. While this mindset requires practice and the gumption to get off the couch, the rewards are well worth the effort.

Ultimately, achieving happiness isn't merely a matter of chance. It requires action and a steadfast commitment to seizing control of one's life. It involves choosing to be an active participant in shaping one's destiny rather than succumbing to a victim mentality.

> *Remembering that you are going to die is the best way I know to avoid the trap of thinking you have something to lose. You are already naked. There is no reason not to follow your heart.* —Steve Jobs.

Retirement

Retirement is a relatively modern concept that didn't exist worldwide 150 years ago. Originating as a Euro-American construct, it's not universally embraced and is absent in many cultures, including those with some of the longest-living citizens. Initially crafted for political reasons, retirement has evolved but remains a culturally specific notion rather than a universal truth.

Researchers suggest that retirement may lead to accelerated biological decline, particularly in Western cultures, where retirement often equates to *living short and dying long*. The medical community has long promoted the principle of 'use it or lose it,' emphasizing the importance of staying active and engaged to maintain good health. When retirees become sedentary and stop thriving, they accelerate the process of decline. These individuals become increasingly isolated (a significant killer), fail to maintain adequate exercise to sustain good health, indulge in being selfish consumers rather than selfless producers, and remove themselves from a working lifestyle—work is a critical factor in longevity. Fortunately, an increasing number of individuals recognize the limitations and downsides of inactivity and are embracing more active and engaged retirement lifestyles.

> *A thriving new beginning can be and should be a time for amazing engagement, growth, connections, contributions, and amazing possibilities.* —Lee M. Brower, author, and business family coach.

Formulating a well-defined plan to cultivate a healthy and fulfilling post-work life of longevity is prudent. Without a plan, we drift without finding purpose, and unfocused time can lead us to accelerated deterioration. Our plan should detail how we'll spend our free time and who we'll spend it with, as well as strategies for achieving financial stability to support our hobbies and interests throughout our remaining years.

The friends we surround ourselves with in retirement can significantly impact our happiness and overall health. Spending time with individuals who exhibit negative or depressing behavior or have resigned themselves to a passive existence can harm our attitudes and well-being. Conversely, cultivating relationships with positive, vibrant, and engaged individuals can enhance our happiness and contribute to our overall health and vitality throughout retirement. It may be time for a change if conversations with friends predominantly revolve around health complaints or fail to inspire personal growth.

> *You rise to the average of the five people you spend the most time with.* —John Rohn, American entrepreneur, author, and motivational speaker.

Retirees often find fulfillment by engaging with younger generations, whose youthful energy and creativity offer fresh perspectives and opportunities for learning. Conversely, younger individuals can benefit from the wisdom and experience of older generations. Cultivating a sense of purpose and direction in retirement is essential to maximizing the talents, skills, and energy still within us.[269]

Many baby boomers are extending their careers beyond the traditional retirement age in America. Some find it difficult to gracefully transition out of the workforce, especially if they still find fulfillment in their jobs. Work offers income and a sense of purpose, community, and structure. For some, their identity is closely tied to their profession. While mandatory retirement at 65 was once commonplace, a significant portion of the population can now work well into their 70s or beyond.[270]

However, when work becomes one's sole identity, it can have profound consequences. Frustration, impatience, and unhappiness may intensify as individuals realize their work does not bring them the fulfillment they hoped for. This realization can lead to existential crises for some and a sense of being trapped in a vicious cycle for others.

Our identities are often shaped by how we present ourselves to others, and tying one's identity to wealth, achievement, and influence can result in a dependency on a high-paying career. Transitioning can be distressing, as individuals feel unable to escape the socioeconomic class they have become a part of. For many, breaking free from this cycle can seem daunting, if not impossible.[271]

Unfortunately, many experienced workers are thrust into retirement unexpectedly, often through layoffs late in their careers. When companies consider staff reductions, the highest-paid employees are typically targeted, leaving senior workers vulnerable. Ageism is a persistent obstacle for older job seekers, making it challenging to secure new employment after job loss. Consequently, many are forced into retirement ahead of their plans before they're financially prepared.

The best time to start thinking about your retirement is before the boss does. —Unknown.

Adjusting to retirement takes time and requires gradually developing a new routine. Like any worthwhile endeavor, success in retirement comes through incremental progress, starting with small steps and repeatedly building upon incremental achievements. Reconnecting with non-work friends and family is essential, as they form the support network in retirement. Additionally, reevaluating what truly matters in life through what experts call *value clarification* can prove helpful.

In our final years, time becomes ever more precious. New and old friendships are the elixir that treats loneliness and sadness. Learning and contributing, when combined with adventure, can provide meaning, purpose, and personal satisfaction.[272]

In spite of illness, in spite even of the arch-enemy, sorrow, one can remain alive long past the usual date of disintegration if one is unafraid of change, insatiable in intellectual curiosity, interested in big things, and happy in small ways. —Edith Wharton, American novelist, short story writer, and interior designer.

Courage to Engage

At the time of this writing, the world appears to be at a crossroads. America is gripped by the most polarized and, frankly, terrifying political culture wars of the modern era.

We are constantly reminded of the critical role of truth, character, ethics, and leadership morality in the functioning of our government and society. Many issues in the public arena stem from individuals choosing self-interest over integrity. They opt for the path of least resistance, prioritizing personal agendas, party loyalty, and politics over collective well-being, often with detrimental consequences.

Our reliance on each other is fundamental to nurturing and upholding accepted cultural norms, which serve as the bedrock of stability for our society and democracy. Each individual plays a role in shaping our future, where engagement and activism are essential for ensuring sustainability, whether it pertains to American democracy or global conservation efforts. We cannot afford to retreat from discussions, reflection, or action on pressing issues, disagreements, and divergences. We must collectively and individually strive to coexist harmoniously, as our survival hinges on our ability to stand united.

> *The government you elect is the government you deserve.* — Thomas Jefferson, American statesman, planter, diplomat, lawyer, architect, philosopher, founding father, and 3rd president of the United States.

For our long-term prosperity as a society, we must demonstrate the courage to confront the divisive issues tearing us apart and illuminate the facts and truths behind current political controversies whenever possible. We must engage in open discussions and debates about political, ideological, and philosophical concepts without succumbing to tribalism or dogma. Embracing difficult and uncomfortable conversations is necessary to move forward and achieve meaningful progress.

> *The world is in greater peril from those who tolerate or encourage evil than from those who actually commit it.* —Albert Einstein, German theoretical physicist, educator, and author.

It's necessary to acknowledge that politics and business have become inseparable. At their core, institutions are political—committed to democracy, truth, and the rule of law. For example, enterprises expend substantial effort to ensure their public statements are truthful. They also follow the applicable laws that regulate their operations.

In contrast, extremist politicians today are venturing beyond distorting the truth, inventing *alternative facts,* and fueling conspiracy theories. Their actions undermine the foundations of our social stability, which endangers our economic growth and national security.

Business leaders have a profound financial, moral, and ethical obligation to defend, reinforce, and buttress the principles underpinning America's ability to thrive, progress, and evolve.

While some politicians seek to erode institutions in pursuit of personal gain, authoritarian power, and retribution, business leaders possess the unique power and influence to counter these threats. By boldly stepping into the arena, they can challenge bad actors, defend democracy, and champion a future prioritizing fairness, opportunity, and sustainability for all Americans. Courageous engagement is a moral imperative and a commitment to enhance society where businesses and citizens alike can thrive.

Positive Intent

Despite society's various challenges, I remain hopeful and optimistic. The human experiment, particularly that of democracy, is a complex and often messy journey characterized by slow but steady progress. It's shaped by the competing ideologies that clash along the way, resulting in numerous twists and turns. Each of us is responsible for contributing to this ongoing experiment with positive intentions and a constructive mindset.

As we engage in debate and citizenship, rather than contributing to the *problem*, we must focus on being part of the *solution*. Acting with good intentions and taking positive actions are essential in counteracting the harmful deeds of those who may seek to undermine our collective well-being. As good people, we must actively engage in efforts that promote progress and contribute to a better future for all.

Jeff Bezos departed from his role as CEO of Amazon with two leadership principles that resonate profoundly and merit acknowledgment. In my view, he encapsulated the essence of effective leadership with remarkable clarity:

> "Strive to be Earth's Best Employer—Leaders work every day to create a safer, more productive, higher performing, more diverse, and more just work environment. They lead with empathy, have fun at work, and make it easy for others to have fun. Leaders ask themselves: Are my fellow employees growing? Are they empowered? Are they ready for what's next? Leaders have a vision for and commitment to their employees' personal success, whether that be at Amazon or elsewhere."

And...

> "Success and Scale Bring Broad Responsibility—We started in a garage, but we're not there anymore. We are big, we impact the world, and we are far from perfect. We must be humble and thoughtful about even the secondary effects of our actions. Our local communities, planet, and future generations need us to be better every day. We must begin each day with a determination to make better, do better, and be better for our customers, our employees, our partners, and the world at large. And we must end every day knowing we can do even more tomorrow. Leaders create more than they

consume and always leave things better than how they found them."[273]

By cultivating a culture of positive intent, leaders and employees can create supportive and innovative workplaces that transcend organizational boundaries, promoting societal well-being. This approach enhances collaboration and personal fulfillment and drives sustainable success and community impact. We contribute to a more compassionate and interconnected world by driving social change for the better.

You want to be the pebble in the pond that creates the ripple for change. —Tim Cook.

CHAPTER 14

Dent the Universe

If your presence doesn't make an impact, your absence won't make a difference. —Trey Smith, American author.

Like many, I closely followed Steve Jobs and Apple's miraculous journey, especially after his return to the helm in 1997. Coincidentally, that period overlapped with my wife Elaine's tenure at Apple. With her firsthand experiences, Apple's endeavors, struggles, obstacles, and eventual triumphs felt intimately connected to our lives.

When Jobs coined the phrase "Put a dent in the universe," it struck a chord with me, particularly as an entrepreneur. Witnessing Apple's rapid resurgence from the brink resonated deeply. Jobs' words aimed to inspire us to pursue our passions relentlessly, especially endeavors with the potential to impact the world profoundly.

Beyond mere purpose, Jobs' wife, Laurene, explained that his phrase symbolizes faith in humanity's capacity to effect change and manipulate current circumstances. Jobs inspires us to expand our imagination beyond mere products, consider the structures and systems that govern and influence our society, and change them fundamentally.

We often struggle with the notion that our individual actions can significantly impact the world. While many support philanthropy and helping those in need, there's frequently a nagging doubt about whether our efforts are significant. The fear of failure or falling short can prevent us from making a difference, especially in areas where we lack experience or familiarity.[274]

Life consists of two dates with a dash in between. Make the dash count. —Stuart Scott, American sportscaster, and TV anchor.

When we reflect on those who have driven substantive change in the world, we often think of industry giants who have created or revolutionized entire sectors. Figures like Bill Gates, Steve Jobs, Richard Branson, and Jeff Bezos come to mind. However, while these individuals possess unique skills and advantages, much of their impact stems from the collaborative efforts of the teams within their companies and foundations. Therefore, the most direct path to making a substantial impact often lies in contributing to team efforts throughout our careers, especially when they are expertly directed and inspired by true visionaries. These collective endeavors are what give our work meaning and purpose.

As individuals, we possess the potential to enact change in the world through our actions and endeavors. When I seek motivation to take personal initiative, I often draw inspiration from the remarkable work of my grandmother, Helen M. Roberts. Widowed in her mid-50s, she was driven by a lifelong aspiration to educate the underprivileged. In 1953, she embarked on her mission by assisting migrant camp adults and children in Santa Clara Valley, offering worship services and teaching skills like sewing, crafts, and literacy.

Her efforts blossomed into a more significant endeavor when, in 1958, she journeyed to Africa to combat illiteracy, beginning in Kenya and later Rhodesia (now Zimbabwe and Zambia). At that time,

Africa faced staggering illiteracy rates, with eight out of every ten adults unable to read or write.

Initially assisting with English language classes for literate Africans, she then learned Swahili to teach a range of subjects to illiterate adults. She authored books on language, health, finance, and religion in Swahili while training numerous teachers in the *Laubach Method* to address adult illiteracy.[275]

During her missionary work in Kenya and Rhodesia, my grandmother encountered numerous talented and inspired Africans, many of whom displayed remarkable intelligence and immense potential. Alongside her literacy associate, Betty Mooney Kirk, she played a pivotal role in facilitating the journey of many of these students to the United States for further education. The aim was for these college-educated individuals to return to Africa equipped to contribute to the literacy cause and enhance governmental leadership in the region.

Their efforts were part of a much larger campaign known as the "Airlift to America," which coordinated the transportation of gifted African students to various American universities. That initiative, supported by influential figures such as John F. Kennedy, Harry Belafonte, Jackie Robinson, and Sidney Poitier, aimed to empower African students with education and skills. Many participants in those airlifts achieved remarkable success, eventually holding significant positions within African governments and society. Among those outstanding individuals was Wangari Maathai, who later became the first African woman to receive the Nobel Peace Prize. [276]

One promising young man who crossed paths with Helen and Betty was Barack Hussein Obama. Initially hired as a clerk for their literacy program, Obama began drafting reading primers in his native Luo language as part of their initiative to publish learning materials in tribal languages. Helen and Betty deeply supported Obama's educational journey, assisting him with completing his correspond-ence school certificate and facilitating his application to the Univer-sity of Hawaii. Once accepted, Obama became the first African student ever admitted to the college.

When Obama missed the first airlift to America, Helen and Betty rallied to raise funds so that he could travel on a separate flight. Betty covered his entire first year of tuition expenses, while Helen commit-ted to financially supporting Obama's family in Nairobi during his absence. Despite her limited income, Helen accepted this responsibil-ity without hesitation.[277]

At the University of Hawaii, Obama met Stanley Ann Dunham, whom he married in 1961. Their son, Barack Hussein Obama II, was born that same year. Young Obama later became the first African American president of the United States.

> *Your impact in the world doesn't depend on how you make a living. It derives from how you live your values.* —Un-known.

Stories like this serve as powerful reminders that each of us has the potential to make a meaningful impact on the world. Whether our contributions are minor or significant, they can create positive change. Much like my grandmother's extraordinary efforts, the influ-ence of our philanthropic and charitable endeavors can unfold unex-pectedly and may only become apparent long after we're gone.

Each of us contributes to the intricate tapestry of humanity, creat-ing ripples that intersect with countless others, shaping the course of human history. Our actions and contributions can leave a lasting im-pact on the world around us. Just as the principle of "Leave no trace" is ingrained in scouting, we can strive to leave our environment and society better and cleaner than we found it, ensuring a positive legacy for future generations.

We all can embrace truth, reject falsehoods, offer support and healing to those in need, and actively engage in political discourse and self-governance rather than remain idle and apathetic. By modeling morality, ethics, and decency, we can set an example for future generations and demonstrate the importance of doing what is *right* for the well-being of society as a whole. Every action we take contributes to the interconnected pool of ripples that shape our future.[278]

Each day offers new opportunities for us to make a positive impact. Despite our overwhelming challenges, I remain hopeful that humanity will continue evolving toward empathy, selflessness, tolerance, and kindness. Our planet is a precious gift that requires our care and protection, and we all have a role in shaping our future. I am optimistic about the possibilities ahead and look forward to witnessing the positive changes that will unfold in the years to come.

> *Action is the foundational key to all success.* —Pablo Picasso, Spanish painter, sculptor, printmaker, ceramicist, and theatre designer.

CHAPTER 15

Conclusion: Leading the Way Forward

It is better to take many small steps in the right direction than to make a great leap forward only to stumble backward. —Louis Sachar, American author.

As we contemplate the many topics and discussions within the multifaceted scope of career intelligence, it is important to reflect on the broader context in which we operate. Today's business landscape is not isolated from the societal challenges we face. From the pressing issues of social justice to environmental sustainability, the choices we make in our careers are intertwined with the world around us.

At a time when the influence of leadership, both ethical and otherwise, profoundly impacts our work environments, we must emphasize the need for integrity and accountability. While challenges such as misinformation and the degradation of public trust persist, the business world has a unique opportunity to lead by example. By prioritizing the health and vitality of our planet and embracing clean water and renewable energy, companies can contribute to a more sustainable future, ensuring that our actions today do not threaten or compromise the well-being of future generations.

Despite the daunting challenges we face, there is reason for optimism. Ethical leadership, a commitment to doing the right thing, and celebrating our differences can pave the way for a brighter future. With its vast resources and influence, the business community must lead the way in this endeavor.

Success should not be measured solely by profit but by our positive impact on society. By creating diverse, inclusive, innovative, and ethical work environments, businesses can drive the transformation needed to address today's challenges.

> *Discover the joy of embracing diversity. When people become more open to the strange, to the unusual, to the radical, to the 'other,' we become more nourished as a species. Currently our ability to do that is being manipulated, diversity is being looked upon as a source of evil rather than as a source of joy and development. We must recapture the profound benefits of seeing the joy in our collective diversity, not the fear.* —Harry Belafonte, American singer, actor, and civil rights activist.

Each of us plays a critical part in this modernization effort within our respective roles. The call to action extends beyond boardrooms and executive offices; it involves every employee, from entry-level to senior management. By upholding integrity, practicing empathy, and striving for excellence in daily interactions, we can build a workplace culture that excels in performance and offers a beacon of hope for the broader society.

Amidst the challenges, remarkable advancements offer hope for a better future. Breakthroughs in medicine and treatments enhance human health and extend life expectancies, allowing us to live healthier, more fulfilling lives. Artificial intelligence can potentially revolutionize innovation, education, and human experience. These advancements and ongoing technological and scientific innovations provide a solid foundation for optimism and progress.

Equally important is the courage to speak the truth to power. Individuals who stand up against bullies who lie and spread anger, hate, and misinformation, whether whistleblowers, executives, politicians, or media personalities, play a critical role in maintaining the integrity of our institutions and communities. Our bravery and commitment to truth are essential for nurturing a healthy, informed society.

> *The further a society drifts from Truth, the more it will hate those who speak it.* —George Orwell (Eric Arthur Blair), English novelist, poet, essayist, journalist, and critic.

Reading is our superpower for overcoming today's most pressing challenges and equipping us to migrate to a better place. As I prepared to publish this book, I had a conversation with Guy Kawasaki, who remarked that, in his observation, most people don't seem to be reading books anymore. Bill Gates recently commented on the importance of reading, saying, "If there's just one piece of advice I could give, then I would urge people to foster a love of reading…It gets you involved… It allows your curiosity to follow its course…Books and reading are the most important things." Reading begets knowledge, which fuels understanding.

As we conclude this exploration of career guidance, let us move forward with a renewed sense of purpose and hope. By embodying the principles of excellence, acceptance, and ethical behavior, we can overcome our challenges and pave the way for a brighter future. Our professional lives are not separate from the world around us; they are an integral part of the fabric that binds us as a society. Through our collective efforts, we will forge a future marked by prosperity, equity, and sustainability. Let this be our legacy and our gift to the generations that follow.

> *The past is to be learned from, not lived in.* —Jeffrey R. Holland, American educator, and religious leader.

Acknowledgements

Writing a book is often a journey fraught with sleepless nights, self-doubt, and the relentless challenge of turning a nebulous idea into a tangible reality. It's easy to get lost in the depths of our own thoughts, overwhelmed by the weight of our aspirations and the intricacies of our work.

In these moments, stepping back and seeking the support of trusted friends, colleagues, and family members becomes not just a comfort but a critical step toward clarity and success. Their insights, encouragement, and unwavering belief provide the perspective and strength to navigate the rough patches and bring our vision to life.

I am profoundly grateful to those involved with this book. The editing, organizing, restructuring, and redacting that took place were influenced substantially by several individuals. Substantial discussion and behind-the-scenes effort influenced the scope, content, coverage, and graphic design. The individuals listed below were deeply supportive and influential:

My daughter and son. Cori and Kyler served as my inspiration for writing this book, and provided the persistent encouragement that fueled my multi-year venture. They offered critical insights and advice on the content and cover design, and urged me onward whenever I needed a jump-start.

Michael Ainscow. My friend Michael provided substantial input and guidance on the cover design. His creativity, unique concepts, and patient encouragement led me to the final design. Bravo!

MK Cornfield. Many thanks to MK for her publishing expertise and moral support.

Mike Eneboe. My "Best Man," Mike provided shrewd advise on book content, and consistently counseled me on the value of brevity as I marshalled through multiple phases of redactions, first with a machete, and finally a scalpel. Every piece of advice that Mike provided was spot-on, although it often took me time and contemplation to expose and recognize his genius.

Guy Kawasaki. Tech titan Guy took a chance on me, when he returned an email request for publishing advice. Since our first phone call, he has expertly advised and mentored me on publishing strategy, cover design, title, and scope of content. His willingness to provide a "Foreword" to my first book, *General Career Intelligence*, was a testament to his faith in my writing and commitment to helping others. Most importantly, our relationship has expanded beyond this project. The entire day that we spent in my woodshop, crafting his custom surfboard balance-trainer, is a memory I'll never forget. Guy is truly "Remarkable", in every sense of the word.

My wife. Elaine has been central to my ability to pursue this project. While her direct influence on book content and cover design was invaluable, the patience she exhibited as a writer's "widow" for several years enabled this book in the most fundamental sense. Words are not enough, but thank you Elaine for supporting my passion—I love you, and owe you big time!

About the Author

Ray Blasing is an engineering leader, technologist, inventor, serial entrepreneur, and author of *General Career Intelligence*. His expansive career charts a course from spacecraft antenna engineering to spearheading the development of the now-ubiquitous millimeter wave full-body scanner, a recognizable security fixture at airports worldwide. Awarded more than 40 patents, Ray's work spans industries and reflects a lifelong dedication to innovation. His expertise in founding and leading tech startups, mentoring and coaching diverse teams, and navigating the intricacies of space, military, commercial, and consumer electronics provides him with profound insights into the domains of engineering innovation, product development, and high-tech leadership.

Notes

Executive Leadership

[1] **Below is an abbreviated:** 8 business leaders give their best pieces of advice for new CEOs. https://www.vistage.com/research-center/business-leadership/advice-for-new-ceos/ (accessed 5/28/2021).

[2] **Storytelling: They possess:** Quora. 5 Qualities That Set Truly Great Leaders Apart From Everyone Else. https://www.inc.com/quora/5-qualities-that-set-truly-great-leaders-apart-from-everyone-else.html (accessed 5/12/2020).

[3] **When searching for:** Marcel Schwantes. Warren Buffett Says Find a Great Leader to Work For (Like These 3 Execs). https://www.inc.com/marcel-schwantes/warren-buffett-says-youre-wasting-your-time-building-perfect-career-find-a-great-leader-to-work-for-instead-like-these-3-execs.html (accessed 3/1/2020).

[4] **When a biographer asked:** Justin Bariso. Steve Jobs and Elon Musk: Brilliant or Brutal? Management Lessons From Two CEOs Bent on Changing the World. https://www.inc.com/justin-bariso/brilliant-or-brutal-management-lessons-from-steve-jobs-elon-musk.html (accessed 7/24/2020).

[5] **That said, leadership:** Ramon Henson. The Leadership of Steve Jobs. https://www.business.rutgers.edu/business-insights/leadership-steve-jobs (accessed 3/23/2021).

[6] **When we think about:** Paul Leinwand and Joachim Rotering. How to Excel at Both Strategy and Execution. https://hbr.org/2017/11/how-to-excel-at-both-strategy-and-execution. (accessed 12/17/2019).

[7] **Nobel laureate Daniel:** Chris Bradley, Martin Hirt, Sven Smit. Strategy to beat the odds. https://www.mckinsey.com/business-functions/strategy-and-corporate-finance/our-insights/strategy-to-beat-the-odds (accessed 7/5/2021).

[8] **In my experience, the companies:** Anna Meyer. Are Unpopular CEOs Bad for Business? Two Founders Weigh In. https://www.inc.com/magazine/202004/anna-meyer/ceo-likable-boss-popularity-away-steph-korey.html (accessed 4/1/2020).

[9] **Unfortunately, in today's public:** John F. Harris. Why So Many Politicians Are Such A--holes. https://www.politico.com/news/magazine/2021/03/11/andrew-cuomo-likable-politicians-475284 (accessed 3/11/2021).

[10] **How does one reach:** Elena Lytkina Botelho, Kim Rosenkoetter Powell and Nicole Wong. The Fastest Path to the CEO Job, According to a 10-Year Study. https://hbr.org/2018/01/the-fastest-path-to-the-ceo-job-according-to-a-10-year-study (accessed 3/7/2020).

[11] **Some individuals may embark:** Thomas Koulopoulos. How Real Leaders Step Up to the Plate During a Crisis. https://www.inc.com/thomas-koulopoulos/how-real-leaders-step-up-to-plate-during-a-crisis.html (accessed 3/21/2020).

[12] **Unsurprisingly, many:** Engineers Are Exceptional Leaders. https://gineersnow.com/magazines/construction-magazines/engineers-are-great-leaders (accessed 12/28/2022).

[13] **While many experts suggest:** Hristina Yordanova. 66 percent tech company CEOs are engineers. https://www.englishforums.com/news/66-tech-company-ceos-engineers/ (accessed 12/28/2022).

[14] **While 33% of S&P:** Thomas Anderson. Why Engineers Make Great CEOs. https://engineeringmanagementinstitute.org/engineers-great-ceos/ (accessed 12/28/2022).

[15] **Selecting the right leader to:** Sierra Ventures. How to Hire Your First Head of Engineering. https://www.sierraventures.com/blog/how-to-hire-your-first-head-of-engineering/ (accessed 10/23/2021).

[16] **The VP of Engineering is:** VP of Engineering vs. CTO - The Difference and Why It Matters. https://www.morganlinton.com/vp-of-engineering-vs-cto-the-difference-and-why-it-matters/ (accessed 12/29/2022).

Mentorship and Coaching

[17] **For example, mentors:** Marcel Schwantes. 3 Rare Strategies Great Leaders Use to Hire Top Talent. https://www.inc.com/marcel-schwantes/3-rare-strategies-great-leaders-use-to-hire-top-talent.html (accessed 3/19/2020).

[18] **Research consistently shows:** Mark Horoszowski. How to Build a Great Relationship with a Mentor. https://hbr.org/2020/01/how-to-build-a-great-relationship-with-a-mentor (accessed 6/23/2021).: Mark Horoszowski. How to Build a Great Relationship with a Mentor. https://hbr.org/2020/01/how-to-build-a-great-relationship-with-a-mentor (accessed 6/23/2021).

[19] **Professional role models demonstrate:** Professional Role Models: Definition, Traits and Benefits. https://www.indeed.com/career-advice/career-development/role-model (accessed 3/19/2023.

[20] **There are many good reasons:** Uthra Ramachandran. 6 Reasons Why Mentorship is Rewarding. https://www.linkedin.com/pulse/6-reasons-why-mentorship-rewarding-uthra-ramachandran (accessed 5/26/2021).

[21] **Successful leaders, including:** Marcel Schwantes. 6 Signs to Instantly Identify Someone With True Leadership Skills. https://www.inc.com/marcel-schwantes/6-signs-to-instantly-identify-someone-with-true-leadership-skills.html (accessed 3/16/2021).

[22] **While you may actively:** Brian Kurtz. Your mentors choose you.. https://www.briankurtz.net/your-mentors-choose-you/ (accessed 5/30/2020).

[23] **When seeking a mentor:** Vineet Chopra and Sanjay Saint. What Mentors Wish Their Mentees Knew. https://hbr.org/2017/11/what-mentors-wish-their-mentees-knew (accessed 1/12/2020).

[24] **Sometimes, engaging multiple:** Julia Fawal. The 5 types of mentors you need in your life. https://ideas.ted.com/the-5-types-of-mentors-you-need-in-your-life/ (accessed 2/3/2021).

[25] **Mark Cuban and other:** Jeff Haden. Why Mark Cuban Follows the 'No Mentors' Rule. https://www.inc.com/jeff-haden/why-mark-cuban-follows-no-mentors-rule.html (accessed 2/20/2021).

[26] **For most, mentoring:** Uthra Ramachandran. 6 Reasons Why Mentorship is Rewarding. https://www.linkedin.com/pulse/6-reasons-why-mentorship-rewarding-uthra-ramachandran (accessed 5/26/2021).

[27] **Managers mentor their:** Stav Ziv. Good Bosses Remember to Do These 11 Things Every Day. https://www.inc.com/the-muse/good-bosses-remember-to-do-these-11-things-everyday.html (accessed 12/3/2019).

[28] **Accept and acknowledge:** Beth Birenbaum. Mentoring: Definition, Examples, & Best Practices. https://www.berkeleywellbeing.com/mentoring.html (accessed 6/3/2024).

Conflicts, Influence and Negotiations

[29] **Statistics show that:** Michael Zipursky. How to become a consultant Study & Guide (2023). https://www.consultingsuccess.com/how-to-become-a-consultant (accessed 10/7/2023).

[30] **Initially, it's helpful to:** Michael Zipursky. How To Become A Consultant: Quit Your Job & Get Your First Client. https://www.consultingsuccess.com/how-to-become-a-consultant (accessed 5/12/2020).

[31] **You might find:** Michael Zipursky. How To Become A Consultant: Quit Your Job & Get Your First Client. https://www.consultingsuccess.com/how-to-become-a-consultant (accessed 5/12/2020).

[32] **Balance: Consultants value:** How to Work Effectively With Consultants. https://www.mindtools.com/pages/article/working-with-consultants.htm (accessed 11/14/2022).

[33] **A recent study found that 20%:** Why Business Partnerships Fail & How to Avoid Bad Partnerships. https://exitconsultinggroup.com/insights/why-business-partnerships-fail/ (accessed 1/6/2023).

Work Culture

[34] **I'll never forget:** Reid Hoffman. How to Think Like an entrepreneur, According to Reid Hoffman. https://www.entrepreneur.com/article/365727 (accessed 3/9/2021).

[35] **Tim Denning defines:** Tim Denning. Entrepreneurship is More Than Being a Founder. https://www.linkedin.com/pulse/entrepreneurship-more-than-being-founder-krishna-pushp-shukla/ (accessed 9/15/2019).

[36] **Startups provide a chance:** Adam Toren. 10 Quotes to Get You Through the Marathon of Entrepreneurship. https://www.entrepreneur.com/article/232683 (accessed 2/27/2021).

[37] **Recent studies reveal that:** Michael Callahan. Out the Other Side. https://www.magzter.com/stories/Business/Inc/Out-the-Other-Side (accessed 2/10/2022).

[38] **Before embarking on a new:** Matt Mansfield. Startup Statistics—The Numbers You Need to Know. https://smallbiztrends.com/2019/03/startup-statistics-small-business.html (Accessed 8/15/2019).

[39] **Studies on business unicorns:** Ali Tamaseb. What Data Reveals About Why Some Startups Reach Billion-Dollar Valuations. https://www.inc.com/ali-tamaseb/super-founders-billion-dollar-valuation-unicorn-startup.html (accessed 5/22/2021).

[40] **Don't be misled into:** Who is the entrepreneur? New Entrepreneurs in the United States, 1996-2021. https://www.kauffman.org/entrepreneurship/reports/who-is-the-entrepreneur-united-states-1996-2021/ (accessed 11/7/2022).

[41] **Business success is rarely:** Richard Branson. Five rough guidelines for creating a successful business. https://www.virgin.com/richard-branson/five-rough-guidelines-creating-successful-business (accessed 11/6/2019).

[42] **The following is an:** Pros and Cons of Working at a Startup (Plus Tips). https://www.indeed.com/career-advice/career-development/working-at-a-startup (accessed 1/1/2023).

[43] **When launching a startup:** Tim Denning. Chase Your Dream, not The Money. Better Marketing. https://medium.com/better-marketing/chase-your-dream-not-the-money-2f43734e39c (accessed 9/2/2019).

[44] **Warren Buffett is an excellent:** Mindo Zetlin. One of the greatest lessons Warren Buffett taught his son: 'Wealth Ethic' isn't the same as 'work ethic'. https://www.cnbc.com/2020/03/24/warren-buffett-greatest-lesson-difference-between-work-ethics-wealth-ethics-that-most-fail-to-realize.html (accessed 6/5/2020).

[45] **Corporate leaders and venture:** Erin Griffith. Silicon Valley Is Trying Out a New Mantra: Make a Profit. New York Times. https://www.nytimes.com/2019/10/08/technology/silicon-valley-startup-profit.html (accessed 11/1/2019).

[46] **Many leaders mistakenly:** Kent Billingsley. From Entrepreneur to Millionaire: How to Build a Highly Profitable, Fast-Growth Company and Become Embarrassingly Rich Doing It. https://www.entrepreneur.com/article/367319 (accessed 3/22/2021).

[47] **Achieving profitability:** Bill Fotsch. How to Base Your Company on Value. https://www.inc.com/bill-fotsch/how-to-base-your-company-on-value.html (accessed 6/16/2022).

Consulting and Partnerships

[48] **It's also necessary:** Peter Thiel with Blake Masters. Zero to One, pp 48-50.

[49] **Guy Kawasaki reinforces:** Guy Kawasaki. American Express. What I learned From Steve Jobs. https://www.americanexpress.com/en-us/business/trends-and-insights/articles/what-i-learned-from-steve-jobs/ (accessed on 9//11/2019).

[50] **It's important to direct:** Marcel Schwantes. Steve Jobs; Advice on Becoming More Productive Is Quite Brilliant. https://www.inc.com/marcel-schwantes/steve-jobs-advice-on-becoming-more-productive-is-quite-brilliant.html (accessed 4/16/2019).

[51] **When seeking inspiration:** Vishal Noel. Leadership skills and qualities of Steve Jobs, which everyone should learn from. https://vishalnoel7.medium.com/top-6-attributes-of-steve-jobs-that-make-him-a-great-leader-1175eba08e0c (accessed 3/23/2021).

[52] **The NDA basically says:** Steve Strauss. How to Prevent Someone from Stealing Your Million-Dollar Idea. https://gusto.com/blog/growth/protect-business-idea (accessed 3/10/2021).

[53] **More specifically, the NDA is:** Michael Guta. Non-Disclosure Agreements: When Does Your Business Need Them? https://smallbiztrends.com/2019/07/non-disclosure-agreements.html (accessed 8/6/2019).

[54] **It's important to distinguish:** Ironclad. NDA vs Confidentiality Agreement: Understanding the Difference. https://ironcladapp.com/journal/contracts/nda-vs-confidentiality-agreement/ (accessed 1/3/2023).

[55] **If you're seeking venture:** Synvest Capital. Why VCs Don't Sign NDAs, and Why You Shouldn't Worry About It. https://synvestcapital.com/why-vcs-dont-sign-nda/ (accessed 1/3/2023).

[56] **While patents can be:** Frances Dodds. Patent the Boring Stuff. https://www.magzter.com/stories/business/Entrepreneur-US/PATENT-THE-BORING-STUFF (accessed 8/10/2024).

[57] **Disruption is an overused:** Facebook business. Defining disruption in the age of startups. https://www.facebook.com/business/m/emerging-disruptors (accessed 11/8/2019).

[58] **Focusing solely on:** Peter Thiel with Blake Masters. Zero to One, pp 57, 58.

[59] **When preparing your:** Maria Tabaka. Success Is Hard Because You Overcomplicate It. Keep Your Strategy Simple With These 7 Questions. https://www.inc.com/marla-tabaka/success-is-hard-because-you-overcomplicate-it-keep-your-strategy-simple-with-these-7-questions.html (accessed 12/7/2019).

[60] **Great teams operate:** Mike Bloomberg. Build a great team. https://www.linkedin.com/pulse/build-great-team-mike-bloomberg/ (accessed 2/3/2020).

[61] **Entrepreneurs should prioritize:** Peter Thiel with Blake Masters. Zero to One, pp 109-125.

[62] **Focus on your team's:** Axel Unger. Lead as We, not Me. https://www.linkedin.com/pulse/lead-we-me-axel-unger/ (accessed 8/1/2019).

[63] **The business mantra:** Imran Tariq. 4 Painful Realities Your Scaling Startup Must Accept In Order to Grow. Entrepreneur. https://www.entrepreneur.com/article/337813 (accessed 9/12/2019).

[64] **Cash is the lifeblood:** Alie Fulton. What are some common misconceptions people have about raising capital? https://www.forbes.com/sites/quora/2019/06/04/what-every-founder-needs-to-know-about-startup-funding/#1cacb8173675 (accessed 11/9/2019).

[65] **There are three primary:** Chip Conley. Hard Lesson: When Co-Investors Disagree. https://www.gsb.stanford.edu/insights/hard-lesson-when-co-investors-disagree (accessed 5/22/2020).

[66] **When seeking funding from venture:** David Kolodny. Founders, Stop Obsessing Over Venture Funding. https://news.crunchbase.com/startups/founders-vc-david-kolodny-wilbur-labs/ (accessed 11/24/2021).

[67] **When pitching to investors:** Quora. What Are The Most Important Things VCs Look For When They Invest https://www.forbes.com/sites/quora/2019/05/30/what-are-the-most-important-things-vcs-look-for-when-they-invest/#7c59f0025ac9 (accessed 11/22/2019).

[68] **Investors invest in:** Justin Kan. What are the most common mistakes founders make when they start a company? Quora. https://www.quora.com/What-are-the-most-common-mistakes-founders-make-when-they-start-a-company/answer/Justin-Kan?share=7d46ad41 (accessed 10/8/2019).

[69] **The pitch deck is your tool:** Guy Kawasaki. The Only Pitch Guyde You'll Ever Need. https://guykawasaki.substack.com/p/the-only-pitch-guyde-youll-ever-need (accessed 7/3/2024).

[70] **When seeking venture capital:** Mandela Schumacher-Hodge Dixon. Will anybody invest in someone like me? https://www.entrepreneur.com/article/363312 (accessed 2/28/2021).

[71] **Be realistic as to:** Alie Fulton. What are some common misconceptions people have about raising capital? https://www.quora.com/What-are-some-common-misconceptions-people-have-about-raising-capital (accessed 2/26/2020).

[72] **After securing your investment:** Mandela Schumacher-Hodge Dixon. Will anybody invest in someone like me? https://www.entrepreneur.com/article/363312 (accessed 2/28/2021).

[73] **Statistically, over one-third:** Friends and Family Investors: The Dangers Startups Must Know. https://www.upcounsel.com/friends-and-family-investors (accessed 1/6/2023).

[74] **Angel investors, typically:** Bob Pavey. Embracing Angels: A VC's Perspective. http://www.morgenthaler.com/press-releases/Embracing%20Angels.pdf (accessed 10/21/2022).

[75] **As a CEO, navigating:** Lou Shipley. Top Five Mistakes First-Time CEOs Make. https://www.loushipley.com/writings-blog/top-five-mistakes-first-time-ceos-make (accessed 11/24/2021).

[76] **Stock options permit employees:** Ed Keible and Bob Pavey. Foolishness over stock options. https://www.cnet.com/culture/foolishness-over-stock-options/ (accessed 7/10/2022).

[77] **Don't worry; be crappy:** Guy Kawasaki. The Art of Innovation. https://www.linkedin.com/pulse/20140310151443-2484700-the-art-of-innovation/ (accessed 9/15/2019).

[78] **Ultimately, business is all:** Marcel Schwantes. Warren Buffett Says You Can Have Success by Following This Rule. https://www.inc.com/marcel-schwantes/warren-buffett-says-anyone-can-achieve-success-by-following-this-1-personal-rule-he-lives-by.html (accessed 6/17/2020).

[79] **If a customer isn't a good fit:** Monel Amin. The First 1000 Days. https://www.linkedin.com/pulse/why-1000-days-monel-amin/ (accessed 7/31/2019).

[80] **Entrepreneurs are notorious:** Pat Flynn. 7 Common Entrepreneurial Traps. https://www.msn.com/en-us/money/smallbusiness/7-common-entrepreneurial-traps/ar-BB1agnpJ (accessed 2/23/2021).

[81] **Flexibility and adaptability:** Holger Seim. Lessons for the New CEO From 5 Great Leaders of History. https://www.entrepreneur.com/article/246388 (accessed 2/27/2021).

[82] **When you change:** Making big changes in times of big change. https://www.magzter.com/stories/Business/Entrepreneur-magazine/MAKING-BIG-CHANGES-IN-TIMES-OF-BIG-CHANGE-or-Why-Amazon-Created-the-Kindle (accessed 2/28/2021).

[83] **Salespeople who go:** Jason Feifer. Want Something From Someone? Do the Work for Them. https://www.msn.com/en-us/money/smallbusiness/want-something-from-someone-do-the-work-for-them/ar-BB1fBJZu (accessed 4/14/2021).

[84] **Significant time and effort:** Bill Murphy Jr. 37 Years Ago, Warren Buffett Explained a Brutal Truth That Most People Never Actually Learn. https://www.inc.com/bill-murphy-jr/37-years-ago-warren-buffett-explained-a-brutal-truth-that-most-people-never-learn.html (accessed 4/10/2021).

[85] **Branding is a strategic:** Liam Farrell. Blog. The difference between MarCom and branding. https://www.unisonoagency.com/branding-and-marcom-differences/ (accessed 1/10/2023).

[86] **Branding is a startup:** James Vincent. 5 lessons I learned from a decade working with Steve Jobs (and advising other rock-star founders). https://www.fastcompany.com/90666283/5-lessons-i-learned-from-a-decade-working-with-steve-jobs-and-advising-other-rock-star-founders (accessed 8/18/2021).

[87] **Statistically, ninety-five percent:** Logan Chierotti. Harvard Professor Says 95% of Purchasing Decisions Are Subconscious. https://www.inc.com/logan-chierotti/harvard-professor-says-95-of-purchasing-decisions-are-subconscious.html (accessed 4/2/2020).

[88] **The most successful companies:** Gary Vaynerchuk. The Key Difference Between Sales and Branding: One Is Way More Effective than the Other. https://www.inc.com/linkedin/gary-vaynerchuk/sales-vs-branding-gary-vaynerchuk.html (accessed 7/14/2022).

[89] **As you grow and scale:** Imran Tariq. 4 Painful Realities Your Scaling Startup Must Accept in Order to Grow. https://www.entrepreneur.com/article/337813 (Accessed 4/12/2019).

[90] **When pricing your products:** Albert Yuen. Bill & Dave's Memos. pp 84-89.

[91] **In a startup, it's important:** Richard Branson. Five rough guidelines for creating a successful business. https://www.virgin.com/richard-branson/five-rough-guidelines-creating-successful-business (accessed 11/6/2019).

[92] **Every company cultivates:** Lindsay McGregor and Neel Doshi. How Company Culture Shapes Employee Motivation. https://hbr.org/2015/11/how-company-culture-shapes-employee-motivation (accessed 12/16/2019).

[93] **Culture can be defined:** Michael Watkins, Rose Hollister, Kathryn Tecosky, Cindy Wolpert. Why Every Executive Should Be Focusing on Culture Change Now. https://sloanreview.mit.edu/article/why-every-executive-should-be-focusing-on-culture-change-now/ (accessed 8/17/2021).

[94] **Leaders who prioritize:** Tomas Chamorro-Premuzic. How to Spot an Incompetent Leader. https://hbr.org/2020/03/how-to-spot-an-incompetent-leader (accessed 3/11/2020).

[95] **Some describe the work:** Douglas Ready. Does your company suffer from broken culture syndrome? https://mitsloan.mit.edu/ideas-made-to-matter/does-your-company-suffer-broken-culture-syndrome (accessed 7/13/2022).

[96] **Studies have shown that *why*:** Kate Tuck. How Company Culture Shapes Employee Motivation. https://strategicleaders.com/how-company-culture-shapes-employee-motivation/ (accessed 11/24/2023).

[97] **The corporate landscape is:** Kalilur Rahman. Culture Vs Strategy—Who eats who for Breakfast, Lunch or Dinner? https://www.linkedin.com/pulse/culture-vs-strategy-who-eats-breakfast-lunch-dinner-kalilur-rahman (accessed 11/8/2019).

[98] **Some leaders prioritize:** Norman Murray. Work at your culture or it will build itself, and you won't like the results!. https://www.linkedin.com/pulse/work-your-culture-build-itself-you-wont-like-results-norman-murray (accessed 4/16/2020).

[99] **A mission statement:** Deborah Sweeney. How to Create a Mission Statement and Why Startups Need One. https://www.score.org/blog/how-create-mission-statement-and-why-startups-need-one (accessed 7/10/2022).

[100] **A third important:** Doug Cantor. The Value of Values. https://www.inc.com/magazine/202205/doug-cantor/values-mission-leadership-advice.html (accessed 5/29/2022).

[101] **Aligning values with:** Jamey Austin. How to make values-based leadership your North Star. https://www.atlassian.com/blog/leadership/values-based-leadership-patagonia (accessed 3/15/2021).

[102] **When crafting your vision:** Brenden P. Keegan. Choosing the Words That Can Change Your Company. https://www.entrepreneur.com/growing-a-business/choosing-the-words-that-can-change-your-company/454703 (accessed 8/8/2023).

[103] **As employees increasingly:** Alvaro Lleo De Nalda, Alex Montaner, Amy C. Edmondson, Phil Sotok. Unlock the Power of Purpose. https://sloanreview.mit.edu/article/unlock-the-power-of-purpose/ (accessed 7/19/2022).

[104] **The most purpose-driven:** Christian Busch and Lisa Hehenberger. How to Evaluate the Impact of Corporate Purpose. https://sloanreview.mit.edu/article/how-to-evaluate-the-impact-of-corporate-purpose/ (accessed 9/28/2022).

[105] **When we're not being:** Mike Rucker. 3 reasons not to bring your authentic self to work. https://www.msn.com/en-us/health/wellness/3-reasons-not-to-bring-your-authentic-self-to-work/ar-AAVe1jd (accessed 3/27/2022).

[106] **When we're encouraged to be:** Jessica Stillman. The 3 Biggest Lessons From a New Harvard Business School Class on How to Be a 'Badass' at Work. https://www.inc.com/jessica-stillman/harvard-business-school-authenticity-office-personality.html (accessed 5/28/2021).

[107] **Some researchers have:** Li Huang. Being your authentic self is actually not ideal for creativity. https://qz.com/work/2035693/being-your-authentic-self-is-not-ideal-for-creativity/ (accessed 7/30/2021).

[108] **Being authentic at work:** Jamey Austin. Why we don't bring our whole selves to work. https://www.atlassian.com/blog/teamwork/why-we-dont-bring-our-whole-selves-to-work (accessed 4/22/2021).

[109] **Like systemic racism:** Rani Molla. American motherhood vs. the American work ethic. https://www.vox.com/recode/22605612/working-mothers-pandemic-childcare-ideal-parent-worker-remote (accessed 8/12/2021).

[110] **Leadership plays an essential:** Joan C. Williams and Sky Mihaylo. How the Best Bosses Interrupt Bias on Their Teams. https://hbr.org/2019/11/how-the-best-bosses-interrupt-bias-on-their-teams (accessed 2/1/2022).

[111] **Mental health in the workplace:** Nina Tomaro. 5 Ideas From Leading Companies to Support Workplace Mental Health. https://thriveglobal.com/stories/5-ideas-from-leading-companies-to-support-workplace-mental-health/ (accessed 3/21/2021).

[112] **Just as great leaders:** Clarice Metzger. Verizon Media CEO Guru Gowrappan Shares His Top DE&I Advice for Leaders. https://thriveglobal.com/stories/guru-gowrappan-verizon-media-mental-health-employees-black-brown-communities/ (accessed 3/21/2021).

[113] **Men's mental health:** Maggie Hureau. Why Supporting and Prioritizing Employee Mental Health Is So Important Right Now. https://thriveglobal.com/stories/support-prioritize-employee-mental-health-coronavirus-covid-pandemic/ (accessed 3/21/2021).

Work-Life Balancing Act

[114] **In today's fast-paced world:** Dropbox. How Work Became a Mess. https://stateofwork.dropbox.com/ (accessed 12/14/2019).

[115] **The pandemic has worsened:** Pandemic-Related Burnout Is Real and Mental Wellness Benefits Are Key to Treating It. https://blog.tasclargemarkets.com/blog/pandemic-related-burnout-is-real-and-mental-wellness-benefits-are-key-to-treating-it (accessed 4/22/2021).

[116] **Work life balance (WLB):** Shalini Govil-Pai. Your Career Is Not a Race—Use These Guideposts to Make It a Mindful and Successful Journey. https://thriveglobal.com/stories/your-career-is-not-a-race-use-these-guideposts-to-make-it-a-mindful-and-successful-journey/ (accessed 6/1/2021).

[117] **A recent study by the World:** Olafimihan Oshin. Who study finds increased risk of death from working 55 or more hours per week. https://www.fr24news.com/a/2021/05/who-study-finds-increased-risk-of-death-when-working-55-or-more-hours-per-week-fr.html (accessed 5/17/2021).

[118] **Modern workers increasingly seek:** Marcel Schwantes. 8 Work Habits Found in Extremely Valuable Employees. https://www.inc.com/marcel-schwantes/7-work-habits-found-in-extremely-valuable-employees.html (accessed 4/5/2020).

[119] **Balancing work and life:** Wanda Thibodeaux. 3 harsh Truths to Accept if You Want to Be Successful. https://www.inc.com/wanda-thibodeaux/3-harsh-truths-to-accept-if-you-want-to-be-successful.html (accessed 4/26/2021).

[120] **As an alternative to WLB:** Pete Wilkins. The Secret of Work-Life Balance for Entrepreneurs (hint...it's different than you think). https://thriveglobal.com/stories/the-secret-of-work-life-balance-for-entrepreneurs-hint-its-different-than-you-think/ (accessed 11/22/2019).

[121] **Jeff Bezos offers:** Katie Canales, Zoë Bernard. Jeff Bezos says work-life balance is a 'debilitating phrase.' He wants Amazon workers to view their career and lives as a 'circle'. https://www.businessinsider.com/jeff-bezos-work-life-balance-debilitating-phrase-career-circle-2021-7?op=1 (accessed 7/3/2021).

[122] **"Work-life harmony,":** Leon Ho. Ditch Work Life Balance and Embrace Work Life Harmony. https://medium.com/the-mission/ditch-work-life-balance-and-embrace-work-life-harmony-62cc68a52bf7 (accessed 3/31/2022).

[123] **It's important to distinguish:** Harvey Deutschendorf. 5 ways emotional intelligence can help prevent workaholism. https://www.fastcompany.com/90615209/5-ways-emotional-intelligence-can-help-prevent-workaholism (accessed 3/24/2021).

[124] **Research finds that highly:** Bourree Lam. Being a Go-Getter Is No Fun. https://www.theatlantic.com/business/archive/2015/05/being-a-go-getter-is-no-fun/393863/ (accessed 2/8/2021).

[125] **It's often difficult to say:** Matthias Schreck. This is how to say "yes" at work without spreading yourself too thin. https://www.atlassian.com/blog/productivity/how-to-avoid-getting-spread-too-thin (accessed 2/7/2021).

[126] **Stress arises from:** Nicholas Petrie. Pressure Doesn't Have to Turn into Stress. https://hbr.org/2017/03/pressure-doesnt-have-to-turn-into-stress (accessed 3/16/2017).

[127] **As a manager:** Mithu Storoni. Smart Leaders Prevent Burnout With 3 Golden Rules. https://www.inc.com/mithu-storoni/3-golden-rules-that-make-a-team-exceptionally-resilient.html (accessed 3/1/2020).

[128] **Recent research suggests that clutter:** Justin Bariso. Science Confirms It: Beginning Your Day With this 1 Simple Task Will Help You Think and Feel Better. https://timesnowbusiness.com/science-confirms-it-beginning-your-day-with-this-1-simple-task-will-help-you-think-and-feel-better/ (accessed 7/17/2022).

[129] **Mindfulness involves being:** Lillian Xiao. Digital wellness aims to cater to the true needs of users, rather than competing for their attention. https://www.editorx.com/shaping-design/article/digital-wellness (accessed 4/14/2021).

[130] **If you're constantly looking:** Theodore Kinni. Bringing Mindfulness to Your Career. https://www.gsb.stanford.edu/insights/bringing-mindfulness-your-career (accessed 5/22/2020).

[131] **The *type* of break:** Stephanie Vozza. This is the exact type of break you should be taking when working from home. https://www.fastcompany.com/90582261/this-is-the-exact-type-of-break-you-should-be-taking-when-working-from-home (accessed 1/17/2021).

[132] **Science has shown that periods:** Jessica Stillman. Steve Jobs, Albert Einstein and Neuroscience All Agree: Your Daily Routine Needs More 'Non-time'. https://www.inc.com/jessica-stillman/steve-jobs-albert-einstein-steven-kotler-non-time.html (accessed 3/4/2021).

[133] **Experts claim that when we go:** Deborah Grayson Riegel. Don't Underestimate the Power of a Walk. https://hbr.org/2021/02/dont-underestimate-the-power-of-a-walk (accessed 3/9/2021).

[134] **Breathing fresh air:** Betsy Morris. Being Outside Is Good for Your Health—but Does Golf Count? https://www.wsj.com/articles/being-outside-is-good-for-your-healthbut-does-golf-count-11615213969 (accessed 4/30/2021).

[135] **It's healthy to break:** John Rampton. You're Not Crunched For Time, You're Just Making these 8 Time-Management Mistakes. https://www.entrepreneur.com/article/358983 (accessed 12/4/2020).

[136] **Experts have uncovered:** Catherine Price. How to Break Up With Your Phone. Page 11.

[137] **Neuroscience research:** Annemarie Dooling. How Being More Productive Starts With Doing Nothing. https://www.wsj.com/articles/why-doing-nothing-can-make-you-more-productive-11615911969 (accessed 4/26/2021).

[138] **Many workers mistakenly:** Shawn Achor. Are the People Who Take Vacations the Ones Who Get Promoted? https://hbr.org/2015/06/are-the-people-who-take-vacations-the-ones-who-get-promoted (accessed 4/26/2023).

[139] **According to experts, the benefits:** Sarah Todd. Going On Vacation Won't Cure Your Burnout. https://qz.com/work/1660743/going-on-vacation-wont-cure-job-burnout/ (accessed 8/5/2020).

[140] **People often spend more:** John Boitnott. How to Stop Sunday From Turning Into Your New Monday. https://www.inc.com/john-boitnott/how-to-stop-sunday-from-turning-into-your-new-monday.html (accessed 2/20/2020).

[141] **To succeed with this:** John Boitnott. How to encourage Your Employees to Leave Work at the Office and Embrace Time Off. https://www.inc.com/john-boitnott/how-to-encourage-your-employees-to-leave-work-at-office-embrace-time-off.html (accessed 2/20/2020).

[142] **Some countries have:** Amy Hunt. How to Increase Productivity by Switching Off and Getting Cozy. https://www.dumblittleman.com/how-to-switch-off-from-work/ (accessed 12/4/2019).

[143] **Many companies nationwide:** Soo Youn. America's workers are burned out. https://www.washingtonpost.com/business/2021/06/28/employee-burnout-corporate-america/ (accessed 6/29/2021).

[144] **Unfortunately, some leaders:** Justin Bariso. When Not to Send an email—A Lesson From Elon Musk. https://thriveglobal.com/stories/when-not-to-send-an-email-a-lesson-from-elon-musk/ (accessed 11/15/2019).

[145] **Research has revealed that burnout:** Zorana Ivcevic Pringle, Robin Stern, Julia Moeller. The truth about burnout: It doesn't look how we expect it to. The Hill. https://thehill.com/opinion/healthcare/458906-the-truth-about-burnout-it-doesnt-look-how-we-expect-it-to (accessed 8/30/3029).

[146] **Mental illness, depression:** Mandy Oaklander. Millennial Employees Are Getting Companies to Radically Rethink Workers' Mental Health? https://time.com/collection/davos-2020/5764680/mental-health-at-work/ (accessed 5/2/2022).

[147] **The pandemic has ushered:** Jaclyn Chen. Parents aren't OK right now. Here's how companies can support them. https://www.protocol.com/workplace/parental-leave-support-companies (accessed 2/10/2022).

[148] **Managers and leaders have faced:** Camille Preston. Feel like you're stretched thin? Here's how to be more intentional as a leader. https://www.fastcompany.com/90624292/feel-like-youre-stretched-thin-heres-how-to-be-more-intentional-as-a-leader (assessed 4/29/2021).

[149] **For millions of workers:** Kate Rockwood. The 9-to-5 Workweek Is Dead. Here's What's Next. https://www.inc.com/magazine/201612/kate-rockwood/tipsheet-productivity.html (accessed 2/20/2020).

[150] **Another recent study revealed that productivity:** David Prosser. Is It Time For The Four-Day Working Week? https://www.forbes.com/sites/davidprosser/2019/03/18/is-it-time-for-the-four-day-working-week/?sh=7bb85ef64faa (accessed 11/18/2019).

[151] **Microsoft experimented with:** Lisa Eadicicco. Microsoft experimented with a 4-day workweek, and productivity jumped by 40%. https://www.businessinsider.in/tech/news/microsoft-experimented-with-a-4-day-work-week-in-its-japan-office-and-productivity-jumped-by-40/articleshow/71901595.cms (accessed 11/12/2019).

[152] **The traditional notion:** Charlie Warzel and Anne Helen Petersen. How to Care Less About Work. https://www.theatlantic.com/ideas/archive/2021/12/how-care-less-about-work/620902/ (accessed 12/6/2021).

Tackling Toxicity

[153] **A recent study found that 56%:** Mary Abbajay. What to Do When You Have a Bad Boss. https://hbr.org/2018/09/what-to-do-when-you-have-a-bad-boss (accessed 1/1/2019).

[154] **Other research has found that toxic:** Christine Porath. How to Avoid Hiring a Toxic Employee. https://hbr.org/2016/02/how-to-avoid-hiring-a-toxic-employee (accessed 2/9/2019).

[155] **In the most toxic:** Brigette Hyacinth. A Toxic Work Culture is forcing your Best Employees to Quit! https://brigettehyacinth.com/a-toxic-work-culture-is-forcing-your-best-employees-to-quit/ (accessed 11/22/2019).

[156] **It's important to recognize:** Tracy Brower. How to manage a domineering employee when you're an introvert leader. https://www.fastcompany.com/90664204/how-to-manage-a-dominating-employee-when-youre-an-introvert-leader (accessed 8/12/2021).

[157] **Executives, in particular:** Valerie Soleil. 10 Traits of Genuinely Smart People (That Have Nothing to Do With Intelligence). https://www.learning-mind.com/traits-genuinely-smart-people/ (accessed 6/25/2020).

[158] **Recently, bullies have:** Rachel Chase. You Asked For It: Are we a nation of bullies? https://www.yahoo.com/news/asked-nation-bullies-132541763.html (accessed 4/3/2022).

[159] **To combat bullying:** Shirley Li. When Meanness Was Celebrated. https://www.theatlantic.com/culture/archive/2021/04/scott-rudin/618569/ (accessed 4/9/2021).

[160] **Psychologists have studied this:** Jeff Haden. Here's How to Tell Within 5 Minutes If Someone Isn't as Smart as They Think. https://www.inc.com/jeff-haden/heres-how-to-tell-within-5-minutes-if-someone-isnt-as-smart-as-they-think.html (accessed 5/1/2019).

[161] **Narcissists often justify:** Sarah Dillon. Narcissists usually end up with this job title, according to science. https://www.theladders.com/career-advice/narcissists-usually-end-up-with-this-job-title-according-to-science (accessed 1/26/2021).

[162] **According to recent research, narcissists:** Beth Ellwood. Narcissists are more likely to gain power at work because they act like they already have it, study suggests. https://www.psypost.org/2021/07/narcissists-are-more-likely-to-gain-power-at-work-because-they-act-like-they-already-have-it-study-suggests-61563 (accessed 7/21/2021).

[163] **When a coworker copies:** Geoffrey James. The Best Response to a Passive-Aggressive Coworker. https://www.inc.com/geoffrey-james/how-to-totally-own-a-passive-aggressive-coworker.html (accessed 11/19/2019).

[164] **They exhibit narcissistic:** Marcel Schwantes. 5 Signs that Instantly Identify Someone With Bad Leadership Skills. https://www.inc.com/marcel-schwantes/6-signs-to-instantly-notice-someone-with-bad-leadership-skills.html (accessed 11/25/2019).

[165] **They fixate on:** J.T. O'Donnell. Are You a Toxic Boss? Google's management Study Will Tell You. https://www.inc.com/jt-odonnell/googles-detailed-management-study-reveals-8-signs-youre-a-toxic-boss.html (accessed 1/7/2020).

[166] **Working in a toxic:** Alison Green. The Workplace Where It Was Normal for Colleagues to Bite Each Other. https://slate.com/human-interest/2018/06/bad-jobs-can-warp-your-sense-of-whats-normal.html (accessed 4/13/2021).

[167] **Toxic individuals often:** Travis Bradberry. 12 Ways Successful People Handle Toxic People. https://www.entrepreneur.com/slideshow/299696 (accessed 3/8/2020).

[168] **The solution to a:** Brigette Hyacinth. A Toxic Work Culture is forcing your Best Employees to Quit! https://brigettehyacinth.com/a-toxic-work-culture-is-forcing-your-best-employees-to-quit/ (accessed 11/22/2019).

[169] **Research suggests that a significant:** Tamara Star. 7 Habits of Highly Miserable People. https://thriveglobal.com/stories/7-habits-of-highly-miserable-people/. (accessed 9/1/2019).

[170] **The following are some additional:** Justin. How to Stop Being Toxic: 19 Steps to Not Be Bitter Or Blame Others. https://lbibinders.org/stop-being-toxic/ (accessed 10/28/2022).

Supercharging Innovation

[171] **Arguing with someone:** Allstate. How Do We Build a Better Society? Have Better Arguments. https://www.theatlantic.com/sponsored/allstate-2020/better-arguments/3475/ (accessed 12/7/2020).

[172] **Have you ever noticed:** Jeff Haden. 10 Signs You're More Persuasive and Influential Than You Think. https://www.inc.com/jeff-haden/10-signs-youre-more-persuasive-influential-than-you-think.html (accessed 11/25/2019).

[173] **Communication, whether speech:** Chloe Noor Khosrowshahi. Here's how Aristotle can help you master the power of persuasion. https://bigthink.com/personal-growth/aristotle-persuasion (accessed 11/14/2020).

[174] **Persuading others can:** John Bowe. Aristotle was a key figure in public speaking—he said the most persuasive people do these 3 things. https://www.cnbc.com/2021/01/12/aristotles-3-most-important-rules-for-being-more-persuasive-in-public-speaking.html (accessed 1/16/2021).

[175] **Offering a choice:** Carmine Gallo. How to Change Anyone's Mind Without Persuading Them. https://www.inc.com/carmine-gallo/change-anyones-mind-without-persuading-strategy-leadership.html (accessed 3/21/2020).

[176] **People are more easily:** Jeff Haden. 10 Signs You're More Persuasive and Influential Than You Think. https://www.inc.com/jeff-haden/10-signs-youre-more-persuasive-influential-than-you-think.html (accessed 11/25/2019).

[177] **If you seem doubtful:** Jeff Haden. 10 Signs You're More Persuasive and Influential Than You Think. https://www.inc.com/jeff-haden/10-signs-youre-more-persuasive-influential-than-you-think.html (accessed 11/25/2019).

[178] **If you have good:** Daniel Pink. The most persuasive people use these 3 timing methods to get what they want, says human behavior expert. https://www.cnbc.com/2020/11/17/the-most-persuasive-people-use-these-timing-methods-to-get-what-they-want-behavior-expert.html (accessed 12/19/2020).

[179] **Everyone negotiates, often:** Carmine Gallo. Win People Over With 2 Simple, Powerful FBI Tactics. https://www.inc.com/carmine-gallo/win-people-over-with-2-simple-powerful-fbi-tactics.html (accessed 4/14/2021).

[180] **When negotiating, arbitrators:** Brian Kurtz. The Power of 100-0. https://www.briankurtz.net/the-power-of-100-0/ (accessed 5/30/2020).

[181] **"Forced Empathy" is:** Derek Beres. "Forced empathy" is a powerful negotiation tool. Here's how to do it. https://bigthink.com/personal-growth/forced-empathy (accessed 12/4/2020).

[182] **Prepare thoroughly:** Roger Fisher, William Ury, Bruce Patton. Getting to Yes: Negotiating Agreement Without Giving In. Chapters 1, 3, 4, 5.

[183] **Lead with a compelling:** Chris Voss. Never Split the Difference: Negotiating As If Your Life Depended On It. Chapters 3,4,7.

[184] **Leverage data:** Deepak Malhotra, Max H. Bazerman. Negotiation Genius: How to Overcome Obstacles and Achieve Brilliant Results at the Bargaining Table and Beyond. Chapters 4, 6, 8.

[185] **Establish clear and:** G. Richard Shell. Bargaining for Advantage: Negotiation Strategies for Reasonable People. Chapters 2, 4.

[186] **Manage your emotions:** Douglas Stone, Bruce Patton, Sheila Heen. Difficult Conversations: How to Discuss What Matters Most. Chapters 3, 5.

[187] **Clarify and codify:** Jim Camp. Start with No: The Negotiating Tools That the Pros Don't Want You to Know.

[188] **Mastering negotiation skills:** Jeff Haden. Here's How to Tell Within 20 Seconds If Someone Isn't as Great a Negotiator as They Think. https://www.inc.com/jeff-haden/heres-how-to-tell-within-20-seconds-if-someone-isnt-as-great-a-negotiator-as-they-think.html (accessed 2/21/2021).

[189] **Maintaining healthy interactions:** Marla Tabaka. How to Deescalate an Argument Using Emotional Intelligence. https://www.inc.com/marla-tabaka/how-to-deescalate-an-argument-using-emotional-intelligence.html (accessed 1/19/2021).

[190] **When faced with a disagreement:** Lisa B. Marshall. How to Tactfully Disagree with Someone. https://www.quickanddirtytips.com/relationships/etiquette-manners/how-to-tactfully-disagree-with-someone (accessed 3/9/2020).

[191] **Despite the benefits:** Angela Dewan. This pandemic risks bringing out the worst in humanity. https://www.cnn.com/2020/03/15/world/coronavirus-humanity-global-response-intl/index.html (accessed 3/15/2020).

Entrepreneurship

[192] **In the ideal sense:** Daniel Wörle. Innovation Vs Invention: Definition, Difference & Importance. https://digitalleadership.com/blog/innovation-vs-invention/ (accessed 6/6/2022).

[193] **Successful companies embed:** Kimberly Eynon. Companies that outperform don't dabble in innovation at the edges." https://sifted.eu/articles/lunar-design-john-edson/ (accessed 5/31/2020).

[194] **Someone once said:** Jeff Haden. 7 Things Steve Jobs Said That You Should Say Every Single Day. https://www.inc.com/jeff-haden/7-things-steve-jobs-said-that-you-should-say-every-single-day.html (accessed 12/10/2019).

[195] **Most importantly, innovation:** Steve Blank. What it's like for a new CTO trying to bring innovation to a company. https://www.msn.com/en-us/news/technology/what-it-s-like-for-a-new-cto-trying-to-bring-innovation-to-a-company/ar-AAYsfSc (accessed 6/14/2022).

[196] **Selling one's startup:** Tomio Geron. Why startups can't innovate inside big companies. https://www.protocol.com/newsletters/pipeline/do-acquisitions-stifle-innovation?rebelltitem=2#rebelltitem2 (accessed 2/20/2021).

[197] **Creativity and innovation go hand:** Liz Lewis. We Can All Learn Creativity: An Interview With Allen Gannett. https://www.indeed.com/lead/learn-creativity-allen-gannett (accessed 3/20/2020).

[198] **While solitude can:** Liz Lewis. We Can All Learn Creativity: An Interview With Allen Gannett. https://www.indeed.com/lead/learn-creativity-allen-gannett (accessed 3/20/2020).

[199] **Creative ideation often:** Dr. Art Markman. Stop Putting Creativity on your Calendar. https://sponsored.qz.com/citrix/wx107/index.html?utm_campaign=Citrix-Q12020-WX107&utm_medium=qz-paid&utm_source=facebook&utm_content=Copy2/ (accessed 4/28/2020).

[200] **Creativity and innovation demand:** David Robson. How the 'creative-cliff illusion' limits our ideas. https://www.bbc.com/worklife/article/20210331-how-the-creative-cliff-illusion-limits-our-ideas (accessed 3/18/2021).

[201] **Encouraging creativity and:** Atlantic Re:think. Three Agency Essentials to Innovate With Purpose. https://www.theatlantic.com/sponsored/accenture-2020/the-government-agencies-that-moved-with-speed/3508/ (accessed 12/13/2020).

[202] **Research indicates that individuals:** David Robson. Why we gloss over great ideas—and invest in bad ones. https://www.bbc.com/worklife/article/20210430-why-we-gloss-over-great-ideas-and-invest-in-bad-ones (accessed 5/18/2021).

[203] **Innovation is a state:** Heidi Zak. The Innovator's Checklist: 4 Ways to Stay Ahead Of the Curve. https://www.inc.com/heidi-zak/the-innovators-checklist-4-ways-to-stay-ahead-of-curve.html (accessed 1/5/2021).

[204] **It is important to include:** uspto.gov. https://www.uspto.gov/web/offices/pac/mpep/s2109.html (accessed 4/12/2024).

[205] **Effectively timing new:** Antonio Nieto-Rodriguez and Whitney Johnson. 6 Questions to Ask Before Starting a Big Project. https://hbsp.harvard.edu/product/H05F6J-PDF-ENG (accessed 5/7/2020).

[206] **E. M. Rogers':** Citizendium. Diffusion of innovations. https://en.citizendium.org/wiki/Diffusion_of_innovations (accessed 9/14/2020).

[207] **For example, during my time:** Bill Comisky, Ray Blasing. Create a Supercomputer For Design and Optimization. Microwaves & RF, May2000.

[208] **While many consider:** Hila Lifshitz-Assaf and Sarah Lebovitz. How Maker Tools Can Accelerate Ideation. https://sloanreview.mit.edu/article/how-maker-tools-can-accelerate-ideation/ (accessed 11/12/2021).

[209] **Innovation sprints offer:** Jonathan Thompson. How to get past "shiny object syndrome" and build what your customers really want. https://www.atlassian.com/blog/teamwork/what-is-an-innovation-sprint (accessed 4/22/2021).

[210] **A company's culture:** Loizos Heracleous and David Robson. 'Positive Deviants': Why rebellious workers spark great ideas. https://www.bbc.com/worklife/article/20210528-positive-deviants-why-rebellious-workers-spark-gr-ideas (accessed 6/8/2021).

[211] **Rebels are a relatively:** Sunny Bonnell and Ashleigh Hansberger. Companies fire employees for these personality traits, but maybe they should be getting bonuses. https://www.fastcompany.com/90645863/companies-fire-employees-for-these-personality-traits-but-maybe-they-should-be-getting-bonuses (accessed 6/11/2021).

Teamwork Unleashed

[212] **The following abbreviated list:** Jo Nash. Neurodiversity in the Workplace: A Strengths-Based Approach. https://positivepsychology.com/neurodiversity-in-the-workplace/ (accessed 6/1/2024).

[213] **Brainstorming encourages diverse:** A. F. Osborn. Applied Imagination: Principles and procedures of Creative Problem-Solving. 1953.

[214] **It breaks mental blocks:** P. B. Paulus. Group Creativity: Innovation Through Collaboration. 2003.

[215] **It reveals hidden talents:** R. K. Sawyer. Explaining Creativity: The Science of Human Innovation. 2012

[216] **It generates unexpected:** T. M. Amabile. Creativity in Context: Update to the Social Psychology of Creativity. 1996

[217] **It encourages ownership:** S. G. Isaksen, K. B. Dorval, D. J. Treffinger. Creative Approaches to Problem Solving: A Framework for Innovation and Change. 2011.

[218] **Cooperative criticism: While:** Jared R. Curhan. Improve Creative Brainstorming With Constructive Criticism. https://sloanreview.mit.edu/article/improve-creative-brainstorming-with-constructive-criticism/ (accessed 7/19/2022).

[219] **I agree with Jeff:** Bill Murphy Jr. Jeff Bezos Uses This Simple Leadership Trick to Overcome Toxic Mindsets. https://www.inc.com/bill-murphy-jr/jeff-bezos-uses-this-leadership-trick-overcome-toxic-mindsets.html (accessed 9/6/2021).

[220] **The best employees refuse:** Myelle Lansat. A former Facebook employee who's now the president of Nylon Media says a corny poster he saw in the Facebook office taught him how to stand out at big companies. https://www.businessinsider.com/former-facebook-employee-corny-poster-how-to-stand-out-2018-11?op=1 (accessed 2/3/2025).

[221] **Below is a list of strategies:** Noah Miller. Laziness in The Workplace: Learn How to Deal with Lazy Employees. https://learndrive.org/laziness-in-the-workplace/ (accessed 12/30/2024).

[222] **It's important to ensure:** John Rampton. What Should You Do When Team Members Aren't Pulling Their Weight? https://www.entrepreneur.com/article/362195 (accessed 2/23/2021).

[223] **The proliferation of:** Ethan Bernstein and Ben Waber. The Truth About Open Offices. https://hbr.org/2019/11/the-truth-about-open-offices (accessed 2/19/2020).

[224] **Understanding human behavior:** Pam Holloway. What if everything we think we know about collaboration is wrong? https://www.linkedin.com/pulse/what-everything-we-think-know-collaboration-wrong-pam-holloway (accessed 4/16/2020).

[225] **Collaboration within large:** Rob Cross and Inga Carboni. When Collaboration Fails and How to Fix It. https://sloanreview.mit.edu/article/when-collaboration-fails-and-how-to-fix-it/ (accessed 1/7/2021).

[226] **Whether a team operates:** Robert Hooijberg and Michael Watkins. The Future of Team Leadership Is Multimodal. https://sloanreview.mit.edu/article/the-future-of-team-leadership-is-multimodal/?og=Frontiers+Editors+Picks (accessed 3/14/2021).

[227] **There are many important considerations:** The 7 Aspects of High-Performing Teams. https://www.linkedin.com/learning/building-high-performance-teams/the-seven-aspects-of-high-performing-teams-2 (accessed 4/26/2021).

[228] **Team building requires:** Patrick Lencioni. Summary: The Five Dysfunctions of a Team. https://www.american.edu/spa/key/upload/execsummaries-five_dysfunctions_of_a_team.pdf/ (accessed 01/13/2025).

[229] **Leaders nurture genuine:** Jeff Haden. Why Smart Bosses Don't Make Employees Engage in Virtual Team Building or Happy Hours. https://www.inc.com/jeff-haden/why-smart-bosses-dont-make-employees-engage-in-virtual-team-building-or-happy-hours.html (accessed 1/21/2021).

Project Mastery

[230] **According to a "Pulse:** Kalilur Rahman. Project management Dilemma—What is your favorite from the Tetrahedron—Scope, Time, Cost or Quality for a smooth delivery? https://www.linkedin.com/pulse/project-management-dilemma-what-your-favorite-from-scope-rahman/ (accessed 11/8/2019).

[231] **While "project management":** Program Management Career Path. https://www.vp-programming.com/program-management-career-path/ (accessed 6/14/2022).

[232] **The following list further delineates:** Rachel Wells. Project Manager Vs. Product Manager Vs. Program Manager. https://www.forbes.com/sites/rachelwells/2023/10/16/project-manager-vs-product-manager-vs-program-manager/ (accessed 1/2/2025).

[233] **The Technical Program Manager:** The Secret Ingredient Driving Facebook's Product Teams. https://www.facebook.com/careers/life/the-secret-ingredient-driving-facebooks-product-teams (accessed 11/6/2019).

[234] **If you're considering:** The technical program manager resume bible (with Google examples). https://igotanoffer.com/blogs/tech/technical-program-manager-resume (accessed 6/15/2022).

[235] **Every successful PM:** Project management triangle (Wikipedia). https://en.wikipedia.org/wiki/Project_management_triangle (accessed 7/30/2020).

[236] **Statistically, most projects:** Clinton M. Padgett. 10 Proven Steps For Project Success. https://www.forbes.com/sites/forbesbooksauthors/2021/01/06/10-proven-steps-for-project-success/?sh=1edae30f26e1 (accessed 1/13/2021).

[237] **Consider the following guidelines:** Kat Boogaard. What is Parkinson's Law and why is it sabotaging your productivity? https://www.atlassian.com/blog/productivity/what-is-parkinsons-law (accessed 8/31/2021).

[238] **The project Kick-Off:** Jonathan Thompson. 5 science-backed team activities that will actually improve performance. https://www.atlassian.com/blog/teamwork/5-science-backed-team-activities (accessed 3/25/2021).

[239] **Leading by example often fosters:** Brian Kurtz. The Power of 100-0. https://www.briankurtz.net/the-power-of-100-0/ (accessed 5/30/2020).

Philanthropy and Citizenship

[240] **Many of us aspire:** Raymond James. Create a legacy that will echo in your community. https://www.raymondjames.com/retirementbydesigninc/resources/living-your-legacy/community (accessed 10/29/19).

[241] **The concept of giving:** Glenn Geher. The Case Against Self-Actualization. https://www.psychologytoday.com/us/blog/darwins-subterranean-world/202005/the-case-against-self-actualization (accessed 6/2/2020).

[242] **At their core:** Mike Bloomberg. You're in Charge: Be selfish give back. https://www.mikebloomberg2020.com/news/youre-in-charge-be-selfish-give-back (accessed 1/25/2020).

[243] **The butterfly effect:** Kalilur Rahman. Are you a Positive Butterfly? Effects of Positive Mental Model and #PayItForward. https://www.linkedin.com/pulse/you-positive-butterfly-effects-mental-model-kalilur-rahman (accessed 11/8/2019).

[244] **Another impactful way:** https://en.wikipedia.org/wiki/Donald_Van_Norman_Roberts (accessed 8/19/20204).

[245] **Microsoft's Brad Smith, for**: Romesh Ratnesar. How Microsoft's Brad Smith is Trying to Restore Your Trust in Big Tech. https://time.com/5669537/brad-smith-microsoft-big-tech/ (accessed 10/1/2019).

[246] **Some leaders have started:** Ikujiro Nonaka, Hirotaka Takeuchi. Strategy as a Way of Life. https://sloanreview.mit.edu/article/strategy-as-a-way-of-life/ (accessed 10/10/2021).

[247] **Google is set to become:** Roland Li and D.K. Dineen. Apple, Google, And Facebook Committed $4.5 Billion for Housing. Now Comes The Hard Part. https://www.sfchronicle.com/business/article/Apple-Google-and-Facebook-committed-4-5-billion-14809347.php. (accessed 11/15/2019).

[248] **Of particular significance:** Terri Gerstein and Jane Flanagan. Major companies have to prioritize workers in new corporate missions. https://thehill.com/opinion/finance/458525-major-companies-have-to-prioritize-workers-in-new-corporate-missions (accessed 9/1/2019).

[249] **While the benefits**: John Mackey. Rethinking the Social Responsibility of Business. https://reason.com/2005/10/01/rethinking-the-social-responsi-2/ (accessed 2/5/2019).

Joyful Living

[250] **Those who weaponize:** Kimberley Richards. Trump Promoted This Disputed Racial Theory In His Inaugural Speech. Here's Why It Doesn't Work. https://www.msn.com/en-us/news/politics/trump-promoted-this-disputed-racial-theory-in-his-inaugural-speech-heres-why-it-doesnt-work/ar-AA1xCio6 (accessed 1/26/2025).

[251] **Business mogul Kevin:** Melissa Koenig. Kevin O'Leary rips 'nuts' Costco for boldly defying Trump order. https://www.dailymail.co.uk/yourmoney/article-14353191/Kevin-OLeary-Costco-DEI-Trump.html (accessed 2/2/2025).

[252] **The meritocracy myth:** Addressing Common Myths About Diversity and Equity in Faculty Recruitment and Hiring. https://academicpersonnel.ucsc.edu/academic-employment/diversity-equity-and-inclusion/common-myths-about-diversity-and-equity-in-faculty-recruitment-and-hiring/ (accessed 2/10/2025).

[253] **These behaviors reflect:** David Smith. Wrecking ball: Trump's war on 'woke' marks US society's plunge into 'dark times.' https://www.theguardian.com/us-news/2025/feb/02/trump-woke-dei-culture-wars/ (accessed 2/10/2025).

[254] **While DEI has largely:** Diversity, Equity, and inclusion. https://en.wikipedia.org/wiki/Diversity%2C_equity%2C_and_inclusion/ (accessed 2/17/2025).

[255] **Unfortunately, these steps:** Mokhtech, Jagsi, Vega, Brown, Golden, Juang, Mattes, Pinnix, Evans. Mitigating Bias in Recruitment: Attracting a Diverse, Dynamic Workforce to Sustain the Future of Radiation Oncology. https://pmc.ncbi.nlm.nih.gov/articles/PMC9436705/ (accessed 2/10/2025).

[256] **How often do we pause:** Marcel Schwantes. Bill Gates Says He Now Asks 4 Questions that He Would Never have Asked at Age 25. https://www.inc.com/marcel-schwantes/bill-gates-says-you-should-ask-4-crucial-questions-to-assess-quality-of-your-life-1-is-from-warren-buffett.html (accessed 11/11/2019).

[257] **Interestingly, artificial intelligence:** Lydia Dishman. AI can explain the meaning of life and the answer will surprise you. https://www.fastcompany.com/90844587/ai-can-explain-the-meaning-of-life-and-the-answer-will-surprise-you (accessed 2/4/2023).

258 **As I spent more time:** Marcel Schwantes. Bill Gates Says His Level of Happiness Is Much Higher at 63 Than at 25 Because He Chooses to Do These 4 Things. https://www.inc.com/marcel-schwantes/bill-gates-says-his-level-of-happiness-is-much-higher-at-63-than-25-because-he-chooses-to-do-these-4-things.html (accessed 3/29/2021).

259 **Success can be defined:** Missy Yost. 19 Definitions Of Success You Should Never Ignore. https://www.lifehack.org/articles/communication/the-new-definitions-success.html (accessed 2/17/2021).

260 **Success isn't a mere:** Benjamin Hardy, Ph.D. 34 Things You Need to Give Up to Be Successful. https://www.inc.com/benjamin-p-hardy/34-things-you-need-to-give-up-to-be-successful.html (accessed 4/6/2020).

261 **Work success, whether:** Jeff Haden. Here's How to Tell in 20 Seconds If Someone Will Never Be Successful. https://www.inc.com/jeff-haden/heres-how-to-tell-in-20-seconds-if-someone-will-never-be-successful.html (accessed 2/28/2021).

262 **Success can be challenging:** Joe De Sena. Want to be really successful? You have to learn 2 hard lessons. https://www.cnbc.com/2021/04/22/hard-lessons-to-learn-if-you-want-to-be-really-successful.html. (accessed 6/21/2021).

263 **When we explore:** Arthur C. Brooks. How to Buy Happiness. https://www.theatlantic.com/family/archive/2021/04/money-income-buy-happiness/618601/ (accessed 4/15/2021).

264 **Beyond a certain point, money:** Jeff Haden. How Happier People Spend Their Money, Backed by Considerable Science. https://www.inc.com/jeff-haden/how-happier-people-spend-their-money-backed-by-considerable-science.html (accessed 1/23/2021).

265 **Some people assume that:** Arthur C. Brooks. If You Want Success, Pursue Happiness. https://www.theatlantic.com/family/archive/2022/10/prioritizing-happiness-before-success/671714/ (accessed 10/16/2022).

266 **Research has determined:** Arthur C. Brooks. The Seven Habits That Lead to Happiness in Old Age. https://www.theatlantic.com/family/archive/2022/02/happiness-age-investment/622818/ (accessed 2/19/2022).

267 **Psychologists have found:** Laurie Santos. How to be Happier. https://www.newsweek.com/2021/01/08/laurie-santos-yale-happiness-professor-5-things-that-will-make-you-happier-1556182.html (accessed 1/10/2021).

268 **Experts have explored:** Kathleen Rellihan. The Secrets to happiness Around the World. https://www.newsweek.com/2021/01/15/secrets-happiness-around-world-1559664.html (accessed 1/10/2021).

269 **Retirement is a relatively:** Gary Foster. What three things should a person avoid once they are past 70 years old? https://www.quora.com/What-three-things-should-a-person-avoid-once-they-are-past-70-years-old/answer/Gary-Foster-60?share=1 (accessed 3/30/2021).

270 **Many baby boomers:** Betsy Morris. How to Know When to Quit Your Job. https://www.wsj.com/articles/how-to-know-when-to-quit-your-job-11611507600 (accessed 1/27/2021).

271 **However, when work:** Janna Koretz. What Happens When Your Career Becomes Your Whole Identity. https://hbr.org/2019/12/what-happens-when-your-career-becomes-your-whole-identity (accessed 3/17/2022).

272 **Unfortunately, many experienced:** First Republic Bank. The Power of Purposeful Aging. https://www.firstrepublic.com/articles-insights/life-money/plan-your-legacy/the-power-of-purposeful-aging (accessed 4/16/2021).

[273] **Jeff Bezos departed:** Minda Zetlin. In Jeff Bezos' Final Days as Amazon CEO He Created 2 New Rules Every Leader Should Follow. https://www.inc.com/minda-zetlin/jeff-bezos-new-amazon-leadership-principles-employees-climate.html (access 7/31/2021).

Dent the Universe

[274] **When Jobs coined:** Lisa Eadicicco. Laurene Powell Jobs says people have been misinterpreting one of Steve Jobs' most famous quotes for years (AAPL). https://markets.businessinsider.com/news/stocks/steve-jobs-famous-quote-misunderstood-laurene-powell-2020-2-1028950313 (accessed 3/2/2020).

[275] **Laubach Method:** Helen M. Roberts. Champion of the Silent Billion.

[276] **Their efforts were part:** Tom Shachtman. Airlift to America: How Barack Obama, Sr., John F. Kennedy, Tom Mboya, and 800 East African Students Changed Their World and Ours. Pages 4-9.

[277] **One promising young man:** https://en.wikipedia.org/wiki/Helen_M._Roberts (accessed 8/19/2024).

[278] **Each of us contributes:** Peter Wehner. Don't Succumb to MAGA Fatalism. https://www.theatlantic.com/ideas/archive/2022/08/political-extremism-fatalism-maga-threat/671234/ (accessed 8/27/2022).